THE SWORD AND THE DOLLAR

Imperialism, Revolution, and the Arms Race

THE SWORD AND THE DOLLAR

Imperialism, Revolution, and the Arms Race

Michael Parenti

St. Martin's Press   *New York*

Editor: Larry Swanson
Project Editor: Laura Ann Starrett
Production Supervisor: Julie Toth
Cover Design: Tom McKevney
Cover Art: Tom McKevney

Library of Congress Catalog Card Number: 88-60536
Copyright © 1989 by St. Martin's Press, Inc.
Manufactured in the United States of America.
32109
fedcba

For information, write:
St. Martin's Press, Inc.
175 Fifth Avenue
New York, NY 10010

ISBN: 0-312-01167-9

To Si Gerson, Sophie Gerson, and Sender Garlin,
longtime warriors in the struggle against imperialism

Contents

Acknowledgments

I would like to thank Kathleen Lipscomb, Lisa Moore, and Cathy Newton for the assistance they rendered in the preparation of this book. Once again Marvin Gettleman and Victor Wallis came through with materials and suggestions that were most useful. A special expression of gratitude is owed to Kathleen McGuire and Colleen McGuire, who provided selfless succor in the early stages of writing and valuable criticisms of the manuscript. In addition, the staff at St. Martin's Press has my thanks, specifically Larry Swanson, Elizabeth Caldwell, and Laura Ann Starrett.

An abundance of helpful suggestions were provided by James F. Petras of State University of New York, Binghamton; Donald R. Culverson of Macalester College; and Ronald T. Fox of California State University, Sacramento.

THE SWORD AND THE DOLLAR

Imperialism, Revolution, and the Arms Race

1

A Policy neither Fainthearted nor Foolish

Why does the United States support right-wing autocracies around the world? Why is it antagonistic toward revolutionary movements and most socialist countries? Why does the United States intervene in other countries with military aid, embargoes, surrogate counterrevolutionary forces, and the US military? Why does the United States have military bases all around the world? Why does it spend hundreds of billions yearly on military appropriations? Why do Washington and Moscow have nuclear arsenals that can blow up the world many times over? In this book, I propose to answer these and other such questions and show that they are very much related to each other.

The debate over US foreign policy, as conducted in the political mainstream by liberals and conservatives, is a narrow one that evades the great realities of political economy. Conservatives argue that our policy has been "no-win" and fainthearted, that we too often play the "helpless giant" pushed around by third-rate powers, that we fail to stand up sufficiently to the "Soviet challenge" and have fallen dangerously behind the USSR in military capability, and that the Communist tide will soon be lapping at our borders—as Ronald Reagan put it—unless we squelch revolutionary movements in this hemisphere and elsewhere.

According to conservatives the world is inhabited by terrorist hit squads, evil empires, Communist aggressors, and other such mortal threats. Like the bloodthirsty savages of some Hollywood western or jungle epic, or the alien creatures of a science fiction film, these "enemies" are motivated not by any concern for their own welfare, but by a mindless impulse to destroy or subjugate us. So we must draw the Free World wagon train in a circle, a defensive perimeter that includes almost all of Europe, Asia, Africa, Latin America, and North America. Should we falter in our resolve, slip in military strength, or try to appease or placate the predatory forces, they will be at our throats.

Liberals share much of this same ideological imagery. Like conservatives, they show concern about what is perceived to be the "Soviet challenge" and the "growing Communist influence." They usually dare not utter a positive word about existing socialist countries. They may not necessarily believe a global Red Menace is about to engulf us, but they are terrified about being portrayed as wimps who are soft on Communism. So they end up acting as wimps to the conservatives, toeing the conservative line on most foreign-policy issues.

However, some liberals (and some fewer conservatives) believe an accommodation can be reached with the Soviet Union, to avoid blowing up the world. Liberals also argue that if we were to improve relations with Moscow, we then could better concentrate on preventing the spread of Communism in the Third World. Like conservatives, liberals want a strong military. They tend to vote for gargantuan defense budgets that are only about 10 percent less than what conservatives want. Many (but not all) liberals are more reluctant to intervene with force and violence against revolutionary movements in other lands. They argue that the best way to stop Communism is by less reliance on military measures and more emphasis on reformist, nonmilitary means. Like conservatives, liberals never for a moment ask what is so urgent about stopping the Communists. They treat it as a point beyond debate (and therefore beyond rational examination) that Communism is a dreadful evil that must be contained and, if possible, eradicated.

As just noted, liberals suffer from the wimp factor, the nagging fear that they might be seen as soft on Communism. As a consequence, most of them jump on cue when the issues of anticommunism and anti-Sovietism come up. Back in 1947, when President Harry Truman initiated the loyalty programs—his own witch-hunt against "subversives" in government—he remarked, "Well, that should take the Communist smear off the Democratic Party."[1] He was hoping that his imitative effort at repression would relieve Democrats of the charge of being soft on Communism—which it did not. Liberals do not seem to realize that conservatives try to stigmatize them on the Communism issue *not only because conservatives don't like Communists but because they don't like liberals.* Conservatives fear Communist revolution, but even more immediately they detest liberal reforms, which they see as taking the country down the slippery slope to socialism. So all the liberals' efforts at Soviet-bashing will not save them from being labeled "soft on Communism" by conservatives.

Neither liberals nor conservatives seem to have anything to say about economic imperialism as practiced throughout the world by the corporate and financial interests in the United States and other capitalist countries. Most liberals and conservatives, be they political leaders, academics, or media commentators, do not believe imperialism exists—at least not since Rudyard Kipling's day or not since the Spanish-American War. If they use the term "imperialism" to describe a contemporary event, it is usually in reference to something the Soviet Union is doing. They never consider whether capitalism as a global system has any integral relationship to US foreign policy. These remarkable omissions are a central focus of this book.

Just as they concur that Communism is bad, so do liberals and conservatives seem to agree that the US government acts with benign intent in the world. While they allow that the United States sometimes must do unsavory things because that is the kind of world we live in, they generally leave the goals and premises of US policy unexamined.

Most disagreements between liberals and conservatives are over tactics. Hence, during the Vietnam War, the questions debated in the mainstream political arena were: Are we relying too heavily on military means? Can we see the light at the end of the tunnel? Are we winning or is it a lost cause? Can we expect to build democracy in "a land that has no capacity for it"? Left unexamined was the idea that the USA was in Vietnam for reasons other than those stated by its leaders, or was pursuing anything but laudable, well-intentioned goals. The antiwar movement raised basic moral questions about the war and about the underlying class interests, but the debate as framed in the major media and in mainstream political life was mostly between those who said we could win the war and those who said we could not—the implication being that if the United States *could* have won, then the war's terrible devastation would have been justified. After US withdrawal from Vietnam, in conformity with this perspective, public discussion was confined to the idea that US intervention had been a well-meaning but unsuccessful effort to help the

Vietnamese install a Western-style democracy in their land. In fact, a vigorous effort to rewrite the history of the war was conducted in the post-Vietnam years, evidenced by the outpouring of academic apologies and media statements that have transformed the US Indochina intervention into a noble effort to defend democracy.[2]

Liberals and conservatives agree that there is something in the world called "US interests," which, while seldom defined, are always thought of as being in urgent need of defense and morally defensible. It is implicitly understood that these "interests" are linked in some way to the freedom and salvation of humanity. Liberals and conservatives also seem to agree that something called "stability" in the Third World is better than "instability"—that is, better than agitation and change, even though it is sometimes admitted that change is needed in one or another oppressively impoverished country.

Liberals—and, to a far lesser extent, conservatives—recognize that much "instability" is due to poverty, but they give little recognition to imperialism and capitalism as a cause of poverty, and any attempt to do so is treated as ideological posturing.

Liberals frequently complain that US policy is often misguided, or overextended, or prone to backing the wrong persons and wrong interests abroad, or given to self-defeating pursuits. Conservatives frequently complain, as already noted, that US policy suffers from timidity and faintheartedness, an unwillingness to commit American military power and stand up to the Russians. In this book, I will argue that US policy is neither fainthearted nor foolish, beset by neither folly nor failure. Rather it is powerful and coercive, and usually effective in its undertakings. And while it makes mistakes and suffers defeats, it is quite rational in its goals and resourceful in its methods. Many of the official explanations given to justify American policies abroad may be false, but this does not mean the policies themselves are senseless. Many of the arguments made in defense of such policies may be confusing—and are meant to be—but this does not mean the policies or policymakers themselves are confused.

The great realities about capitalism, imperialism, interventionism, militarism, and the East-West conflict, left unexamined and undebated in the conservative-liberal mainstream, are what I invite you to explore in the pages ahead. Such an exploration will reveal that US foreign policy has suffered defeats and made mistakes but has generally been consistent and successful. It may not be serving the interests of Third World peoples, nor even of the American people, but it serves well those who know how to be well served.

This book is devoted to a critical treatment of both American imperialism and the US-USSR "rivalry." I will try to show a linkage between US interventionism in the Third World and the East-West arms race. (Some attention also is given to past imperial practices of other nations.) *The criticism of United States foreign policy found herein is not to be mistaken for a criticism of the United States as a nation, nor a criticism of the American people.* If anything, it is my view that Americans deserve something better than what their leaders have been giving them. In Chapter 7, I take pains to show how Americans themselves are victims of US policies abroad. It is my contention that such policies do not represent the interests of the American people. Nor do these policies coincide with the opinions registered by most Americans regarding issues like overseas interventionism, increased military spending, and arms buildups, as we shall see. No matter how many times one makes the point, however, some people cannot understand that a criticism of our nation's leaders and policies is not a criticism of our nation as such, not an attack on our country's moral worth as a nation. To criticize our leaders—the people in the White House, the National Security Council, the Central Intelligence Agency, and members of Congress—is to do the American thing; it is our hard-won democratic right and remains part of what it means to be an American. To raise our voices in protest against imperialism and militarism is not to sell out to our enemies but to better locate them.

In the pages ahead, I will use terms such as the "ruling class," the "propertied class," the "owning class," the "dominant interests," and the "corporate interests." When I do so, I am referring to the rich and powerful who own most of the land, capital, and technology of this nation, who employ most of its labor, and who translate their immense economic power into a lion's share of political power, occupying the top policymaking positions of both boardroom and government, regardless of which political party or personality occupies the White House. It is no great conspiratorial secret as to who they are. They are described in fairly specific detail in Chapter 16.[3]

Finally, if there is any lesson to be drawn from this book, it is that while the history of imperialism is filled with dreadful injustices and atrocities, we, the people, can make a difference and can win victories. The ruling class rules, but not quite in the way it might want to, for it must make concessions to popular protest and, at crucial points, it must suffer some of the constraints imposed by popular power at home and abroad. US imperialist policy is increasingly limited by resistant social forces around the globe and within our own country. So even as the destructive capacity of the US military grows, the ability of Washington policymakers to control the world is declining. Those who rule cannot always use their power with indifference to the countervailing forces of socialism, revolution, and democratic protest and resistance.

To those readers who will be quick to apply one or another label to my efforts, let me say that this book does not represent an extremist viewpoint. Its message is quite moderate and democratic; it is a critique of military buildup, police-state oppression, and economic exploitation. There is nothing "extremist" about that. The extremists are already in power. They have turned much of the world into a military garrison and an economic purgatory. Most of the people in the United States and throughout the entire world want an end to the arms race, an end to huge military spending programs, an end to nuclear confrontations, and an end to US interventionism on behalf of the rich and powerful; in effect, they want an end to imperialism— even if they don't call it imperialism. The sentiments and perspective found herein, therefore, do not represent the viewpoint of a fringe minority but of the great majority of the world—at least on basic points. The fringe minority is composed of those who need all the bayonets and bombs to keep the world as they want it. The majority of the earth's people are ready for something else, something better. And therein lies our hope.

Notes

1. Quoted in David Horowitz, *The Free World Colossus* (New York: Hill and Wang, 1965), p. 101.

2. Noam Chomsky and Edward S. Herman, *After the Cataclysm: Postwar Indochina and the Reconstruction of Imperial Ideology* (Boston: South End Press, 1979).

3. For a study of class power in the American political system see Michael Parenti, *Democracy for the Few*, 5th ed. (New York: St. Martin's Press, 1988).

2

Imperialism and the Myth of Underdevelopment

We in the United States live in a capitalist society, and this fact has significance not only for us but for the rest of the world. So let us take a moment to dwell upon the nature of capitalism. The essence of the capitalist system is the accumulation of capital, the making of profits in order to invest and make still more profits. The first law of capitalism is: make a profit off the labor of others or go out of business. And the best way to accumulate capital is not to work hard but to get others to work hard for you. Private gain, not social need, is the central imperative of our economic system. As an erstwhile chairman of Castle and Cooke put it: "We are in the business of making a profit. We are not in business primarily to satisfy society. We're not going to satisfy society very long if we go out of business. So profits are the number-one consideration."[1]

Money itself has no value unless it can command the serviceable things produced by labor. Capital does not grow of itself; it must be mixed with labor to create marketable value. Certainly one can make money by mere speculation—but only because there is a small stratum of people accumulating enough money off the labor of others to invest in speculative things at increasingly higher prices.

One's money must be either spent on direct consumption or invested to accumulate new value from labor. There is a third way, you might say. Money can just be "saved," and one can earn interest on the savings. But savings are a form of investment. And the interest earned on savings are but a portion of the profits once removed. The only reason the bank will give you 7 percent interest on your savings is because it then lends those same funds out to a business at 12 percent. And the only reason the business pays 12 percent interest to the bank is because it is making, say, 30 percent off the labor of its employees (and using your money to do it).

Wealth comes from two sources: from the natural resources of the environment and from the labor that is mixed with those resources—the mental and physical labor that produces the commodities and services of our society. Profits are the money you make *without working*. (As just noted, the interest you "earn" on your bank deposit is a form of profit under a different name.) Investment earnings are wealth created by people who work and distributed to people who take no part in the work, the stockholders. For small owners who both work in their own businesses and employ others, it can be said that some of their income must represent the value produced by their own labor and some portion, usually the larger if they are doing well, represents the value produced by the labor of their employees. Corporate managers also work; they administer and supervise and can be considered employees of the firm, albeit highly paid ones who represent the large investor's interests. Often they themselves are also large investors.

Capital as such does not produce anything. Capital is produced by labor. You could be as rich as Rockefeller but you could never build anything with your wealth. You may have noticed that when labor takes off—be it for a weekend, a holiday, or a strike—nothing is produced. Capital is the surplus value created by labor. "Putting one's money to work" means mixing it with labor to extract more capital from that labor. Capitalists are always running advertisements telling us how capital creates jobs, commodities, factories, and prosperity. The truth is, purely on its own without labor, capital is incapable of making a pencil, let alone building a pencil factory.[2]

Capital is dead labor, the accumulation of past mental and physical effort. It must constantly be mixed with labor to realize its value and increase its sum. As corporate managers themselves will tell you: investors will not put their money into anything unless they can extract more than they invested. Increased earnings can only come with an increase in the size of the corporate operation. So the system must continually expand. A central law of capitalist motion and development is *expansion*. The capitalist is engaged in a ceaseless, restless search for profitable enterprise, for ways of making still more money. (Expansion per se is not a bad thing; it is the exploitative nature of capitalist expansion for private profit that concerns us here.) Ironically enough, those with great surpluses of money have a most pressing problem of always having to find things to put that money into so as to protect or augment its value.

Furthermore, a capitalist economy is an unplanned and competitive one in which security is guaranteed to no one, not even the corporate giants. A corporation searches for security by increasing its hold over resources, developing new technologies (through the application of mental and physical labor), searching out cheaper labor markets, getting government to subsidize everything from production to exports, capturing a competitor's market, merging with other companies, devising new sales networks and techniques, and the like. The problem is that all the other big companies are doing the same thing. So not even the giant corporations can rest secure for very long.

Grow or die: that's the unwritten rule. To stand still amidst the growth of competitors is to decline, not only relatively but absolutely, causing a firm's financial structure to collapse. The dynamics of a market economy—the accumulation of profit and the need to invest surplus capital, the demand for strategic overseas materials and new markets, the fluctuations in consumer spending, the instabilities of old markets, the threat of recession and depression, the pressures of domestic and foreign competition—all these things force corporations into a restless, endless drive to expand, compelling them to gather as much strength as they can. Those ecologists who dream of a "no-growth capitalism," better to preserve the environment, do not seem to realize that the concept is an oxymoron.

I once heard a corporate executive explain why his company was expanding overseas: he noted that the regional firms in New England that years ago decided not to pursue *national* markets are now extinct. He could not even recall their names. The same fate awaits those companies that today do not go *international*, he concluded. Whether it really is all that drastic, the point remains that the history of capitalism is a history of expansion from local to regional to national to international arenas. About 140 years ago, Marx and Engels noted the phenomenon, describing a bourgeoisie that "chases . . . over the whole surface of the globe. It must nestle everywhere, settle everywhere, establish connections everywhere."[3] Given its expansionist nature, capitalism can never stay home.

The attractions of Third World investments are evident: a relative lack of competition, a vast cheap labor pool, the absence or near absence of environmental and safety regulations and corporate taxes, and the opportunity to market products at monopoly prices. As the practical limitations of investments are reached in one country and the margin of profit narrows, outlets are sought in other less advantaged and more vulnerable lands. As Harry Magdoff states:

> What matters to the business community, and to the business system as a whole, is that the option of foreign investment (and foreign trade) should remain available. For this to be meaningful, the business system requires, as a minimum, that the political and economic principles of capitalism should prevail and that the door be fully open for foreign capital at all times. Even more, it seeks a privileged open door for the capital of the home country in preference to capital from competing industrial nations. . . .[4]

The quality of products and services, the safety of commodities, the protection of the natural environment, the conditions supportive of community life and human development, the opportunity to do gratifying and socially useful work, the care of the vulnerable and handicapped, in sum, a whole range of values that might be basic to human happiness, are considered in the capitalist mode of production, if at all, only to the extent they advance or retard pecuniary gain.

Capital has no attachment to any particular place or people. It has no loyalty to God or country, nor any disloyalty, for that matter. "Merchants have no country," observed Thomas Jefferson way back in 1814. "The mere spot they stand on does not constitute so strong an attachment as that from which they draw their gains."[5] (However, merchants will also grow attached to the country that protects their gains.)

Along with expansion and growth comes the increasing concentration of capital. There are more than 200,000 corporations in the USA today, but 100 companies control more than half the nation's industrial assets. Fifty of the largest banks and insurance companies own half of all the financial assets. Ten firms make 22 percent of all the profits.

Of special interest to us is the international scope of this capital concentration. Some 400 corporations control about 80 percent of the capital assets of the entire nonsocialist world. One-third of the assets of US industrial corporations are located outside the United States. Eight of the nation's nine largest banks now rely on foreign sources for over 40 percent of their total deposits. Many of these holdings—often the larger portions—are in other industrial countries. But more and more investment is going into the Third World. Citibank, for instance, earns about 75 percent of its profits from overseas operations, mostly in the Third World.[6] American and other Western corporations have acquired control of more than 75 percent of the known major mineral resources in Asia, Africa, and Latin America. The USA is South Africa's largest trading partner and its second-largest foreign investor, with investments amounting to about $2 billion as of 1986. US banks provide the apartheid regime with one-third of its international credit.[7]

Given the low wages, low taxes, nonexistent workers benefits, and nonexistent occupational and environmental protections, *US multinational profit rates in the Third World are 50 percent greater than in developed countries.*[8] Hence, giant companies like Exxon, Cargill, Coca-Cola, IBM, Honeywell, Woolworth, Upjohn, Mobil, ITT, Gillette, and Reynolds make more than half their total profits abroad. As early as 1963 *Business Week* noted the trend:

> In industry after industry, U.S. companies found that their overseas earnings were soaring, and that their return on investment abroad was frequently much higher than in the U.S. As earnings abroad began to rise, profit margins from domestic operations started to shrink. . . . This is the combination that forced development of the multinational company.[9]

Where business goes so goes government—as we shall see. In the service of big business, the governments of capitalist nations, including the United States, have striven mightily to create and maintain the conditions of investment and accumulation in other lands. This may not be the only function of US foreign policy, but it is the function that is often ignored by those who would minimize the role played by international capitalism in the affairs of nations.

IMPERIALISM

For some 500 years the nations of Western Europe, and later North America, plundered the wealth of Asia, Africa, and Latin America. *This forceful expropriation of one country's land, labor, markets, and resources by another is what is here meant by imperialism.* Imperialism is of course older than capitalism. Neither Alexander the Great, nor the emperors of Rome, nor the Spanish conquistadores were capitalists. They did not systematically accumulate capital through the rationalized exploitation of free labor and the expansion of private markets. But these earlier plunderers all had one thing in common with capitalists: the desire to expropriate the wealth of other peoples' land and labor. They were all imperialists. Capitalist imperialism differs from these earlier forms in the systematic ways it invests in other countries and shapes the productive forces, penetrates the markets, and transforms the economies and cultures of the colonized nations, integrating their financial structures and trade into an international system for the extraction of wealth.

When the merchant capitalists replaced the mercantilist monarchs, the process of expropriation accelerated and expanded. Along with gold and silver, they took flax, hemp, indigo, silk, diamonds, timber, molasses, sugar, rum, rubber, tobacco, calico, cocoa, coffee, cotton, copper, coal, tin, iron, and later on, oil, zinc, columbite, manganese, mercury, platinum, cobalt, bauxite, aluminum, and uranium. And of course there was that most dreadful of all expropriations—of human beings themselves—slaves. Millions of people were abducted from Africa, while millions more perished in the hellish passage to the New World.

The stupendous fortunes that were—and still are being—extracted by the European and North American investors should remind us that there are very few really poor nations in what today is commonly called the Third World. Brazil is rich; Indonesia is rich; and so are the Philippines, Chile, Bolivia, Zaire, Mexico, India, and Malaysia. Only the people are poor. Of course in some areas, as in parts of Africa south of the Sahara, the land has been so ruthlessly plundered that it too is now impoverished, making life all the more desperate for its inhabitants.[10]

In a word, the Third World is not "underdeveloped" but overexploited. The gap between rich and poor nations is not due to the "neglect" of the latter by the former as has been often claimed. For forty years or more we have heard how the nations of the North must help close the poverty gap between themselves and the nations of the South, devoting some portion of their technology and capital to the task. Yet the gap between rich and poor only widens because investments in the Third World are not designed to develop the capital resources of the poor nations but to enrich the Western investors.

From 1970 to 1980, the flow of investment capital from the United States to the Third World amounted to about $8 billion. But the return flow from the Third World to the United States in the form of dividends, interest, branch profits, management fees, and royalties was $63.7 billion.[11] Together, all the multinational corporations and banks in the world take as much as $200 billion every year from the Third World nations.[12] Nor should this come as a surprise since, as we already noted, the first rule of capitalism is that sooner or later more must be taken out than put into any business venture. Why else would companies and banks invest, except to make more than they started with?

Third World nations would have been only too grateful if they could have escaped the attentions of the Western self-enriching nations that exploited them throughout their history. Consider India: As late as 1815, India exported £1.3 million of textile goods to Britain and imported only £26,000 from that country. But Britain placed prohibitive tariffs on Indian imports, and used its armies and gunboats in India to prevent that country from taking retaliatory protective measures. By 1830 the trade balance was reversed. As British textile goods flooded India, Indian industrial centers like Dacca fell into decay, and Indian weavers, spinners, and metal workers were driven out of business.

But "you cannot continue to inundate a country with your manufactures, unless you enable it to give you some produce in return," observed Marx.[13] Only then will it have some funds to purchase the finished goods dumped on its markets. Thus, to complete the imperialistic relationship, Britain promoted the large-scale production of agricultural raw materials in India, especially cotton plantations. Hence "a people who formerly had exported cotton goods to all parts of the world now exported only raw cotton to be worked up in Britain and sent back to India as textile goods!"[14] Yet India's earnings from this arrangement proved insufficient and by 1853 India had accumulated a national debt of £53 million. This was financed from the labor of the common people and had an additionally regressive effect upon the economy. From 1850 to 1900, India's per capita income dropped by almost two-thirds.[15] India was forced deeper into poverty and denied the opportunity of its own development so that it might serve as a provider for British capitalism.

In the nineteenth century, British industrialists similarly transformed China and Egypt from exporters of manufactured goods into providers of raw materials for British industry. In 1856, Engels remarked on the baneful effects of Britain's colonization of Ireland: "How often have the Irish started out to achieve something, and every time they have been crushed politically and industrially. By consistent oppression they have been artificially converted into an utterly impoverished nation. . . ."[16] So too did the industrialists and financiers of France, Belgium, and the Netherlands "artificially convert" the economies of various Third World countries, retarding their economic development for centuries.[17]

In the early 1900s, British firms appropriated about two-thirds of India's economic surplus and one-tenth of Malaya's. In other words, British investments did not finance the colonial territories, rather the colonies provided finance for Britain. Likewise, before World War II, Dutch capitalism annually extracted an amount of economic surplus from what is now Indonesia equal to about one-sixth of Holland's national income.[18]

Africa has been one of the lands most often misrepresented as "primitive" and "underdeveloped" by imperialism's image makers. The truth is, as early as the 1400s, Nigeria, Mali, and the Guinea coast were making some of the world's finest fabrics and leathers. Katanga, Zambia, and Sierra Leone produced copper and iron, while Benin had a brass and bronze industry. As early as the thirteenth century, finely illuminated books and manuscripts were part of the Amharic culture of Ethiopia, and impressive stone palaces stood in Zimbabwe.[19] Yet Africa under colonial rule soon was exporting raw materials and importing manufactured goods from Europe, like other colonized places.

The advantages Europeans possessed in seafaring and warfare proved decisive. "West Africans had developed metal casting to a fine artistic perfection in many parts of Nigeria, but when it came to the meeting with Europe, beautiful bronzes were far less relevant than the crudest cannon."[20] Arms superiority also allowed the Europeans to impose a slave trade that decimated certain parts of Africa, set African leaders against each other in the procurement of slaves, and further retarded that continent's economic development.

Attempts by African leaders at development, including the area of arms technology, were suppressed by the British, French, and other colonizers. From the seventeenth to the twentieth centuries, Europe imposed imperialist trade relationships, forcing Africa to sell its raw materials and buy manufactured goods on increasingly disadvantageous terms. As Walter Rodney points out: "There was no objective economic law which determined that primary produce should be worth so little. Indeed, the [Western capitalist] countries sold certain raw materials like timber and wheat at much higher prices than a colony could command. The explanation is that the unequal exchange was forced upon Africa by the political and military supremacy of the colonizers. . . ."[21]

The investors exploit not only the Third World's land and natural resources but also its labor. United Brand, Standard Fruit, Del Monte, and Cargill no doubt are in El Salvador for the sugar, bananas, and other such agribusiness export products. But they, along with Alcoa, USX, Westinghouse, Phelps-Dodge, American Standard, Pillsbury, Proctor & Gamble, Chase Manhattan Bank, Bank of America, First National Bank, Standard Oil of New Jersey, Texaco, and at least twenty other major companies, are in that tiny country also for the cheap labor. They reap enormous profits by paying Salvadoran workers subsistence wages to produce everything from aluminum products and baking powder to computers and steel pipes—almost all for export markets.[22]

If Third World nations are impoverished, then, it is not because of their climate or culture or national temperament or some other "natural condition" but because of the highly unnatural things imperialism has been doing to them. It is not because they have lacked natural wealth and industries but, quite the contrary, because the plenitude of their resources proved so inviting to the foreign pillagers, and the strength of their industries so troublesomely competitive to foreign industrialists.

Nor is overpopulation the cause of Third World poverty. The most desperately impoverished areas of the Third World, such as Northeast Brazil and the various famine regions of Africa, are among the more sparsely populated. Countries like India, Pakistan, and Indonesia, whose poverty is often blamed on their supposedly excessive human fertility, actually have less people per square mile than England, Wales, Holland, Japan, Belgium, West Germany, Italy, and a few other industrialized countries.[23] Cuba, with a population of only 5 million people in the 1950s, suffered widespread poverty and hunger; today with a population of 11 million no one is starving.

This does not mean that population growth is never a problem. It is and will become even more serious if populations continue to grow at present rates. Thus, while China today under Communist rule seems able to feed its enormous population of over 1 billion, it may have reached something of an "absolute" demographic limit. At least its own leaders seem to think so and have tried to impose a draconic limitation of one child per family—the only country in history to have done so. For other countries, such as Japan and Barbados, and places like West Bengal and Kerala in India and Java in Indonesia, a substantial increase in population could lead to a serious worsening of already difficult social conditions. In any case, it can be argued that, whatever the social conditions, women in any part of the world should have access to birth control information and devices if they so wish.

The truth is that "the amount of food crop produced in the world at present is sufficient to provide an adequate diet to about 8 billion people—more than twice the world population."[24] The problem is not in food production but in the distribution and uses to which so much of the land is put. There is evidence suggesting that people are not poor because they have large families; rather they have large families because they are poor. A peasant who had land but no children would have to hire laborers to work the fields and thereby suffer a serious reduction of income. Similarly, landless peasants can increase their income if they have more children, that is, more hands to hire out. And as some of the children reach maturity they can be sent into the cities to work so that they might send back part of their earnings—but only if the family is large enough to spare them. As one Third World peasant puts it: "You think I am poor because I have too many children. If I don't have my sons, I wouldn't have half the prosperity I do. And God knows what would happen to me and their mother when we are too old to work and earn."[25]

As the level of prosperity advances, and people achieve a more secure and varied life and accumulate a modest surplus, large families are no longer functional. More likely they are a hinderance to opportunities for schooling and careers.[26] That we are so ready to think of people, per se, as the cause of hunger says a great deal about how we are conditioned to regard people: as an economic liability, a drain on society, when actually they are the creative source of all social wealth. The wealth of any nation begins with its people, with its human labor.[27]

Nor can we blame poverty on the allegedly low productivity, slovenly work habits, and fatalistic cultural passivity of Third World peoples, most of whom admittedly have never heard of the Protestant work ethic. In fact, millions manage to stay alive in the Third World only by driving themselves to the limits of exhaustion, often traveling long distances to work, toiling twelve and fourteen hours each day.

Even in their own homes they labor hard to compensate for the absence of services and amenities more affluent persons take for granted.

Observing the Lever House on New York's fashionable Park Avenue, W. Alpheus Hunton mused: "You look at this tall, striking glass and steel structure and you wonder how many hours of under-paid Black labor and how many thousands of tons of underpriced palm oil and peanuts and cocoa it cost to build it."[28] Hunton's comment graphically makes the point: Third World poverty and multinational industrial wealth are directly linked to each other. The large companies invest not to uplift impoverished countries but to enrich themselves, taking far more out than they ever put in.

Publications on both the Right and the Left, along with the United Nations itself, describe the Third World as composed of "developing" countries. This terminology creates the misleading impression that these countries are escaping from Western economic exploitation and emerging from their impoverishment. In fact, most of them are becoming *more* impoverished. Third World nations are neither "underdeveloped" nor "developing"; they are overexploited and maldeveloped.

Notes

1. Chairman of Castle and Cooke of Dole Standard Fruit Co., interviewed in the documentary film *Controlling Interests* (San Francisco: California Newsreel, 1978).

2. See Karl Marx, *Capital*, volume 1 (Middlesex, England: Penguin Books, 1976), for a full exposition of this.

3. Karl Marx and Frederick Engels, *Manifesto of the Communist Party*, reprinted in *Selected Works*, volume 1 (Moscow: Progress Publishers, 1969).

4. Harry Magdoff, *The Age of Imperialism* (New York: Monthly Review Press, 1969), pp. 20–21.

5. Letter to Horatio Spafford, March 17, 1814.

6. Jonathan Aronson and Elliot Stein, Jr., "Bankers Milk the Third World," *Progressive*, October 1977, pp. 49–51.

7. *New York Times*, June 19, 1986.

8. *Monthly Review*, December 1983, p. 58.

9. *Business Week*, April 20, 1963.

10. F. Polyansky, *An Economic History, The Age of Imperialism (1870–1917)* (Moscow: Progress Publishers, 1973) available from Imported Publications, Chicago; see also Eduardo Galeano, *Open Veins of Latin America, Five Centuries of the Pillage of a Continent* (New York: Monthly Review Press, 1973).

11. Paul Sweezy and Harry Magdoff, in *Monthly Review*, November 1983, p.

37. The $8 billion is a net figure from which about $5 billion in repatriated capital has been subtracted.

12. J. J. Joseph, "Foreign Investment and Profits in Developing Countries," *Political Affairs*, July 1982, p. 12. For earlier data see Pierre Jalee, *The Pillage of the Third World* (New York: Monthly Review Press, 1968).

13. Karl Marx and Frederick Engels, *On Colonialism* (selected writings) (New York: International Publishers, 1972), p. 52.

14. Ernest Mandel, *Marxist Economic Theory*, volume 2 (New York: Monthly Review Press, 1968), p. 447; also L. S. Stavrianos, *Global Rift, The Third World Comes of Age* (New York: William Morrow, 1981), pp. 230–255. Engels, *On Colonialism*, pp. 51–52.

15. Marx and Engels, *On Colonialism*, p. 53; also V. D. Zotov, *The Marxist-Leninist Theory of Society* (Moscow: Progress Publishers, 1985), p. 67.

16. Marx and Engels, *On Colonialism*, p. 319.

17. Mandel, *Marxist Economic Theory*, p. 447, and sources cited therein.

18. E. L. Wheelwright, "Historical Appraisal: Colonialism Past and Present," in S. A. Shah, ed., *US Imperialism in Modern Asia* (Montreal: Afro-Asian Latin American Solidarity Committee, 1972).

19. Walter Rodney, *How Europe Underdeveloped Africa* (Washington, D.C.: Howard University Press, 1974).

20. Ibid., p. 78.

21. Ibid., p. 160; also Stavrianos, *Global Rift*, pp. 196–204, 278–308.

22. For an excellent selection of readings on El Salvador see Marvin Gettleman et al., *El Salvador: Central America and the New Cold War* (New York: Grove Press, 1981).

23. Erland Hofsten, "The Family Planning Controversy," *Monthly Review*, November 1974, p. 19.

24. Barry Commoner, "How Poverty Breeds Overpopulation [and Not the Other Way Around]" in Gary Olson, ed., *How the World Works* (Glenview, Ill.: Scott, Foresman, 1984), p. 43; also Keith Schneider, "Scientific Advances Lead to Era of Food Surplus Around World," *New York Times*, September 9, 1986.

25. Mamhood Mandini, *The Myth of Population Control* (New York: Monthly Review Press, 1972), p. 111.

26. Commoner, "How Poverty Breeds Overpopulation . . ." pp. 33–43.

27. Frances Moore Lappe and Joseph Collins, *World Hunger: Ten Myths*, 4th ed. (San Francisco: Institute for Food and Development Policy, 1979), pp. 10–11.

28. Quoted in Rodney, *How Europe Underdeveloped Africa*, p. 149.

3

Maldevelopment and a "Sharp Philanthropy"

Have we not overlooked all the progress the industrial nations have brought to the Third World? Some people argue: "Western countries did extract wealth from their colonies, but that's only part of the story. Today these countries, especially the United States, invest large sums of capital which help advance the technology and productivity of backward societies. True they take out more than they put in, since they must make something on their investment, but they also create wealth that benefits the recipient country. It is not a simple zero-sum situation; both parties benefit. And since these poor nations do not produce enough for their own needs, then foreign investments are very much welcomed by them."

In response to that argument, I would note that indeed there have been large foreign investments in the poorer nations and these are growing larger all the time. Such investments may increase production and profits but they seldom benefit the ordinary people. The "trickle down" theory works even less in the Third World than in the United States. Investments are usually welcomed by the small upper class of the recipient nation, the people who benefit directly from favorable contracts, payoffs, and kickbacks. Investments do not go into a country, as such, but into a particular set of activities that are beneficial to the investor and to those who service investor interests, such as strong-arm rulers who keep the work force in line. Left out of this arrangement, and often victimized by it, are the bulk of the populace.

Consider agricultural production. There is the notion that the people of poor nations would no longer be hungry if—with some help from rich nations—they learned how to produce more food. The truth is that most Third World nations already produce enough grain and other foods to feed themselves. Many of them are actually food *exporters*. However, their own people do not get in on the distribution. In Mexico, where about 80 percent of the children in rural areas are undernourished, livestock—raised by big landowners for profitable exports—consume more basic grains than the country's entire rural population. At the same time, tons of fresh produce are shipped annually from Mexico to the USA.

Throughout much of the Third World the choice land is owned by major landowners and corporate agribusiness and is either left underutilized or is used for livestock or cash crop exports that bring enormous profits to a few. With "development," or what more accurately should be called "maldevelopment," countries like Indonesia, Ceylon, and Malaysia, which were easily self-sufficient in food production as late as the 1950s, now suffer shortages as their land comes increasingly under the control of multinational agribusiness. Similarly, Africa has become both less self-sufficient in food and more active as a commercial food exporter. Land once used to grow corn and sorghum for local consumption now produces coffee and cotton for export. Deprived of native grains and unable to afford the imported wheat and rice, the people of Africa suffer increasingly from hunger, even as their lands feed people elsewhere.

When profit considerations rather than human need determines how resources are used, then poor nations feed rich ones. Many of the protein products consumed by North Americans (and their livestock and domestic pets) come from Peru, Mexico, Panama, India, Costa Rica, and other countries where grave protein shortages exist. Even as large numbers of children in these countries die from malnutrition, food production is increasingly geared to the export market. Under capitalism, money is invested only where money is to be made.

The problem is neither poor lands nor unproductive populations but foreign exploitation and class inequality. A mere 2.5 percent of landowners (mostly absentee owners including agribusiness firms) control almost 75 percent of the world's land.[1] In Northeast Brazil 1 percent of the population owns 45 percent of the land—the choice land. Vast, lush sugar plantations—owned by "farmers" who spend most of their time in Rio de Janeiro beachfront luxury apartments—are surrounded by scrubby dirt farms too small to feed the families that work them. Deprived of the fertile lands by agribusiness, the peasants in various countries are driven to the hillsides and less fertile terrain, where they work soil that is so poor it will bear a crop for only a year or two. The overcultivated and depleted soil is soon transformed into barren land by both the greedy rich and the needy poor, inviting more famine.

If poor nations are so hamstrung as to be unable to help themselves, it is equally difficult for them to band together and help each other. Trade among them has actually declined. As they all export more to the rich nations in order to pay off their astronomical debts, they also buy less from each other and become increasingly locked into the imperialist system. Due to the maldevelopment imposed on them by foreign investors, many Third World countries have not had the chance to develop natural markets with each other. Instead, they often produce the same export products—which further stymies trade between them.

Meanwhile, trade between the imperialist and Third World nations is set in terms that are favorable to the former, allowing them to sell high and buy cheap. As Carlos Andres Perez, then-president of Venezuela, stated in an open letter to the president of the United States in 1974:

> Each year we, the countries which produce coffee, meat, tin, copper, iron or petroleum, have been handing over a larger amount of our products in order to obtain imports of machinery and other manufactured goods, and this has resulted in a constant and growing outflow of capital and impoverishment of our countries.
>
> In Latin America, as in the other developing countries, we can assert that the developed countries have been taking advantage of the fundamental needs of the Latin American, Asian or African [people]. To cite the particular case of Venezuela, petroleum prices showed a steady decline for many years, while our country was obliged to purchase manufactured goods from the United States at ever-higher prices, which, day after day, restricted even further the possibilities of development and well-being for Venezuelans.[2]

If capital investment were intended not only to profit the investor but to uplift poor nations, then why do Third World peoples grow poorer and why do their nations go ever deeper into debt? Private foreign investment does not develop Third World countries, it maldevelops them. In 1982, a United Nations special committee studying the impact of multinational corporations on development found that a "host country" may experience high rates of growth while its income distribution does not improve and even deteriorates.

High income accrues "largely to domestic elites associated with foreign interests," while "basic needs of the population such as food, health, education, and housing" are left unattended.[3]

One such host country is Brazil. In 1964, soon after the reformist government of President Joao Goulart announced its plans to distribute millions of acres of land to the poor and nationalize seven US oil companies, it was overthrown by a US-trained and financed right-wing military. The new regime immediately created a most inviting climate for business investment: labor unions were tightly restricted; strikes were outlawed; and generous tax rebates and tax-free export earnings were granted to foreign investors. Within the next ten years there emerged the "Brazilian miracle," as it was described on the financial pages of US newspapers. The gross national product tripled, growing faster than any in the world including Japan's. But the growth reached only a small segment of the population. The real income of the poorest 80 percent *declined by over half* in the decade after Goulart. One-third of the population had tuberculosis; one-half of the children had no schools; and the infant mortality rate climbed to the second highest in the hemisphere. Hunger and starvation increased as vast acreages of farmland were converted to export crops.

Two multinational corporations controlled 80 percent of Brazil's electronics industry, as Brazilian firms were driven out of business. American and other foreign companies controlled 60 percent of heavy industry, 90 percent of pharmaceuticals, and 95 percent of automobile production. All this new investment was of no benefit to Brazilian workers. Under the military dictatorship the twelve-hour day was instituted; the unemployment rate climbed; and Brazilian workers had the highest industrial accident rate in the world.

Meanwhile, $12 billion a year was spent on the Brazilian army, the most powerful in Latin America. Thousands of trade unionists, students, clergy, peasants, and intellectuals were arrested, tortured, and murdered. In 1975, eighteen Catholic bishops and clerics issued a statement—immediately banned by the military—protesting these developments:

> The "Brazilian miracle" has resulted in privileges for the wealthy. It has come as a curse upon those who have not asked for it. The rich become always richer and the poor always poorer in this process of economic concentration. Far from being the inevitable result of natural deficiencies, this tragedy is the consequence of international capitalism. Devel-

opment came to be defined not in terms of the interests of Brazilian society but in terms of the profits made by foreign corporations and their associates in our country. The absence of freedom, the violence of repression, the injustices, the impoverishment of the people—all in favor of foreign capital.[4]

Today in the maldeveloping countries, we find more factories, more exports, more giant agribusiness—and more poverty and hunger than ever before. After a decade of a very good growth rate in the Philippines, according to the *Washington Post*, "the average Filipino is probably worse off than when the decade began."[5] Of the 9 million Filipino children between six months and six years of age, at least one-third are either "moderately" or severely malnourished. Yet the Philippines has become a food exporter in the last two decades, selling abroad large quantities of the very rice and vegetable products needed by Filipino children.[6]

Fifty percent of Guatemala's Indian children die before the age of five from malnutrition and related illnesses. It has been argued that such poverty is historical, an original condition: the Indians have always been poor. In truth, the Mayan Indian population had more abundant food supplies and better lands in the fifteenth century before the Spaniards arrived than they do today. Their staples were corn and beans, supplemented by fruits, vegetables, and wild game. With the arrival of the Europeans the forested plains were cleared for the growth of cotton, sugar, coffee, and the raising of beef for export to more affluent nations. The Indians were forced back into the hills where the land was poor and quickly eroded. Today, the largest landowners and investors in Guatemala are American agribusiness corporations.[7]

Foreign investment has led to the nearly complete extermination of tribal peoples in the tropical rain forests of Brazil, Venezuela, Colombia, Peru, Bolivia, and Ecuador. Land speculators and foreign capital interests, mostly from Great Britain, the United States, and West Germany have grabbed vast tracts of the Amazon interior. One US firm controlled by the Sellig Brothers bought and resold over 3.3 million acres of land in Brazil. What the conquistadores began with their swords is being completed by real-estate companies, and mining and oil corporations with dynamite, napalm, machine guns, and airplanes, as bands of heavily armed men employed by the companies penetrate the interior on extermination expeditions. In the upper Amazon Basin and the Mato Grosso region in Western Brazil not more than 50,000 Indians survive where several decades ago there were upwards of a million. One British-owned corporation alone is held responsible for the death of 30,000 Indians. In the last thirty years, ninety tribes have disappeared in the Amazon basin.[8]

The *Times* of London, in a report entitled "Genocide," provides a glimpse of what "development" has meant for the Indian tribes of Brazil:

> Of the 19,000 Mundurus believed to have existed in the thirties, only 1,200 are left. In Aripuana, the Cintas were attacked by air [with] sticks of dynamite. Only 500 survived out of 10,000. . . . Two tribes of the Patachos were exterminated when they were given smallpox injections. . . . The strength of the Guaranis has been reduced from 5,000 to 300. . . .
>
> Some, like the Taipainas—in the case of a gift of sugar laced with arsenic—have disappeared altogether. . . . The Nhambiquera Indians were mowed down by machinegun fire. The Maxacalis were given fire water by the landowners who employed gunmen to shoot them when they were drunk. . . . To exterminate the tribe of Beicos de Pau, an expedition was formed which went up the Aribos River carrying presents and a great quantity of foodstuffs for the Indians. These were mixed with arsenic and formicides.[9]

Or as *Fortune* magazine (August 1974) proudly proclaimed regarding the Amazon development: "Big Business is moving into the backlands."

Along with foreign investors, the wealthy classes in poor countries have a regressive effect on their countries' economies. They take the money they accumulate from other people's labor (or from payoffs and theft) and spend it on imported luxury goods rather than on locally made products, or they put it into real estate or into foreign bank accounts, rather than invest in local development that would provide jobs and products for mass consumption. When the erstwhile president of the Philippines, Ferdinand Marcos (with an assist from his wife), stashed away hundreds of millions of dollars in Swiss banks, jewelry, and Manhattan real estate, he was doing very little to help develop the Filipino economy and much to retard it. The total wealth he accumulated (much of it taken from the state treasury) has been estimated at anywhere from $6 billion to $10 billion, the better part of which was taken out of the Philippines.

Within the maldeveloped nations, highly unequal income distributions mean that luxury dwellings will be built rather than affordable decent houses for workers, cosmetic surgery clinics for the rich instead of hospitals for the poor, air-conditioned corporate office buildings instead of water-purification projects in the villages, expensive automobiles instead of buses and trains, posh country clubs instead of schools, Coca-Cola plants instead of dairies. For decades the gap between rich and poor has been widening—not only between nations but within them.

THE FOREIGN AID TRAP

Private capital investment has done little to alleviate "underdevelopment" and much to create it, but what of foreign aid and foreign loans? These monies are supposedly invested not for profit's sake but to help the recipient nation develop its agriculture, technology, roads, and ports. But if that nation's economy is in the hands of a small wealthy class and a coterie of multinational companies, then, as with private investment, the "aid" will likely be applied in ways that serve the dominant economic interests. A "sharp philanthropy" is what Marx called the assistance rendered by the colonizer to the colonized.[10] Almost all foreign aid to Third World countries ends up helping the rich at the expense of the poor. The new roads that are built usually go from the big plantations, mines, oil fields, and refineries straight to the ports—in support of extractive industries.

The principal beneficiaries of agricultural technology have been the larger commercial farms.[11] Be they called "modernization" or "Green Revolution," rural-aid programs are designed to upgrade agricultural production through the introduction of pesticides, chemical fertilizers, irrigation, land reclamation, mechanization, and the development of new grains. They raise the capital costs of production and the value of the land, leading to the displacement of the poorer peasants and the expansion of large agribusiness devoted to commercial crops. Because only big landholders have the money to invest in the new technology, they usually are the only ones to profit from it. With their coffers swollen with new export earnings, they acquire— often by force and subterfuge—still more properties for investment and drive more peasants from the land, thereby causing more hunger and deracination. In any case, most US aid is in the form of military assistance. As of 1987, the US government was spending more on the counterrevolution in Nicaragua than on aid to the world's forty poorest nations.[12]

Aid programs launched by the World Bank and its affiliate, the International Development Association (IDA), show the same pattern. Formally linked to the United Nations, but acting independently and dominated by rich donors like the United States, the World Bank gives out loans of relatively modest sums on a piecemeal project basis to countries that face monumental problems of poverty. More than a third of its loans go for energy, transportation, telecommunications, and other such projects that bring little benefit to the poor. Funds slated to help small producers rarely do so. In Bangladesh, for instance, a $12 million World Bank project to install 3,000 deep tubewells for irrigation to serve peasants in arid areas primarily benefited large agribusiness farms. The big landowners were the political bosses who controlled the cooperatives that received the tubewells.[13] The World Bank has been lending money to famine-ridden nations for tourist resorts. The Bank lent Niger $5 million for an airport that, in the words of its own report, would "help stimulate exports of meat and vegetables, which, because they are perishable, must rely on air transport."[14]

US aid is not intended to change the social structures of recipient nations but to shore up existing class relations, creating what our leaders call "stability." Aid is cut off when genuine reforms are attempted, when the reformers tamper with the distribution of class power and wealth. Thus in 1970, as the democratically elected government in Chile, under the presidency of Salvador Allende, initiated social and economic reforms, all US aid was cut off—except for military assistance to the Chilean military, which was increased. President Kennedy spoke accurately when he said that "foreign aid is a method by which the US maintains a position of influence and control around the world. . . ."[15]

The US government compensates corporations for losses due to war, revolution, insurrection, or confiscation by a foreign government, and refuses aid to any country that nationalizes without full compensation of the assets owned by US firms. By the 1980s, it became US policy in places like Africa to make aid contingent upon a country's willingness to dismantle public sectors of the economy and hand them over to private (usually US) firms. US aid is used to denationalize profitable enterprises, and nationalize unprofitable ones. At times, Washington gives funds to Latin American governments for the purpose of having them expropriate unprofitable American companies at above-market prices. Thus, some multinationals are well compensated for ridding themselves of holdings that are losing money, dumping them into the lap of a foreign government in exchange for money provided by the US taxpayer.

US aid usually influences the recipient nation's skills, tastes, and needs so that the dependency on American products continues well after the aid program has ceased. The recipient country must sign an agreement with the Agency for International Development (AID) that commits it to come up with a certain amount (usually 25 percent) in matching funds for any aid project. American monies are allocated often with the express condition that they be used to buy American goods transported in American ships at American prices.[16] This "has meant that three-fourths of U.S. foreign-assistance money remains in the U.S."[17] According to AID administrator Peter Mc-Pherson: "Two-thirds of what we give comes back in 18 months in the form of purchases."[18] Technical assistance grants are a boon to American consulting firms since all aid consultants must come from the USA. Along with aid, the needy nation has to open itself to US capital penetration. Thus in 1966, in a widely publicized instance, India was denied a shipment of US food until it agreed to accept a chemical fertilizer plant run by an American corporation.[19]

Then there are the foreign loans from Western banks and the balance-of-payments support from the International Monetary Fund (IMF) to financially troubled countries. (Member nations control the IMF by a system of weighted voting which ensures dominance by the wealthiest countries, principally the USA.) Since 1973, the Third World debt has grown from $73 billion to more than $1 trillion, that is, $1,000 billion, an unpayable sum. One of the causes of indebtedness is the debt itself. The more a nation borrows, the greater is its payment burden and the greater the pressure to borrow still more to meet expenses—often at higher interest rates and shorter payment terms.

An increasingly larger portion of the earnings of indebted nations goes to servicing the debt, leaving still less for domestic consumption and creating an even greater need to borrow. So the debt increases budgetary deficits, which in turn increase the debt. By 1986, 80 percent of Paraguay's export earnings went to pay the interest on its $2 billion foreign debt. Most other debtor countries must devote anywhere from one-third to two-thirds of their earnings to service debts. By 1983 the money collected by foreign banks in the form of interest payments on Third World debts was three times higher than their profits on direct Third-World investments.[20]

Eventually, to qualify for more loans a country must agree to the

IMF's "stabilization" terms. The terms invariably include cutting back on domestic consumption while producing more for export—thus earning more of the hard currency needed to pay its debt. Countries have had to cut back on their already insufficient spending in the fields of health, education, and human welfare, and penalize the common population "with wage freezes and higher prices while offering generous tax and legislative concessions to foreign investors."[21]

But if these foreign loans have intensified the impoverishment of Third World nations, why do these same nations keep asking for more and more money? Sometimes they have no other means of getting by. In other instances, borrowing serves the private interests of rulers. Nations as such do not make the decisions to borrow money; their leaders do. And these leaders are often outrageously corrupt military and political figures who amass personal fortunes by siphoning off substantial portions of the borrowed funds.[22] The pattern of a growing national debt and a self-enriching elite could be observed in Chile under Pinochet, Nicaragua under Somoza, the Philippines under Marcos, Zaire under Mobutu, and Indonesia under Suharto, to name a few.[23] But the people are not left out entirely. The accumulated national debt becomes theirs to pay. As Marx noted over a century ago: "The only part of the so-called national wealth that actually enters into the collective possession of a modern nation is—the national debt."[24]

In sum, foreign aid and foreign loans may have a philanthropic appearance, but they are not equalizers and were never intended to be. Attempts to augment the incomes of the mass of the people and better their work conditions would increase the cost of labor and cut into profit margins. Aid from rich nations and loans from rich banks are not likely to be granted if the funds will be used to compete against the capital accumulation interests of the donors. As currently dispensed, these monies do their share to aggravate rather than diminish economic inequality.

THE FREE WORLD PURGATORY

Some defenders of capitalism might argue: "References to poverty and cheap labor in the Third World are misleading. By American standards, foreign workers making sixty cents an hour appear terribly underpaid, but such a wage might be quite sufficient given the cost of living in some countries. Stories of peasants driven from the land conjure up images of starving populations, but the displaced peasantry becomes the new proletariat, as happened earlier in Western capitalist nations. What we are describing, then, is the transition—admittedly a sometimes painful one—from traditional society to modern capitalism." Yet as the evidence treated earlier indicates, the "transition" has brought greater impoverishment for the many and more enrichment for the few. Third World wages are not only terribly low by American standards but inadequate in Third World countries.

According to the mainstream theory of development, the backward economic sector in a Third World country releases its workers who then find employment in the modern sector at higher wages. As capital accumulates in the modern sector, business reinvests its profits, thus creating still more jobs. Finally, as traditional and less-productive occupations are destroyed, all the workers are absorbed into the modern economy and come to share in its prosperity.

The reality is something else. The present-day failure of the Irish economy might serve as an example, even though Ireland is not normally thought of as a Third World country. Lacking in industry and development, the Republic of Ireland (composed of the twenty-six poorest counties) offered grants to multinational corporations to locate there, along with tax rates ranging from 0 to 10 percent. It was anticipated that the companies would build in Ireland, hire Irish people, expend funds, and reinvest profits in that country. In fact, after locating, the firms invested little of their own capital and instead took full advantage of the Irish government's grants. They hired a few low-paid Irish workers while importing most of their own professional staffs. They reaped big profits but put hardly any of it back into the country. By 1987, more than 10 percent of Ireland's gross national product (GNP) openly was taken out of the country to the USA or Europe by foreign companies. Another 10 percent was being sneaked out by various means. Thus, some 20 percent of Ireland's GNP—practically all the profits of its nonagricultural sector—was being extracted by the multinationals. Furthermore, the depressed condition of the economy has sustained Irish emigration, including the exodus of young professionals.[25]

As the traditional economic sector collapses in many Third World countries, and people are driven off the land and out of their crafts and trades, they flee to the city in search of work. Some of the more fortunate find employment at subsistence wages in factories, mines, or hotels. Others find seasonal work, odd jobs, or enter into black marketeering. Some are absorbed into the public sector, including the numbers recruited as police or conscripted into the army. But the vast multitude are left scratching out a desperate existence in the teeming slums.[26]

In other words, the displaced peasantry is less likely to be transformed into a new proletariat than into shantytown dwellers, beggars, peddlers, prostitutes, and an unschooled, underfed, underemployed reserve army of labor, desperate enough to work for meager sums under the worst conditions. Capitalism could not exist without a reserve army of labor to help depress wages and bolster profits. In most industrialized countries, social programs cushion some of the misery endured by the poor and underemployed. In the Third World there are no cushions to speak of. Let us look at some of the appalling results:[27]

- Of the world's population of over 4 billion people, about 1 billion suffer from malnutrition and over 500 million are actually starving. Every year some 40 million people, half of them children, die from hunger and malnutrition.
- The International Labor Organization reports that child labor continues throughout much of the world where the earnings of offspring are needed to supplement the incomes of poor families. More than 52 million children, under the age of fifteen, work up to twelve hours daily for less than half the wages adults earn. Specifically criticized for ignoring minimum-age legislation were Thailand, India, Malaysia, South Africa, Guatemala, Spain, and Italy. Harsh conditions have caused a higher rate of sickness among children who work than among those who do not. For instance, a common ailment among working children in Naples is polyneuritis, a paralysis brought on by inhaling poisonous glues used in leather factories.
- According to a 1981 United Nations report, 2 million children in Thailand, many under the age of ten, are employed illegally in factories, working ten hours daily, seven days a week, for fifty cents to seventy cents a day. Thousands, some as young as six years, are sold by their impoverished parents into annual or lifetime work in factories, farms, homes, or brothels.
- The *International Herald Tribune* reports that most of Peru's 16 million people are moving from "malnutrition to the brink

of starvation." Conditions worsened after Peru's military government imposed an austerity program that eliminated food, fuel, and transportation subsidies in order to qualify for further IMF loans.

- According to statistics circulated by UNICEF: 25 to 30 percent of the children in the Third World die before the age of four from malnutrition and related diseases. More than 10 million children under four years are so seriously malnourished that their physical and mental development are at risk.
- Of every ten Bolivians, six cannot read, while half of the children of that country do not attend school. In the cemetary at Catavi thousands of tiny graves are scattered among the larger ones for adults. Of every two children born in the mining camps, one dies soon after opening its eyes. The surviving child, if male, will almost certainly grow up to be a miner and will die from silicosis of the lungs well before his fortieth year.
- Researchers at the University of Witswatersrand in Johannesburg found that about one-third of South Africa's Black children below age fourteen are chronically malnourished. In some of the "homelands" the proportion of malnourished children exceeds 60 and 70 percent.
- The mayor of Fort Liberté, Haiti, says the residents of his town are happy that Baby Doc Duvalier was overthrown but all their problems remain. He notes there is still no electricity or clean drinking water in the town and people are still dying of typhoid fever, intestinal diseases, and malaria. In addition, many people develop eye problems from trying to work in the dim glow of kerosene lamps.
- About 150,000 Bengali children go blind every year because of malnutrition and a lack of Vitamin A in their diet, according to UNICEF.
- Faced with chronic unemployment and impending starvation, many people sell their blood to commercial blood companies. In South India some 40,000 persons so maintain themselves. Blood is one of Haiti's major exports. Given their poor diets, ill health, and excessive blood donations, many donors suffer impairment of the body's natural immunity mechanisms, leaving them susceptible to sometimes fatal viruses. Sold to hospitals in industrialized countries like the United States, their

plasma may sometimes be the source of seriously infectious diseases.

Now consider a few individual cases in some detail:

Alfredo and His Family

On the outskirts of Bogata, Colombia, a brickmaker named Alfredo and his wife and eleven children work from 5 A.M. to 6 P.M. shoveling mud and water to make bricks. Alfredo's children, some as young as four and five years, carry bricks all day long. The bricks get a good price on the market but most of it goes to the supervisor and the absentee landowner. The family is unable to meet its minimal expenses. Its diet consists mostly of gruel. There is no clean water supply. The entire family lives in a one-room hovel with no possessions other than the clothes on their backs and a few pans and utensils. The children are scrawny and underfed. The bricklayer himself suffers from a variety of diseases caused by the poor diet and the constant contact with mud and dampness. He and his wife look twenty years older than they are. The primitive living accommodations provided by the owner stand next to the ovens where the bricks are baked. These ovens let off noxious gases that the family breathes. If it rains and the unbaked bricks are ruined, Alfredo takes the loss, sometimes consisting of two or three days' labor. To survive he must borrow money from the boss at usurious rates. After thirty years of labor, Alfredo has not a peso and is thousands of pesos in debt. He and others like him are not allowed to unionize.

Were they to go on strike they would be evicted and jailed by the police. Alfredo, and others in his family who are old enough, are taken to the polls at election time by the supervisor to vote as instructed, their hands stamped with the appropriate color depending on the party they choose. If they refuse to vote, or do not vote for the party of the owner's choice, they will be kicked off the land. (Colombia is considered by US political leaders to be a "democracy.")

Increasingly, Alfredo has been coming home drunk and beating his wife and children. One day in a drunken fit he threatens to kill his family, causing one of his children to exclaim: "Kill us, Papa, then we will be free of our misery." The misery of Alfredo and his family is shared by millions of other impoverished people in Colombia.

Lee Mi Wha

In Seoul, South Korea, a textile worker, Lee Mi Wha, age nineteen, works twelve hours a day, seven days a week, tending five machines in a deafening mill. For this she gets $65 a month or about eighteen cents an hour. At some of the other mills the shifts are from fourteen to sixteen hours. If she wants a day off she has to earn it by working a twenty-four-hour shift. Living in company barracks with other young women, Lee rarely has the opportunity to go out. Originally from an impoverished farm, she misses her family and the countryside. Because of the endless toil, foul air, unsafe conditions, noise and filth, the women workers suffer from depression, impaired hearing, and other work-connected illnesses. They have no sick leave, no unemployment or disability insurance, no retirement benefits or occupational safety protections. If they are maimed or injured, they are tossed out to fend for themselves. Attempts by Lee and her coworkers to protest these conditions would lead to immediate dismissal—or possible arrest and torture.

It is not true that the mass of people in the maldeveloped countries of the "Free World" get along well on modest but sufficient incomes. What they face is increasingly severe conditions of malnutrition and hunger, chronic sickness, underemployment, cruel and dangerous work conditions, substandard housing, lack of clean drinking water, and the absence of adequate medical, transportational, recreational, and educational facilities.

Even the middle-class people of these nations, far fewer in number and relatively more privileged than what is considered middle class in the United States, are experiencing a sharp decline in their living standards. In the 1980s, as the income gap between rich and poor in the Third World widened, more middle-class people were pushed into poverty.[28]

There is a connection between the maldevelopment of Third World countries and the capital-accumulation process carried out by the multinational corporations. Apologists for capitalism deny the link. For them, underdevelopment is caused by backward traditions and cultures, overpopulation, deficient resources, and the like. By this view, capitalism is the source of development and not the cause of maldevelopment. The poverty of nations is taken as the original condition of all precapitalist countries which can be overcome by adopting capitalist values and capitalist methods of production.[29]

As we have seen, the advanced Western capitalist nations are not the mentors of Third World development but a major cause of under-development. What they introduced into Asia, Africa, and Latin America was a *dependent* capitalism, linking the nonindustrial to the industrial world in an exploitative, one-sided relationship (as opposed to the more equitable and mutually beneficial links that might exist between two industrialized nations such as the United States and Great Britain). This dependent capitalism has the following key traits:

1. The Third World's natural resources are plundered by the advanced capitalist nations, and its industrial development is suppressed or retarded, in some cases for centuries.
2. The Third World's economic infrastructure is distorted, organized around a few extractive industries and export agriculture. Growing capital investments from richer nations bring a limited industrial development whose goal is to use the available cheap labor to produce commodities for affluent Western consumer markets.
3. The needs of Third World people for housing, food, medical care, and education become superfluous to this process of capital extraction.
4. The homegrown capitalist classes of the Third World use their money for high-living consumption and external investment. The more politically influential among them are often engaged in a wide-scale plunder of public monies and resources. Like the foreign investors, they contribute nothing while taking a good deal out of their own nation's economy.

A lot of consciously coordinated effort is required to reproduce the conditions that keep this exploitative system in operation. This brings us to another crucial component: the role of state power in the preservation of imperialism.

Notes

1. Frances Moore Lappe and Joseph Collins, *Food First* (New York: Houghton Mifflin, 1977); also Susan DeMarco and Susan Sechler, *The Fields Have Turned Brown* (Washington, D.C.: Agribusiness Accountability Project, 1975); Gregg Jones,

"On Fertile Negros, Filipinos Die of Malnutrition," *Boston Globe*, September 7, 1986.

2. *New York Times*, September 25, 1974.

3. *New Leader*, August 9–23, 1982.

4. This quotation and much of the information above is from the documentary *Controlling Interests* (San Francisco: California Newsreel, 1978); also James Kohl, "Secret War in Brazil," *Progressive*, August 1977, p. 35.

5. *Washington Post*, October 30, 1980.

6. Ibid.

7. Findings of World Health Organization specialist Dr. Moises Behar, reported in the *New York Times*, August 26, 1975; also Report by the Guatemalan Church in Exile, Washington, D.C., 1985.

8. David St. Clair, *The Mighty Mighty Amazon* (New York: Funk and Wagnalls, 1968); "Brazil's Dead Indians: The Killing of an Unwanted Race," in *Atlas*, January 1970, pp. 22–29; *Der Spiegel*, October 27, 1969, November 3 and November 10, 1969; *Sunday Times* (London), February 23, 1969; PBS special report on the Amazon, July 21, 1987.

9. *Times* (London), February 23, 1975.

10. Karl Marx and Frederick Engels, *On Colonialism* (selected writings) (New York: International Publishers, 1972), p. 49.

11. Frances Moore Lappe and Joseph Collins, *World Hunger: Ten Myths*, 4th ed. (San Francisco: Institute for Food and Development Policy, 1979), pp. 42–44.

12. According to Robin Broad and John Cavanaugh, "Nicaragua: A Barefoot Peril," *Newsday*, August 6, 1987.

13. Penny Lenoux, "The World Bank" in Gary Olson, ed., *How the World Works* (Glenview, Ill.: Scott, Foresman, 1984), p. 121.

14. Annual Report of the International Bank for Reconstruction and Development, Washington, D.C., 1974, p. 28.

15. Teresa Hayter, *Aid As Imperialism* (London: Penguin Books, 1971), p. 5; also Patricia Adams and Lawrence Solomon, *In the Name of Progress, The Underside of Foreign Aid* (Toronto: Energy Probe Research Foundation, 1985); and Frances Moore Lappe et al., *Aid As Obstacle* (San Francisco: Institute for Food and Development Policy, 1981); George Lopez and Michael Stohl, eds., *Development, Dependence, and State Repression* (Westport, Conn.: Greenwood Press, 1985).

16. Hayter, *Aid as Imperialism*, pp. 95–97.

17. Tom Barry, Beth Wood, and Deb Preusch, *The Other Side of Paradise* (New York: Grove Press, 1984), p. 159.

18. Ibid.

19. Michael Sweeney, "From Dustbowl to Saigon: The 'People's Bank' Builds an Empire," *Ramparts*, November 1970, p. 43.

20. Michael Tanzer, "An Invaluable Work," *Monthly Review*, December 1983, p. 58.

21. Cheryl Payer, "The Bretton Woods Twins," in Olson, *How the World Works*, p. 107; see also Payer's *The Debt Trap* (New York: Monthly Review Press, 1975); and her *The World Bank* (New York: Monthly Review Press, 1982).

22. See for instance Janet Page, "Uruguay: Democracy and Debt," *IPS Feature* (Institute for Policy Studies, Washington, D.C., February 25, 1986).

23. See *Washington Post*, April 27, 1986 for a report on Suharto.

24. Karl Marx, *Capital*, volume 1 (Middlesex, England: Penguin Books, 1976), p. 919.

25. Rachel Hoffman's correspondence, *Washington Post*, March 28, 1987.

26. See Juan Garcia Passalacqua in *San Juan Star*, August 1, 1981.

27. All the examples that follow are from: *New York Times*, April 11, 1978;

Wall Street Journal, July 22, 1981; Michael Tanzer, review in *Monthly Review,* December 1983; Report of the International Labor Organization, 1980; Report to the United Nations by the Anti-Slavery Society (London) 1980, cited in the *Guardian,* September 3, 1980; *Washington Post,* July 16, 1986; *International Herald Tribune,* July 11, 1978; *Workers World,* January 16, 1976; UNICEF report, cited in the *Guardian,* April 28, 1976; report of International Conference of National Commissions in *New York Times,* May 11, 1986; Glenn Davis, executive director of UNICEF, on CBS radio, March 21, 1975; *The Brickmaker,* a documentary film (New York: Cinema Guild, 1972); report by UN Economic and Social Commission for Asia and the Pacific, cited in the *Guardian,* January 12, 1983; Associate Press, October 11, 1978.

28. A. Kent MacDougall, "In Third World, All but the Rich Are Poorer," *Los Angeles Times,* November 4, 1984.

29. See James Dietz, "Development and Imperialism," *Monthly Review,* November 1976, pp. 58–59.

4

The Mean Methods of Imperialism (I)

When imperial domination is imposed upon a people, they do not always remain passive victims. Contrary to the image of a mute and mindless multitude, they frequently organize, protest, strike, resist, sabotage, riot, and rebel in the hope of bettering their lot or preventing its further deterioration. In turn, the foreign colonizers and the collaborationist Third World rulers will exercise every measure of control to keep the people in tow—from the subtlest manipulation to the most dreadful violence.

Hollywood provides three basic scenarios, which for many of us serve as our first—and sometimes most lasting—impression of imperialism:

- *The Walt Disney Idyllic.* The White colonizers arrive in what is a fertile but empty land. Seeing nobody around, they stake out a claim. After fighting off some predatory animals and enduring a few hardships, they manage to build nice homes and settle down on their farms.
- *The South Seas Romance.* The White colonizers arrive to be greeted by smiling natives who offer gifts and throw their country open to the wise and beneficial rule of the newcomers. The White leader falls in love with the friendly chief's beautiful daughter and a happy time is had by all.
- *The Thin-Red-Line Heroic Epic.* White colonizers arrive peacefully intended, only to be attacked by shrieking, bloodlusting savages inexplicably bent on committing fiendish acts. In self-defense, the brave, outnumbered White colonizers fight back and eventually exterminate the horrid savages and establish a civilized order.

The real picture is something else. In the history of imperialism we find very few, if any, empty lands and very few, if any, peaceable colonizations. True, there has been much savagery and violence, but almost all of it has been perpetrated by the foreign usurpers. We need to be reminded that *only by establishing military supremacy* were the European and North American colonizers able to eliminate the crafts and industries of Third World peoples, control their markets, extort tribute, undermine their cultures, destroy their villages, steal their lands and natural resources, enslave their labor, and accumulate vast wealth. Military supremacy was usually achieved after repeated and unspeakably brutal applications of armed violence.

Think of what the Spaniards did in South America; the Portuguese in Angola and Mozambique; the British in China, India, and Ireland; the Belgians in the Congo; the Germans in Southwest Africa; the Dutch in the East Indies; the French in North Africa and Indochina; the Japanese in Korea, Manchuria, and China; the Italians in Ethiopia, Somalia, and Libya; and the Americans in the Philippines, Central America, Indochina, and in North America itself (against Native American Indians, Mexicans, and African Americans). Actually it is difficult for most of us to think about it, since imperialism's terrible history is not regularly taught in our schools nor treated by our media.

The colonization of the Third World by European and North American powers is often treated as a "natural" phenomenon, involving "development" and "dependency" and "specialization of markets." But what is most impressive is imperialism's *un*natural quality, its reliance upon force and violence to impose itself upon the world. Empires do not "naturally" develop, nor do they emerge innocently "in a fit of absentmindedness," as was said of the British empire. Rather they are welded together with deceit, fraud, blood, and sorrow. They are built upon the sword, the whip, and the gun. The following is a generalized scenario depicting the methods of colonization over the centuries.

- *Foothold.* A company of investors or "adventurers" seeking wealth, accompanied by small numbers of officials and military from the imperial nation, encamp in the "primitive land." Usually they are chartered and subsidized by their governments. The native population makes contact with the seemingly friendly colonizers and soon learn that the visitors are there to stay.

- *Expansion.* The land companies and mining interests, assisted by government officials connected to the expedition, make claim to ownership of huge territories, minerals, and other resources. European settlers arrive, including farmers, plantation owners, and herders whose migration is usually subsidized by the imperial nation. A "protectorate" is quickly formed by the imperial state, which now assumes responsibility for the security of the land claims and the lives of its nationals.

- *Military Clashes and Build-up.* When the indigenous people refuse to give up their rights to the land, they are subjected to harsh attacks by the colonizers' military force. With desperate courage they fight back. These early clashes do not necessarily go well for the colonizers, who are quick to summon more troops and heavier firepower from the imperial state.

- *Peace Councils and Treaties.* Solemn proclamations of peace and friendship are entered upon with the tribes. Treaties are signed to reassure the indigenous peoples that their interests are to be respected. These agreements often harbor deceptive clauses that expand imperial privileges and diminish native rights. In any case, treaty protections are soon regularly violated. The treaty's real functions are (a) to put the natives off their guard for awhile and (b) lend an appearance of legitimacy to the venture, as something based on a "joint agreement" between the colonizer and the colonized.

- *Divide and Conquer.* The colonizers play on tribal rivalries, encourage tribal wars, arm one side against another, bestow special privileges to some chiefs to stoke the envy and enmity of others. They bribe chiefs and use them as a surrogate influence over the people. (In parts of Eastern Africa where the tribes were ruled by democratic councils that had no chiefs, the British set up puppet chiefs as their instruments.)

- *Use of Mercenaries.* The imperialists enlist natives of dissident or displaced tribes into the ranks of the colonial army, along with mercenaries from other European nationalities (as did the British in India, the French in North Africa and Indochina, and the Germans in Southwest Africa). Attacks against native resistance intensifies.

- *Imperial Cooperation*. While the imperial powers sometimes fight among themselves, they just as often cooperate and co-ordinate their efforts in carving up continents and subduing indigenous peoples.
- *Use of Missionaries*. Missionaries attack the existing value systems and customs that sustain the indigenous peoples. They "domesticate" natives into compounds, teach submission to and love of the White people's God and civil authority. They dissuade natives from pursuing sinful pursuits such as rebellion and armed resistance.
- *Final Solution*. The colonizers engage in all-out military attacks with forces enjoying a vast superiority in numbers and armaments. They exterminate whole villages and tribes, cut off food supplies, deprive natives of water and pasture for their livestock, assassinate native leaders, deliberately spread infectious diseases (in North America and more recently in South America). They introduce and encourage the natives' use of addictives such as alcohol or—as did the British in China—opium. They conduct mass executions of prisoners, use captives for forced labor in mines or on farms, or for building railroads or other such purposes.[1]

In some instances, the indigenous population is almost entirely exterminated or otherwise displaced, as in the Caribbean, North America, Australia, and Hawaii. When portions of the colonized population manage to survive, it is due to several things.

First, there is usually a need for native labor. A European colonizing nation that slaughters the entire indigenous population deprives itself of that most valuable productive force: human labor. It must then import migrant workers from other colonized lands or from Europe.

Second, in past colonizations, the missionaries who worked closely with the imperial authorities developed an interest in the survival of the native populations, as was the case in parts of Africa and Latin America. Policies of extermination, if allowed to go full course, would bring an end to missionary work and the termination of overseas missions for want of wards to whom God's word could be administered.

Third, there is the outrage that arises from anti-imperialists within the colonizing nation and abroad, as reports of atrocities seep back home. This opposition has seldom turned events around but it does sometimes cause the imperialists to act with greater circumspection. In some cases, protests throughout the world and within the imperialist country have exercised a measurable restraint upon policy.

Fourth, the valiant resistance of native peoples sometimes convinces the conquerors that, rather than trying to impose a policy of total extermination, it would be less costly to make some minimal allowances for surviving indigenous communities, usually in the least hospitable locales and on the poorest land. Of these various factors, I think the most important is the need for labor. The conquistador is inclined to put a swift sword to the natives; the capitalist finds it more profitable to work them slowly to death.

IMPERIAL STATE TERRORISM

Ponder the fate of Algeria in the hands of French colonial authorities. In the nineteenth century much of that country was inhabited by Berbers, described by Frederick Engels as "an industrious race, living in regular villages, excellent cultivators, and working in mines, in metals, and in coarse wollen and cotton factories."[2] From the first occupation by the French in 1830 to the time of Engels's report in 1857:

> [T]he unhappy country has been the arena of unceasing bloodshed, rapine, and violence. Each town, large and small, has been conquered in detail at an immense sacrifice of life. The Arab and Kabyle [Berber] tribes . . . have been crushed and broken by the terrible razzias in which dwellings and property are burnt and destroyed, standing crops cut down, and the miserable wretches who remain massacred, or subjected to all the horrors of lust and brutality.[3]

Marshal Thomas Bugeaud, commander of the French forces in Algeria in the early 1840s, reported: "More than fifty fine villages, built of stone and roofed with tiles, were destroyed. Our soldiers made very considerable pickings there." Another army officer wrote: "We have made organized raids in all directions round Bilda. These well-conceived raids have ruined or at least begun the ruin of the country."[4]

A century later the French were still at it in Algeria, this time employing the latest counterinsurgency technology, everything from jet bombers to electroshock torture, against the national liberation movement and the civilian population that supported it. By the

1950s, with an army of 100,000, the French had killed or maimed tens of thousands of Algerians, destroyed hundreds of villages, used torture "on a wide scale," and forced about 1.5 million people into concentration camps where many starved because of the lack of adequate provisions. Another million or more were uprooted from the countryside and forced into the cities.[5]

There is a similar story in Indochina. In precolonial days, villages in Vietnam were ruled by democratically elected local leaders. Some 20,000 one-teacher private village schools had given the population an unusually high literacy rate never again attained once the French moved in and abolished the schools. Popular uprisings in Indochina were mercilessly crushed by the colonizers who, between 1930 and 1932 alone, executed an estimated 10,000 insurgents and their sympathizers. By the eve of World War II, there were more prisons in Indochina than hospitals or schools.[6]

Lest we think this kind of behavior is peculiar to the French, consider what the British did during the sepoys revolt in India in the mid-nineteenth century: torture, widespread executions, "the violations of women, the spittings of children, the roastings of whole villages."[7] "Not a day passes but we string up from ten to fifteen of them [non-combatants]," wrote one British officer. Another exulted: "We hold court-martials on horseback, and every nigger we meet with we either string up or shoot."[8] Today in Northern Ireland, British forces are engaged in military repression and the mistreatment and torture of prisoners. Ireland was England's first colony, used by the British for 800 years as a testing ground for imperialism.

What the Belgians did in the Congo (now Zaire) during the 1890s and into the early twentieth century adds another inglorious page to the history of imperialism: the mass slaughter of whole tribes, the enslavement of populations in order to work them to death in the mines, the imposition of a draconian rule so severe as to have caused Mark Twain angrily to liken King Leopold II to "a wild beast . . . who for money's sake mutilates, murders, and starves half a million friendless and helpless poor natives in the Congo State every year." Twain observed that the slaughter evoked not a murmur of protest from the other "Christian powers."[9]

Along with France and Great Britain, another democracy that has made war against weaker peoples is the United States. Upon taking the Philippines from Spain in 1898, the US then had to fight a bloody three-year war against Filipino rebels. In Luzon alone over

600,000 people were killed by American troops or died from war-related diseases and privations—as the war against the guerrillas became a war against the people who supported the guerrillas.[10] US General Arthur MacArthur issued a proclamation renouncing "precise observance of the laws of war." Among other things, MacArthur's troops tortured and executed prisoners (civilians included), destroyed crops, food stores, domestic animals, boats, and whole villages, and forced tens of thousands of Filipinos into "relocation camps." In 1901 the *Philadelphia Ledger* carried a dispatch from its Manila correspondent:

> Our men . . . have killed to exterminate men, women, children, prisoners and captives, active insurgents and suspected people from lads of 10 up. . . . Our soldiers have pumped salt water into men to "make them talk," and have taken prisoners people who held up their hands and peacefully surrendered, and an hour later . . . stood them on a bridge and shot them down one by one, to drop into the water below and float down, as examples to those who found their bullet-loaded corpses.[11]

A Republican member of Congress gave an eyewitness report on the war:

> You never hear of any disturbances in Northern Luzon . . . because there isn't anybody there to rebel. That country was marched over and cleared out. . . . The good lord in Heaven only knows the number of Filipinos that were put under the ground; our soldiers took no prisoners; they kept no records; they simply swept the country and wherever or however they could get hold of a Filipino they killed him."[12]

The United States intervened repeatedly in Latin America, killing large numbers of Haitians, Mexicans, Nicaraguans, and others in the doing. In 1986, Bill Gandall, aged seventy-seven, recalled how in 1928 he spent two years as a Marine in Nicaragua fighting Augusto Cesar Sandino, the leader for whom the Sandinistas are named: "We never caught him because no matter how we tortured, we could never get people to inform." He remembers how the Marine Corps spread democracy in Nicaragua: "I shot a guy at the polls" in the fraudulent election of 1928. In addition, he busied himself "taking part in rapes, burning huts, cutting off genitals. I had nightmares for years. I didn't have much of a conscience while I was in the Marines. We were taught not to have a conscience."[13]

During the Vietnam War US forces massacred whole villages; murdered prisoners of war; set up "free fire zones" in which all living things were subjected to annihilation; systematically bombed all edifices, including hospitals, schools, churches; and destroyed croplands and work animals. US forces also trained and assisted South Vietnamese police and military in the use of torture and the assassination of suspected National Liberation Front (NLF) sympathizers.[14] The CIA director of that day, Richard Helms, admitted that 20,500 persons were assassinated in the CIA-sponsored Phoenix Program, an undertaking that used death squads to destroy the NLF leadership. Others put the number at twice that.

The total firepower used by the United States in Vietnam "probably exceeded the amount used in all previous wars combined."[15] In Vietnam, the US dropped eight million tons of bombs (leaving 21 million bomb craters), and nearly 400,000 tons of napalm. With a minor assist from troops from other Western nations, the US military killed about 2.2 million Vietnamese, Cambodians, and Laotians, maimed and wounded 3.2 million more, and left over 14 million Indochinese homeless or displaced, with over 300,000 missing in Vietnam alone. The US war effort also left Vietnam with an estimated 83,000 amputees, 40,000 blind or deaf, and hundreds of thousands of orphans, prostitutes, disabled, mentally ill, and drug addicts.[16]

The 18 million gallons of Agent Orange and other such chemical defoliants dumped from US planes poisoned hundreds of thousands of acres and worked their way into Vietnam's food chain, dramatically increasing the number of miscarriages, stillbirths, and birth deformities. The chemical warfare gave Vietnam one of the world's highest rates of liver cancer, a disease virtually unknown in that country in prewar days. The continuous bombings and use of napalm and defoliants rendered two-fifths of Vietnam's land unsuitable for forestry or agriculture.[17]

To achieve this horrendous record of destruction, the US military used B-52 bombers against combatants and civilian populations alike. The "Daisy Cutter," a monster-sized bomb weighing 7.5 tons, when dropped by parachute and detonated above the ground, destroyed everything in an area equal to ten football fields. The AC-47 helicopter gunship was armed with three Gatling guns that together fired 18,000 rounds of 7.62 millimeter ammunition per minute, killing in that time every living thing in an area the size of a city block, and turning heavily vegetated terrain into plowed-up fields.

The US military also used phosphorous bombs, laser-guided bombs, and fragmentation bombs, the latter designated to maximize internal body wounds with flying flechettes that tear into the flesh. "When Vietnamese surgeons became adept at removing the metal flechettes imbedded deeply in the victims' bodies, American scientists redesigned the bombs to use plastic flechettes that could not be detected by X-rays."[18] Those who claim the US military effort failed in Vietnam because "we did not fight to win" are either ignorant of that war's unparalleled savagery or they mean to say that nuclear bombs should have been used.

The United States has extended military aid to right-wing regimes fighting against popular resistance movements in El Salvador, Guatemala, Indonesia, Argentina, Brazil, Malaysia, the Philippines, Zaire, to name some of the recipients. Let us look at El Salvador. That country is wide open to multinational investment; a small number of super-rich families control the bulk of its domestic wealth, while most of its people live on subsistence diets and have no access to medical care. The counterinsurgency, funded and led by the US, is waged today against a broadly based liberation movement. Of the more than 60,000 Salvadorans killed in the war between 1979 and 1987, many thousands are believed to have been murdered by right-wing death squads. Another 540,000 have fled into exile, and another 250,000 have been displaced or forced into resettlement camps within El Salvador, a country of only 4 million people.[19]

The Salvadoran army massacred whole villages suspected of being sympathetic to the guerrillas. On December 11, 1981, a US-trained elite battalion killed more than 1,000 people in the village of Mozote and some nearby hamlets. The survivors fled into the forest and five years later they were still in hiding, subjected to constant aerial attacks.[20] Representative Barbara Mikulski (now a US Senator) interviewed numerous victims; here is a typical account, drawn from an interview with a peasant woman:

> Many members of her family were killed. She personally saw children around the age of eight being raped, and then [the soldiers] would take their bayonets and make mincemeat out of them. With their guns they would shoot at their faces. . . ." The Army would cut people up and put soap and coffee in their stomachs as a mocking, [the woman said]. They would slit the stomach of a pregnant woman and take the child out, as if they were taking eggs out of an iguana. That is what I saw."[21]

By the early 1980s, the US was resorting to an air war against the guerrilla-controlled zones in El Salvador, with daily bombings that included the use of incendiary and fragmentation bombs, and poison chemicals dropped into water streams. Some victims' experiences were reported in the *Christian Science Monitor:*

> We have holes dug in the ground outside our villages to hide in when the planes come and we keep the children near the holes or in them all day. At first the Air Force dropped bombs that knocked down trees and houses, killed people, and made a three-meter crater. Then they began to drop bombs that exploded before hitting the ground and others that made craters eight meters deep to kill us as we hid in our shelters.[22]

Incendiary bombs were used to destroy the soil itself. As one US-trained Salvadoran soldier told an American reporter: "Usually we drop incendiary bombs before we begin operations. . . . By the time we enter the area, the land has been burned over and the subversives pretty well toasted."[23] The army moves in after the bombings to destroy surviving homes, crops, domesticated animals, food stores, and anything else that might sustain life.

The United States not only has funded the Salvadoran war but has played an active role in it. US military "advisors" sometimes have gone along on military forays and directed artillery fire. American pilots have flown observation planes from Honduras into El Salvador, radioed information from their planes directly to a planning room in the Pentagon, near Washington, D.C. There, two thousand miles away, computers analyze the data and pick targets for the evening's bombing run. A teletype from the Pentagon to Ilopango Air Force Base near San Salvador provides that day's targets to the US-trained Salvadoran pilots who then carry out their mission in the A-37 bomber planes provided by the US.[24]

Another right-wing military regime supported by the United States is the one in Indonesia. The recipients of about $2 billion in US military and economic aid over the last ten years, the Indonesian generals came to power in a coup that took the lives of 500,000 to 1 million people in 1965. A decade later, the generals conducted a war of attrition against East Timor, a former Portuguese colony which upon independence had chosen a populist socialist government. The Indonesian military has killed an estimated 100,000 to 200,000 East Timorese, out of a population of only 650,000. Tens of thousands of others have been forcibly relocated into internment camps or have fled the country.[25]

Indonesia and El Salvador are only two of many US client states. By "client state" I mean those nations that are (1) open to US capitalist penetration under conditions highly favorable to US corporate investors and unfavorable to the people of that society; (2) open to US military and political influence; (3) run by a privileged class that is friendly to the US government, sharing Washington's interest in preserving the client state's existing distribution of class power and wealth.

Both client-state leaders and US leaders say that reforms in the Third World must take place within an orderly framework, without disruption of the ongoing social stability. Indeed, they often argue that *before* there can be any change, there must be stability. But for them, stability can only be preserved if change is confined to minor reforms that do not cut into the ubiquitous prerogatives of ruling interests and do not threaten the prevailing social order. Client-state leaders want "stability," equating it with orderly rule, easy access to graft, and secure possession of wealth. Western corporate investors also want "stability," equating it with acquiescent low-paid workers and safe high-profit investments. And the US government wants "stability," equating it with economic, ideological, and strategic dominance. So while they all might give lip service to the need for reform, US political and corporate leaders and client-state leaders strive mightily to solidify the existing social relations that make reform both unlikely and unworkable.

The one social interest in Third World nations that seldom suffers from underdevelopment is the military and police. Between 1973 and 1980, the US government sold $66.8 billion in arms to Third World countries. US technical assistance also plays a role in putting together the relocation camps, undercover intelligence and surveillance networks, detention sites, interrogation and torture centers, death squads and other such essentials of "Free World stability." The CIA has trained and supplied secret police and repressive security forces on every continent, in Chile, Brazil, Argentina, Iran, Israel, South Korea, Japan, South Africa, Australia, West Germany, Italy, Portugal, and Spain. At the CIA training facility in Camp Peary, Virginia, a large section of the base is devoted to training right-wing operatives from various countries in the methods of sabotage and terror bombings. The CIA's assassination program used with such murderous effect in Vietnam has been duplicated in El Salvador. The CIA has been linked directly or indirectly to various right-wing terrorist groups including the MSI in Italy, the Black April group of Vietnamese refugees, General Gehlen's BND in Germany, and organizations in Jamaica, Spain, Greece, Argentina, Brazil, Bolivia, and elsewhere.[26]

After an extensive investigation, the US Senate Intelligence Committee reported that (1) the CIA was involved with the group that assassinated General Rene Schneider (a democratic constitutionalist) in an effort to block the election of President Salvador Allende in Chile, (2) that President Eisenhower authorized the poisoning by the CIA of Congolese liberation leader Patrice Lumumba—although Lumumba was supposedly killed by "rivals," and (3) the CIA made at least eight assassination attempts against Fidel Castro and other Cuban leaders, even using organized crime gangsters as operatives.[27]

More than 80,000 foreign military officers have been trained by the United States at such places as Fort McNair in Virginia and Fort Gulick in Panama. Of these, scores have gone on to become heads of state, ambassadors, and other political leaders; hundreds have become chiefs of staff; and over a thousand have become top-ranking generals. During the 1960s and 1970s, most of the military leaders who were engaged in the coups that overthrew nine democratically elected governments in Latin America were American trained. All the troops were American equipped. Eighty percent of the top officers who conducted the 1964 coup in Brazil were US-trained (while only 20 percent of the officers who did *not* participate were trained in the United States). The entire Chilean junta was the beneficiary of US military training at one time or another.[28] The US training schools help forge close links between Latin America's ruling officers and the US military and intelligence establishment, and among the officers themselves. The Panamanian newspaper, *La Prensa,* described the US school in that country as "the University of Assassins" where "soldiers are being prepared to go kill Salvadoran, Nicaraguan, Guatemalan, Chilean, and Uruguayan brothers."[29]

Assassins they are: the Latino military has been linked to death squads in just about every Latin American client state. In a "democracy" like Colombia, some 100,000 workers, peasants, and intellectuals have died at the hands of US-trained security forces and death squads since the late 1940s.[30] First utilized by the United States in Vietnam to torture and murder tens of thousands of civilians, death squads have enjoyed a wide use in US client states since the 1960s; *their growth closely correlates with US military aid and training.*[31]

The right-wing military do other things besides kill. In Uruguay, during the decade after the military takeover in 1973, one of every fifty inhabitants was imprisoned, one of every sixty-five tortured, and three of every twenty were driven into exile.[32] As of 1987, half of all the political prisoners in South Korea were labor-union people who had agitated for better wages and work conditions. They had been subjected to repeated beatings, electric shock, and other forms of torture.[33]

Consider the fate of Manuel de Conceicao, a peasant leader who lived in a region of Brazil where the best lands belong to big landowners and US corporations. Suffering a grinding poverty, working—when work was available—for barely subsistence wages on the latifundias, seeing their children die of malnutrition, the peasants decided to organize themselves and demand reforms. These efforts were summarily crushed by Brazilian army units that had been trained and equipped by US military-aid programs. Manuel was among those arrested in 1972 and brought before Brazilian security police who had been schooled at US army bases in the latest methods of counterinsurgency and interrogation. For his crime of protesting the economic conditions of his life, Manuel was treated as follows:

> For four months I was heavily tortured by the Army in Rio de Janeiro, and then in the Naval Information Center. . . . Near death, I was taken to the hospital for the sixth time. The beatings had been so severe that my body was one big bruise. The blood clotted under my skin and all the hair on my body fell out. They pulled out all my fingernails. They poked needles through my sexual organs and used a rope to drag me across the floor by my testicles. Right afterwards they hung me upside down.
>
> They hung me handcuffed from a grating, removed my artificial leg, and tied my penis so I could not urinate. They forced me to stand on my one leg for three days without food or drink. They gave me so many drugs that my eardrums burst and I am impotent. They nailed my penis to a table for 24 hours. They tied me up like a pig and threw me into a pool so that I nearly drowned. They put me in a completely dark cell where I remained for 30 days urinating and defecating in the same place where I had to sleep. They fed me only bread soaked in water. They put me in a rubber box and turned on a siren. For three days I neither ate nor slept and I nearly went mad. . . ."[34]

Manuel was not a solitary victim. After the Brazilian military junta overthrew the democratically elected Goulart government, it jailed an estimated 35,000 to 40,000 people, many of whom were subjected to systematic and protracted torture. During these years, the junta enjoyed friendly relations with Washington, and Brazil was hailed as a staunch US ally, a Free World bulwark against the threat of Communism.

The defenders of the West can be quite imaginative in their

methods of torture and terror. Two women who opposed the Brazilian military were arrested by the infamous DOPS, the regime's special counterinsurgency police. Instead of being tortured, which was the usual procedure, they were brought to a hospital where they were subjected to plastic surgery:

> One of the women had her mouth taken away from her. The other lost half her nose. And they were released after several days with the gentle suggestion that they be sure to visit their comrades to show off their "cures." They had been turned into walking advertisements of terror, agents of demoralization and intimidation.... In the case of the woman whose mouth had been shut, the most sophisticated techniques of plastic surgery had been employed. Great care had been taken by her medical torturers to obliterate her lips forever, using cuts and stitches and folds that would frustrate even the best reconstructive techniques. [Luis, a Cuban plastic surgeon] even thought he could detect a "U.S. hand" in this macabre handiwork, or that of a Brazilian schooled in the United States. A small hole had been left in the face to allow the woman to take liquids through a straw and survive....
>
> When Luis and the medical team reopened the hole where her mouth had been, the sight was far more sickening than they had expected: All of the teeth had been removed and two dog fangs—incisors—had been inserted in their place. A little surprise from the fascist madmen....
>
> The other woman had had half her nose removed, skin, cartilage, and all. A draining, raw, and frightening wound was her "treatment," the sign she was to carry around with her to warn people that rebellion was a "disease" and torture the "cure."[35]

El Salvador is another "Free World" bastion. In 1982, *The Other Side*, a religious magazine published in Philadelphia, ran an anonymous testimony from a young man who had deserted the Salvadoran army and fled to Mexico. Part of his training by eight American Green Berets consisted of "teaching us how to torture." He witnessed a boy of about fifteen, suspected of supporting the guerrillas, being subjected to a demonstration torture by the Green Berets. They tore out the youth's fingernails, broke his elbows, gouged out his eyes, and then burned him alive. The author reports that the torture sessions continued into the next day and included a thirteen-year-old girl. Another victim had various parts of his body burned and was then taken up in a helicopter while still alive and thrown out at 14,000 feet. The defector noted that "often the army goes and throws people out over the sea." The editors of *The Other Side* withheld the Salvadoran informant's name "for obvious reasons" but claimed that "the basic outline of his story has been corroborated by independent sources which we believe to be reliable."[36]

Victims and survivors of the fascist coup in Chile in 1973 tell how the Chilean military—trained and financed by the United States—tortured people with electric shock, particularly on the genitals; forced victims to witness the torture of friends and relatives (including children); raped women in the presence of other family members; burned sex organs with acid or scalding water; placed rats in women's vaginas and into the mouths of other prisoners; mutilated, punctured, and cut off various parts of the body, including genitalia, eyes, and tongue; injected air into women's breasts and into veins (causing slow, painful death); shoved bayonets and clubs into the vagina or anus, causing rupture and death.[37]

Elba Vergara, secretary to President Allende (himself murdered by the Chilean generals), was made to witness repeated torture and rapes. At one point her tormentors told her they would show her their "theater."

> Four men came in, bearing a cot with a sheet-covered figure. "Sit down," one ordered. "You're going to see a performance by a bad actor, an actor who has forgotten his part. Help him remember it." They uncovered a body entirely purple, missing a foot. "Come closer," another ordered. "Look at him. You'll know him." And she did. It was 27-year-old "El Gordo" Toledo, with whom she had been 20 days before. He could hardly speak, or scream, any more. When Elba maintained that she did not know him, they said, "Let's see"—they pulled out his nails, cut off his remaining ear, cut out his tongue, gouged out his eyes, and killed him slowly as she watched, thinking, "He could be my son." Then they brought another "actor," 26-year-old Eduard Munoz. It took them five hours to kill him, under her eyes. It was worse than any pain they could have inflicted on her, she said. Later she was forced to watch while her cellmates—aged 16, 17, and 40, nude and drugged, were directed to perform an erotic dance before they were raped. Another girl, back from a dreaded torture center, and pregnant, was so crazy that each time she awoke she screamed that her only desire was for her child to be born so she could kill it.[38]

One could go on. Torture has been used on a systematic basis by US-sponsored autocracies in Guatemala, Greece, Uruguay, Argentina, Indonesia, Zaire, Ecuador, Paraguay, Turkey, Bolivia, Iran (under the Shah), the Philippines, and dozens of other nations. A United Nations official who has talked to former torture victims from various countries in Latin America notes: "All of them . . . still feel the electric shocks, the octagonal beating sticks, the barrels of shit-filled water into which they were dunked, the psychedelic hoods to make them crazy, the lit cigarettes, the rats shoved up into their bodies, the humiliation and isolation. They still feel."[39]

US support of police state terrorism and torture is not an irrational policy. It may foster and feed off irrational and even deranged acts but its goals are rooted in some very rational interests. Edward Herman marshals a great deal of evidence to show that

> as human rights conditions deteriorate, factors affecting the "climate of investment," like the tax laws and labor repression, improve from the viewpoint of the multinational corporation. This suggests an important line of causation. Military dictatorships tend to improve the investment climate. . . . The multinational corporate community and the U.S. government are very sensitive to this factor. Military dictators enter into a tacit joint venture arrangement with Free World leaders: They will keep the masses quiet, maintain an open door to multinational investment, and provide bases and otherwise serve as loyal clients. In exchange, they will be aided and protected against their own people, and allowed to loot public property.[40]

Thus do US policymakers use fascism to protect capitalism, while claiming they are saving democracy from Communism.

Notes

1. For a superb and comprehensive account of colonization of the Third World see L. S. Stavrianos, *Global Rift, The Third World Comes of Age* (New York: William Morrow, 1981.

2. Karl Marx and Frederick Engels, *On Colonialism* (selected writings) (New York: International Publishers, 1972), p. 156.

3. Ibid., p. 158.

4. Both quotations are from Ian Clegg, *Workers' Self-Management in Algeria* (New York: Monthly Review Press, 1971), p. 24.

5. Alf Andrew Heggoy, *Insurgency and Counterinsurgency in Algeria* (Bloomington, Ind.: Indiana University Press, 1972), pp. 213, 236, and passim. On the use of torture in Algeria see Henri Alleg, *La Question* (Paris: Les Editions de Minuit, 1961).

6. See Marvin Gettleman, ed., *Vietnam: History, Documents and Opinions* (Baltimore: Penguin, 1965); also Ngo Vinh Long, *Before the Revolution: The Vietnamese Peasants Under the French* (Cambridge, Mass.: MIT Press, 1973).

7. Marx and Engels, *On Colonialism*, p. 153. The report is by Marx.

8. These several quotations are from ibid., pp. 153–54.

9. Maxwell Geismar, ed., *Mark Twain and the Three R's* (New York: Bobbs-Merrill, 1973), p. 175. For accounts of colonial repression throughout the Third World, over the centuries, see Stavrianos, *Global Rift*.

10. Daniel Schirmer, *Republic or Empire* (Cambridge, Mass.: Schenkman, 1972), p. 231.

11. Quoted in Schirmer, p. 234.

12. Ibid., pp. 236–7; the Congressman preferred to remain unnamed; see also Stuart Creighton Miller, *"Benevolent Assimilation": The American Conquest of the Philippines, 1899–1903* (New Haven: Yale University Press, 1983).

13. Coleman McCarthy, "Doing His Penance for American Sins in Nicaragua," *Tampa Tribune,* March 1, 1986.

14. Marvin Gettleman et al., *Vietnam and America* (New York: Grove Press, 1985), passim.

15. Ibid., p. 461.

16. Indochina Newsletter, Dorchester, Mass., issue #18, November–December 1982.

17. Ibid.; also *Washington Post,* July 16, 1987.

18. Gettleman, *Vietnam and America,* pp. 461–62.

19. Marvin Gettleman et al., *El Salvador: Central America and the New Cold War* (New York: Grove Press, 1981); *Washington Post,* July 11, 1987.

20. Jon Lee Anderson and Lucia Annunziata, "The Lost People of La Joya," *Nation,* June 21, 1986, p. 856. For an eyewitness account by Archbishop John Quinn see *San Francisco Examiner,* May 11, 1986.

21. Report prepared by New England Press (1981); for other accounts see Gettleman, *El Salvador.*

22. *Christian Science Monitor,* April 27, 1984.

23. Ibid.; also Gettleman, *El Salvador;* and *Alert,* publication of the Committee In Solidarity with the People of El Salvador (CISPES) Washington, D.C., 1985.

24. CISPES Bulletin, Washington, D.C., March 1986.

25. William Blum, *The CIA: A Forgotten History* (London: Zed, 1986), pp. 108–12, 217–20; Jose Ramos-Horta, *Funu: The Unfinished Saga of East Timor* (Trenton, N.J.: Red Sea Press, 1986); and *Christian Science Monitor,* April 30, 1986.

26. Sidney Lens, "Perspective," *Progressive,* February 1977, p. 13; also Edward Herman, "U.S. Sponsorship of State Terrorism," *CovertAction Information Bulletin,* Summer 1986, pp. 27–33.

27. Blum, *The CIA: A Forgotten History; New York Times,* November 21, 1975 and June 19, 1975; also John Stockwell, *In Search of Enemies: A CIA Story* (New York: W. W. Norton, 1978).

28. Edward Herman, *The Real Terror Network* (Boston: South End Press, 1982), p. 125; Jeffery Stein, "Grad School for Juntas," *Nation,* May 21, 1977; *Guardian,* February 26, 1978; *Washington Post,* September 24, 1984; Victor Perlo," The Pentagon School," *Daily World,* May 5, 1983.

29. *Washington Post,* September 24, 1984; also Stein, "Grad School for Juntas," p. 624.

30. Marc Frank, "Colombians Fight Right-wing Terror," *People's Daily World,* September 19, 1986.

31. Herman, "U.S. Sponsorship . . ." pp. 32–33; Amnesty International, *Disappearances: A Workbook,* (New York: Amnesty International, 1981); Blum, *The CIA.* On the Phoenix program in Vietnam see Marvin Gettleman et al., *Vietnam and America* (New York: Grove Press, 1985), pp. 403–04.

32. Uruguyan Damian Sroedes, in *People's Daily World,* July 18, 1987.

33. *New York Times* August 19, 1987.

34. Letter smuggled out of prison, *Village Voice,* September 20, 1973, p. 26.

35. Robert Cohen, " 'In Brazil the Women Boast About Their Plastic Surgery,' " *CovertAction Information Bulletin,* Winter 1986, pp. 21–22; also Bernard

Quick, "Toward Abolishing Torture," *The Witness,* September 1986, p. 9–11. *Torture in Brazil, A Report,* (New York: Vintage, 1986).

36. The Editors, *The Other Side,* May 1982.

37. Jose Yglesias, *Chile's Days of Terror: Eye-Witness Accounts of the Military Coup* (New York: Pathfinder, 1974); *Washington Post,* April 1, 1987; A. J. Langguth, *Hidden Terrors* (New York: Pantheon, 1978).

38. Rose Styron, "Chile: 'The Spain of Our Generation,' " *Ramparts,* May/June 1975, p. 29; also Samuel Chavkin, *The Murder of Chile* (New York, Everest House, 1982): and Edward Boorstein, *Allende's Chile* (New York: International Publishers, 1977).

39. Cohen, " 'In Brazil the Women Boast . . .' " p. 22.

40. Herman, "U.S. Sponsorship of State Terrorism," pp. 30–31.

5

The Mean Methods
of Imperialism (II)

From Cuba to Chile, from Ghana to Guyana, from Indonesia to Iran, US leaders have tried to crush insurgencies and subvert governments that have tampered too much with the existing capitalist economic order or have dared to depart from it. When possible, other peoples are used as surrogates to carry out counterrevolutionary tasks. Thus, the United States has given guns and funds to potentially separatist groups such as the Meo tribes in Vietnam, the Miskitos in Nicaragua, the Ogaden and Somali populations in Ethiopia, and Muslim tribes in Afghanistan. Some of these tribes, such as those in Vietnam and Afghanistan, have been heavily involved in the heroin trade and have a direct interest in maintaining the status quo.[1]

The imperialists often attain an impressive degree of international coordination. Thus, Argentine counterinsurgency advisors and Argentine-trained Nicaraguan rightists assisted by the United States were sent to Guatemala to help suppress a popular uprising. Various Latin American governments have sent military officers to Taiwan to be trained in anticommunist ideology, death-squad organization, and other aspects of political repression. The Taiwanese training program was set up with American assistance and funds.[2]

In a number of countries, such as South Africa, Zaire, Guatemala, Chile, Angola, and Haiti, where US policymakers have not always felt politically comfortable about committing American military personnel in noticeable numbers, Israel has been willing to do the dirty work in return for large sums of US aid and other special considerations. Likewise in countries such as Nicaragua (with the contras), El Salvador, Namibia, Taiwan, Indonesia, the Philippines, and Bolivia, Israeli military personnel have worked as advisors in counterinsurgency. According to one Israeli writer: "Consider any third-world area that has been a trouble spot in the past 10 years and you will discover Israeli officers and weapons implicated in the conflict—supporting American interests and helping in what they call 'the defense of the West.' "[3]

Counterrevolutionary forces composed of exiles and mercenaries have been used by the United States in the Bay of Pigs invasion of Cuba and the right-wing counterrevolutionary attacks in Nicaragua (the "contra war"). Assisted by US military advisors and hundreds of millions of dollars, the contras have conducted a war of attrition against the Nicaraguan people. Lacking any popular base in Nicaragua, they behaved just the opposite of revolutionary guerrillas. Instead of going into areas and assisting the people and winning their support, they attacked health clinics, collective farms, agricultural cooperatives, croplands, schools and homes, indiscriminately killing men, women, and children.[4]

As of 1986, the contra war in Nicaragua had claimed some 9,000 people and had left 7,200 children without parents. A reporter for the *San Francisco Chronicle,* who spent the night at an orphanage built by the Sandinista government for children whose parents had been killed in contra attacks, gives this glimpse of the human misery caused by the counterrevolution:

> The children were all small; most of them were under 8 years old. They looked sorrowful and love-starved as they sat in the bare barracks. . . .
> "Usually the Contras murder the whole family," said Amador [an attendant]. "But sometimes the little ones get away and we find them lost and wandering in the jungle. They're the lucky ones. Many of them die before we can find them."
> I went into the barracks, hopped into a top bunk and tried to fall asleep on the thin mattress. . . . There were about 16 children in the room—both boys and girls—and the sounds of their sadness made sleep impossible.
> Some wept in their sleep, or hummed their lonely tunes in a harmony of sorrow that I had never heard before. The little girl who kissed me when I arrived cried in the bunk below me.
> After lying awake listening for a couple of hours, I climbed out of the bunk and went out to the front stoop to smoke my pipe and think about this war and all the little kids who suffer from horrors they don't understand.
> After awhile I heard a soft sobbing behind me. I turned to find a little boy, three or four years old. He kissed me on the cheek, sat down beside me and pulled my arm around him. We sat that way for awhile. Then he put his head in my lap and we both cried.[5]

Another well-publicized instance of destabilization was Chile. The Senate Select Committee on Intelligence found that President Nixon had issued orders to the CIA to "play a direct role in organizing a military coup d'état in Chile to prevent Allende's accession to the presidency."[6] The CIA compiled lists of Chilean leftists to be arrested, and disbursed millions of dollars to antidemocratic opposition parties and media and to right-wing paramilitary organizations.[7] "Not a nut or bolt will be allowed to reach Chile under Allende," said Edward Korry, US ambassador to that country in 1973. "Once Allende comes to power we shall do all within our power to condemn Chile and Chileans to utmost deprivation and poverty."[8] As Nixon himself remarked; "Make the [Chilean] economy scream." In 1971, the United States imposed economic sanctions, cut credits, and stopped aid programs to Chile, but increased US aid to the military.[9]

In Chile, American firms themselves played an active role in destabilization, most notably the International Telephone and Telegraph Corporation (ITT) which, along with several other companies, contributed large sums to Allende's conservative electoral opponent in 1970. A group of business executives organized by David Rockefeller into the Council of the Americas, which included Harold Geneen of ITT and Donald Kendall of Pepsico, proposed covert action in Chile to defeat Allende and elect the right-wing candidate, pledging $500,000 for the campaign.[10] ITT also pressured the White House to oust Allende from office when his government nationalized the telephone company in October 1971.[11]

The Pinochet military dictatorship that murdered Allende and seized power in Chile in 1973 abolished all political liberties, executed about 30,000 Chileans, and arrested, tortured, or drove into exile many thousands more. Pinochet's free-market policies, formulated by conservative economists from the USA, brought runaway inflation, a drastic drop in real wages, a sharp growth in unemployment, deep cuts in human services, and a huge increase in the national debt.[12] But the economy was not a failure for everyone. There was a dramatic upward redistribution of wealth; the top 5 percent doubled their share of the national income in a few years under the US-supported dictatorship, while workers saw their real wages cut almost by half. Big US corporations and banks returned to Chile to recapture enterprises that had been nationalized under Allende, and to enjoy profits and interest payments that were fatter than ever.[13]

Honduras is another imperialist dreamland—or nightmare—

depending on your class perspective. While US investments grew, the standard of living for the average Honduran declined and Honduras sank deeper into foreign debt. Eighty percent of the land in Honduras is owned by foreign companies, most of it by United Brands and Standard Fruit which, backed by the US government, were able to gradually squeeze out the few remaining British firms. (Between 1911 and 1925, US Marines intervened in Honduras six times to protect US investments.) The choice land is used to grow cash export crops such as bananas and coffee, and raise cattle for beef exports. In Honduras, forty children die every day of hunger and disease; over two-thirds are malnourished. Half the country's 4 million inhabitants live without electricity, running water, or decent housing.[14]

In the 1980s, along with a marked increase in US military aid, there was a sharp escalation in state violence against the Honduran people. Critics of the government were labeled "subversivos" and "Sandinista sympathizers," and were treated to mass arrests, death-squad assassinations, and disappearances. Political prisoners who subsequently reemerged from captivity gave dreadful accounts of torture. In Honduras in the 1980s, while much of the economy deteriorated, the technology of state repression made great advances.[15]

The United States has been an active participant in Honduras's maldevelopment, sending counterinsurgency experts and spending hundreds of millions of dollars to bolster the Honduran military. The US built a vast network of forward-deployment bases and airfields for its own forces in Honduras and conducted joint US-Honduran military exercises, transforming that country into a launching pad and backup area for military actions throughout Central America, especially against Nicaragua.

"The lowest priority for current US policy toward Honduras is Honduras," writes Philip Shepherd.[16] The Honduran people seemed to agree with that conclusion. A 1986 survey conducted by the Honduran National Autonomous University found that more than 80 percent of Hondurans rejected the presence of US troops; 75 percent believed that Honduran foreign policy was controlled by Washington.[17]

US policies in Honduras are not without their contradictions. To quote Shepherd again:

> The Reagan administration claims its goals are to help consolidate Honduran democracy, reorganize its economy for greater socioeco-

nomic well-being, and promote social stability. Yet the impact of its policies has been the opposite: democratic institutions and practices have been undermined, human rights abuses have spread, the economy is a shambles, and the stability of Honduras is threatened.[18]

Capital requires protection, as do the institutions through which it operates. As capital expands its operations, the state that is associated with its protection must develop its capacity for autocratic control. Thus, the "Free World" increasingly resembles a dreary string of heartless police states. Yet this system of state terrorism and economic deprivation can undermine the very stability it attempts to impose, for ultimately there is no security of rule without the support of the populace. The repressive stability achieved is nothing more than a surface calm under which the population seethes. In the words of Kenneth Kaunda, president of the Republic of Zambia, "The absence of war does not necessarily mean peace. Peace is something much deeper than that."[19]

OTHER METHODS

To supplement its use of force and violence, the United States has attempted to penetrate the political, cultural, and social institutions of many countries, employing the following methods:

Elections

Washington has financed conservative political parties in Italy, Brazil, Chile, Venezuela, Jamaica, the Dominican Republic, Grenada, and other countries in Latin America, Asia, and Europe.[20] The United States has promoted and funded elections in countries such as Vietnam, the Philippines, El Salvador, Guatemala, and Grenada, usually between carefully selected conservative or reactionary candidates, for the purpose of lending a veneer of popular legitimacy to client states.[21]

Undercover Infiltration

CIA operations abroad have included the infiltration of important political organizations in countries such as Brazil, Ecuador, Italy, and Honduras, to name a few. The CIA has maintained agents at the highest possible levels of various governments, among heads of state, military leaders, and opposition political parties.[22]

Labor Unions

Along with infiltrating existing Third World labor organizations, the United States has coopted workers into tame unions that are more anticommunist than antimanagement. The American Institute for Free Labor Development (AIFLD), funded by the US government and operated by the AFL-CIO, has played this role throughout Latin America. The AIFLD board of trustees contains a number of corporate executives with enormous holdings in Latin America and the Caribbean. AIFLD graduates have been linked to coups in Brazil, Guyana, and to counterinsurgency work in Cuba (under Batista). A similar AFL-CIO enterprise is the African American Labor Center (AALC) which has trained compliant union leaders and organizers from over twenty countries in Africa, providing them with millions of dollars to build organizations and buy followings.[23]

Cultural Imperialism

Along with capital penetration of the Third World there is an increasing cultural penetration. The Ford Foundation and other foundations help maintain Third World universities that produce scholarship supportive of a US ideological perspective. American textbooks, academic programs and courses, American news columnists, news reports and features, American comic strips and comic books, American movies, television shows, magazines, music, fashions, and consumer products inundate Latin America, Asia, and Africa. Polls taken in Mexico in 1982 found that 85 percent of the children questioned recognized the trademark of a brand of potato chips, a distinctly American snack food, but only 65 percent identified Mexico's national emblem.[24] The rich investor nations control the ideational environment as well as the material one. Most of the news published in the Third World is from US media sources. The average Third World nation is better informed about US viewpoints and concerns than about those of neighboring countries or of its own backlands. The CIA alone owns outright over 200 newspapers, magazines, wire services, and publishing houses that operate in countries throughout the world.[25]

The lyrics to a jingle put out by the Coca-Cola Company provides a perfect summary of cultural imperialism: "We'd like to teach the world to sing in perfect harmony / We'd like to buy the world a Coke and keep it company."

Notes

1. *New York Times,* June 18, 1986.

2. Scott Anderson and Jon Lee Anderson, *Inside the League* (New York: Dodd, Mead, 1986).

3. Benjamin Beit-Hallahmi, "Israel's Global Ambitions," *New York Times,* January 6, 1983; also, Jane Hunter, *Israeli Foreign Policy: South Africa and Central America* (Boston: South End Press, 1987); Bishara Bahbah, *Israel and Latin America: The Military Connection* (New York: St. Martin's Press, 1986).

4. For one of many incidents see Orville Schell and Robert Bernstein, "Contra Atrocities or a Covert Propaganda War?" *Wall Street Journal,* April 23, 1985.

5. Tom Weber, *San Francisco Chronicle,* April 24, 1985.

6. *New York Times,* November 21, 1975.

7. Saul Landau and Peter Kornbluh, "Chile: The Ambassador Has Forgotten What Happened," *Washington Post,* October 1, 1983; also James Petras and Morris Morley, *The United States and Chile* (New York: Monthly Review Press, 1976); *New York Times,* September 8, 1974.

8. Quoted in *Controlling Interests,* documentary film (San Francisco: California Newsreel, 1978). Korry himself was critical of US policy in Chile; see his "The Sell-Out of Chile and the American Taxpayer," *Penthouse,* March 1978, pp. 70–74, 88–116.

9. Petras and Morley, *The United States and Chile.*

10. Korry, "The Sell-Out of Chile . . ." pp. 74, 88.

11. Senate multinationals committee investigations as reported in the *Observer* (London) September 16, 1973; William Blum *The CIA: A Forgotten History* (London: Zed, 1986), pp. 232–42.

12. Michael Moffitt, "Chicago Economics in Chile," *Challenge,* September/October 1977.

13. James Petras, "Chile and Latin America," *Monthly Review,* February 1977, pp. 13–24; Isabel Letelier and Michael Moffitt, "Human Rights, Economic Aid and Private Banks: The Case of Chile," IPS Issue Paper (Institute for Policy Studies, Washington, D.C., 1979).

14. For a fuller account see Richard Lapper and James Painter, *Honduras, State for Sale* (London: Latin American Bureau, 1985).

15. Ibid.

16. *World Policy Journal,* Fall 1984.

17. *People's Daily World,* July 10, 1986.

18. *World Policy Journal,* Fall 1984. For an account of US sponsored repression and terror in two other Central American countries see Michael McClintock, *The American Connection,* vols. 1 and 2 (London: Zed, 1985).

19. *New York Times,* April 28, 1975.

62   THE SWORD AND THE DOLLAR

20. *New York Times,* May 13, 1973, January 13, 1978, and May 1, 1985; *Workers World,* December 17, 1976; Kohl, "Secret War . . ." p. 34.

21. Edward Herman and Frank Brodhead, *Demonstration Elections* (boston: South End Press, 1984).

22. Phillip Agree, *Inside the Company: A CIA Diary* (London: Penguin, 1975).

23. *Venceremos,* February 1975, p. 2; Jack Kutz, "AFL-CIO: Scabbing for the U.S. in Central America," *In These Times,* April 15–21, 1987; Obi Bini, "AFL-CIO: A Neocolonial Tool in Africa," *Guardian,* December 14, 1977; Fay Hansen, "AIFLD and Nicaragua," *Economic NOtes,* September 1985, pp. 10–11. Ann Fagin Ginger and David Christiano, *The Cold War Against Labor,* vol. 2 (Berkeley, CA.: Meiklejohn Civil Liberties Institute, 1987), especially pp. 723–768.

24. *New York Times,* January 13, 1982.

25. *New York Times,* December 25, 26, and 27, 1977.

6

A Condominium Empire: Neo-Imperialism

Let us recapitulate a bit: (1) US multinational corporations (along with the firms of other advanced capitalist nations) control most of the wealth, labor, and markets of Asia, Africa, and Latin America. (2) This control does much to maldevelop the weaker nations in ways that are severely detrimental to the life chances of the common people of the Third World. (3) The existing class structure of the Third World, so suitable to capital accumulation, must be protected from popular resistance. Through the generous applications of force and terror and by cultural and political domination, the imperialist nation directly—or through a client-state apparatus—maintains "stability" and prevents changes in the class structure of other nations.

The state's role is to protect not only the capital that has been accumulated but *the accumulation process itself.* The growth of American corporations from modest domestic enterprises to vast multinational giants has been accompanied by a similar growth in the international reach of the US military and the US national security state. Sometimes the sword has intervened in other lands to protect the advantages won by the dollar and sometimes the dollar has rushed in to enjoy the benefits carved out by the sword. In the latter instances, state power stakes out a claim for US capital penetration, which capitalists could not achieve for themselves, as in the Philippines, Cuba, Hawaii, and China. The state thus has acted as initiator and not just protector of investment opportunities, being in the service of American business, taking on the initial risk and cost so that private investors might feel comfortable enough to follow. President Woodrow Wilson made this clear when he observed that the *government* "must open those [overseas] gates of trade, and open them wide, open them before it is altogether profitable to open them, or altogether reasonable to ask private capital to open them at a venture."[1] Most impressive is the way American militarism and American capitalism have kept each other company in their travels abroad.

The United States has about 500,000 military personnel stationed in twenty-one countries and over 330 major military bases costing many billions of dollars yearly to maintain. US carrier-attack fleets patrol every ocean and almost every sea. In addition, the US spends billions yearly on intelligence operations, covert actions, and counterinsurgency. The exact amount is unknown since that portion of the budget is kept secret, even from most members of Congress. But we do know that a huge national security state has developed in the United States since World War II. Its function, as we have seen, is to buttress anticommunist, procapitalist governments and undermine and destroy popular insurgent movements whenever possible.

The US government has given over $200 billion in military aid to some eighty nations since World War II. US weapons sales abroad have grown to about $10 billion a year and compose about 70 percent of all arms sold on the international marketplace.[2] Two million foreign troops and hundreds of thousands of foreign police and paramilitary have been trained, equipped, and financed by the United States. Their purpose has not been to defend their countries from outside invasion but to protect foreign investors and the ruling elites of the recipient nations from their own potentially rebellious populations.

These then are the two fundamental components of empire: First, *the expropriation of the land, labor, markets, and natural resources of other nations.* Second, *the building of a military security system to safeguard the international social order that maintains and expands this capital accumulation process.* By this definition it is fair to say that the United States has an empire, the largest and richest ever known in history, and is an imperialist power, the greatest ever. Most Americans are astonished to hear of it, having been taught that their country, unlike other nations, has escaped the sins of empire and has been a champion of peace and justice among nations. This enormous gap between what US leaders do in the world and what Americans think their leaders are doing is one of the great propaganda accomplishments of the dominant political mythology.[3]

The history of the United States has been one of territorial, commercial, and military conquest. While this statement will jar some readers, we might ask: how else does a nation emerge from an obscure settlement of thirteen coastal enclaves to become the world's greatest power except by conquest and expansion? The American success story craves explanation: in a ruthless, unsavory world, how do the virtuous manage to be so successful?

As our common reading of history would have it, expansion was accomplished by a process of natural accretion: westward settlement, land purchases, defensive wars, reluctant acquisition of spheres of influence to defend weaker peoples, the enforcement of treaty agreements—such were the innocent, almost accidental growing pains whereby the virtuous allegedly became powerful while keeping their virtue intact. Unlike other nations, the United States apparently developed a mighty empire while never being sullied by imperialist practices. If imperialism is admitted, it is most often described as a kind of momentary lapse occurring sometime in that decade from the Spanish-American War to Teddy Roosevelt's "big stick" policy. By this treatment of history, it can be said that the American empire, like the British empire, was acquired in a fit of absentmindedness—an assertion that remains implausible no matter what empire is being considered.

In the early part of our history, the Republic was ruled by persons who suffered quite overtly from expansionist pangs. Drawn exclusively from the landed and merchant classes, this nation's founders saw the necessity for building a strong central government designed to protect the interests of property and commerce at home and abroad. Their desire for territorial and commercial expansion was explicitly and repeatedly stated. As early as 1783, George Washington described the United States as a "rising empire."[4] In 1787, John Adams concluded that the young Republic was "destined" to extend its rule over all of North America, including Canada and Mexico. In 1801 Jefferson, having decided that "the American people was a chosen people ... gifted with superior wisdom and strength" and that "God led our forefathers, as Israel of old," dreamed of a United States encompassing the entire Western hemisphere.[5]

Throughout most of the nineteenth century, the American Republic was busy exterminating Native American Indians, making war against Mexicans, attempting unsuccessful expeditions to conquer Canada, and defeating Southern seccessionism in what was the USA's major mainland war.

As a relative latecomer to the practice of overseas colonialism, the United States could not match the older European powers in the acquisition of far-flung territories. But what it lacked in overseas real estate, it made up for in commercial expansion. By the turn of this century direct annexation of territories was no longer the most expedient way of enjoying the fruits of empire. As experiences in Cuba and Latin America were to teach, a great power could own much of the wealth, exploit the labor and resources, and control the internal markets and policies of neighboring lands without troubling itself with de jure possession. So the United States became an empire of a different sort—or at least of a different appearance.

Under the more traditional forms of colonialism or imperialism (the terms are used synonymously here), the colony is directly possessed by the imperial power. But under neocolonialism (or neo-imperialism), the flag of the imperial power no longer flies over the colony. Unlike "the grandeur that was Rome" with its conquering legions and its ruling consuls extracting tribute from other lands, and unlike the British empire with its omnipresent Union Jack upon which the sun never set, the US empire cannot be seen on a map. The USA was the earliest and most consummate practitioner of neocolonialism, that is, the practice of direct exploitation without the burden of direct rule.

Rather than conquering other lands, the United States "condominiumized" them, so to speak. Consider why a landlord would convert the rental units he owns into condominiums which he sells to others. If he sells you the apartment you once rented from him, and you take out a mortgage with him (an "owner-financed note"), you must pay him a handsome downpayment, easily the equivalent of one or two years' rent, along with monthly mortgage payments that will amount to far more than your rent. And now that you "own" the apartment, you, not he, must look after it and pay the property taxes, fuel, and maintenance. Should you default on your mortgage payments during the twenty years of obligation, he repossesses the condo, gets to keep all the money you sank into it, and can sell it to another buyer. As any banker knows, under capitalism the trick is not to own the asset, but to hold the note on it. In this way one skims the cream without enduring the burdens of ownership.

Also analogous to the transition from imperialism to neo-imperialism is the transition from slave labor to free labor. Under free labor the owner no long directly owns the workers and no longer has to provide for their care. Now he extracts the only thing from workers that interests him: their labor or, more specifically, the profit he can make off their labor power. During afterwork hours or times of sickness, old age, or lay-offs, the laborers must fend for themselves. Instead of owning the assets, which are the workers themselves, the boss buys—on highly favorable terms—their labor. The workers now own themselves but not the wealth created by their labor nor the means of labor, which are also the means of production.

Without straining these analogies too much, I would suggest that the transition from colonialism to neocolonialism is something like the shift from rental ownership to condominiums, or the changeover from slavery to heavily exploited free labor. Almost a half-century before the British thought of giving up the costs of directly administering India—while continuing to exploit that country's land and labor—the United States had perfected this practice in Cuba. Nominal ownership of the island was given to the Cubans in 1902 when President Teddy Roosevelt withdrew American troops. The Cubans now had their own flag, currency, constitution, government, army, and president. They "owned" their country, but even less so than the way the small buyer owns a condominium. US interests retained control of Cuba's choice land, its markets, finances, exports, imports, and foreign relations. A clause inserted in the Cuban constitution gave the US the right to intervene militarily in Cuba at any time to protect US property. The Cubans had few of the prerogatives but many of the burdens of governance, including the task of keeping things orderly for the Yankee investors (who occasionally sent in the Marines to lend a helping hand).

Note how the United States gave the Philippines its "independence" in 1946. Under the Bell Act passed by Congress that year, American citizens were given equal rights with Filipinos in the development of the Philippines's natural resources and the operation of public utilities. A free-trade relationship was set up between the two nations that—given the highly unequal trade balance—worked to the advantage of US exporters. The Philippine peso was fixed in relation to the dollar at the rate of 2 to 1 and any change required the approval of the president of the United States. What occurred in the years that followed resembles a classical imperialist situation—minus the flag. US companies engaged in competitive dumping of commodities. They put up competing factories and drove out scores of pioneering Filipino entrepreneurs. American businesses acquired control of key industries, siphoned off large amounts of local credit to finance their investments, and used US banks to channel Filipino savings to foreigners. American military bases and PX stores became among the biggest importers—free from customs duties and regulations.[6]

It is not quite correct to say that the Philippines have gained political independence but have yet to win economic sovereignty. For if the Filipinos lack sovereignty over their own economy, how politically independent can they really be? Economic power is no less political for being economic. As one American historian put it: the United States retained much of "the economic and military advantages for colonial power, while it was relieved of the burden of administration and of direct responsibility for Philippine welfare."[7]

A country that is granted nominal independence enjoys a somewhat greater legitimacy in the eyes of its populace than one directly and more visibly under imperialist subjugation. The cloak of independence, then, is a cover for neo-imperialism. In countries with de jure independence, nationalist movements are robbed of a major issue. Since struggles for national liberation have a way of evolving into social revolutions, independence can blunt revolutionary appeals. It does seem that the countries kept longest under direct colonial rule are more likely to have social revolutions (for example, Vietnam, Laos, Guinea Bissau, Mozambique, Angola, Zimbabwe, Algeria, South Yemen) than the far more numerous ones that achieved an earlier neo-imperialist "independence."

The major colonizing powers seemed to recognize this when dealing with a number of nationalist struggles in Africa. Within a five-year period, from 1959 to 1965, from Ghana to Gambia, Britain and France gave almost all their former colonies de jure political independence, rather than having them develop a revolutionary experience in the fight for freedom and self-rule. Of course there is no guarantee this ploy will always work: think of revolutionary Cuba, Nicaragua, and Ethiopia. Their nominal independence did not forestall revolution.

Neo-imperialism carries certain risks and costs of its own. The appearance of autonomy fosters expectations of *complete* independence and social betterment among the populace and sometimes even among national leaders. In politics, appearances take on a reality of their own and have an impact of their own, which is why political leaders always try to manipulate appearances. The imperialist has a more difficult time justifying domination and asserting that Third World people are incapable of equality and self-government when, in fact, those same people have attained some semblance of self-rule.

Therefore, the changeover from a world of colonies ruled directly by European and North American powers to a world of distinct, albeit still dependent, nation-states is not without significance and represents a net gain for the democratic forces of the world.

Be that as it may, what we have today is a condominiumized US empire, and quite an empire it is. Judging by the scope and growth of investment, the expropriation of resources, the exploitation of labor, and the range of military power, judging by every imperialist standard except direct political sovereignty, the US empire must be considered a momentous global success. Yet it is one that faces the danger of decline, for like every previous empire it is not anchored in the interests of the subjugated peoples—nor in the interests of its own people, as we shall see.

Notes

1. William Appleman Williams, "American Interventionism in Russia: 1917–20," in David Horowitz, ed., *Containment and Revolution* (Boston: Beacon Press, 1976), p. 28.

2. *New York Times,* September 9, 1975.

3. See Michael Parenti, *Inventing Reality: The Politics of the Mass Media* (New York: St. Martin's Press, 1986) for a discussion of the media's role in bolstering the mythology of US foreign policy.

4. Richard W. Van Alstyne, *The Rising American Empire* (Chicago: Quadrangle, 1965), p. 1.

5. Albert K. Weinberg, *Manifest Destiny* (Chicago: Quadrangle, 1963), pp. 39–40.

6. E. L. Wheelwright, "Historical Appraisal: Colonialism, Past and Present" in S.A. Shah, ed., *U.S. Imperialism in Modern Asia* (Montreal: Afro-Asian Latin American People's Solidarity Committee, 1972), p. 17.

7. Shirley Jenkins, *American Economic Policy Toward the Philippines* (Stanford: Standford University, 1954), p. 69.

7

The Empire Strikes
Back Home

Americans have little cause to take pride in being part of "our" mighty empire, for what that empire does is nothing to be proud of. Furthermore, it is not *our* empire; it does not belong to the American people. The policies of empire benefit the dominant interests within the imperial nation. Few policies represent the interests of all our citizens. More often government policies are the product of some special faction, some combination of particular interests. When we say "our" policy is such-and-such, and "our" interests must be protected, we might question whether all of us are represented by the goals pursued.

What are "US interests"? They are said to include not just the investments of business but the needs of all Americans, our entire way of life. Hence, far-off countries, previously unknown to most Americans, suddenly become vital to "our" interests. To protect "our" oil in the Middle East and "our" resources and "our" markets elsewhere, *our* sons and daughters might have to participate in overseas military ventures, and *our* taxes are needed to finance these ventures.

The next time "our" oil in the Middle East is in jeopardy, we might remember that relatively few of us own oil stock. Yet even portfolio-deprived Americans are presumed to have a common interest with Exxon and Mobil because they live in an economy dependent on oil. It is assumed that if the people of other lands wrested control of their oil away from the big US companies, they would refuse to sell it to us. Supposedly they would prefer to drive us into the arms of competing producers and themselves into ruination, denying themselves the billions of dollars in much needed hard currency they might otherwise earn on the US market.

In fact, nations that acquire control of their own resources do not act so strangely. They are usually more than eager to get in on the US market. A look at existing socialist countries reveals that they are happy to have access to US markets, usually selling at prices equal to or more reasonable than those offered by the giant multinationals. So when Third World peoples, through nationalization, revolution, or both, take over the oil in their own ground, or the copper, tin, sugar, tobacco or whatever, it does not hurt the interests of those of us who live by our own labor. But it certainly hurts the multinational conglomerates that once owned and profited from these resources.

Yet we are made to believe that we, the people of the United States, have a community of interest with the giant multinationals, the very companies that at any time might desert our communities in pursuit of cheaper labor markets abroad. In truth, on almost every issue we, the people, are not in the same boat with the big companies. Policy costs are not equally shared, and benefits are not equally enjoyed. This was as true of ancient empires as of the ones today. In 1919, the conservative economist Joseph Schumpeter described the imperialism of classical Rome in words that might sound familiar to present-day Americans:

> That policy which pretends to aspire to peace but unerringly generates war, the policy of continual preparation for war, the policy of meddlesome interventionism. There was no corner of the known world where some interest was not alleged to be in danger or under actual attack. If the interests were not Roman, they were those of Rome's allies; and if Rome had no allies, then allies would be invented. When it was utterly impossible to contrive such an interest—why, then it was the national honor that had been insulted. The fight was always invested with an aura of legality. Rome was always being attacked by evil-minded neighbors, always fighting for a breathing space. The whole world was pervaded by a host of enemies, and it was manifestly Rome's duty to guard against their indubitably aggressive designs. They were enemies who only waited to fall on the Roman people.[1]

Such a policy can be understood, Schumpeter writes, only by ascertaining what "domestic class interests" benefited from it. Those who gained were the "aristocracy of landlords, agricultural entrepreneurs, born of struggle against their own people" whose dominance rested "on control of the state machine."[2] "No administration in history, the historian Ernst Badian concludes, "has ever devoted itself so wholeheartedly to fleecing its subjects for the private benefit of its ruling class as Rome of the last age of the Republic."[3]

In sum, the "national" policies of an imperialist country reflect the interests of that country's dominant socio-economic class. *Class rather than nation-state more often is the crucial unit of analysis in the study of imperialism.*

The tendency to deny the existence of conflicting class interests when dealing with imperialism leads to all sorts of misunderstandings or half-understandings. For example, liberal writers like Richard Barnet have pointed out that empires cost more than they bring in especially when wars are fought to maintain them.[4] Thus, over a twenty-year period, 1950–70, the US government spent several billions of dollars to shore up a corrupt dictatorship in the Philippines, hoping to protect what amounted to about a billion-dollar US investment in that country. The same pattern holds true in other client states: what our government expends in aid and arms usually exceeds the value of the investments. Barnet concludes that "the costs of maintaining imperial privilege always exceed the gains."[5] From this it has been concluded that empires are "irrational" affairs, not worth the cost and effort.

In fact, however, empires represent a direct transference of capital from poor to rich nations. They are not losing propositions for everyone. The *governments* of imperial nations may spend more than they take in, but the same is not true of the privileged portion of the citizenry. The people who reap the benefits are not the same ones who foot the bill. As Thorstein Veblen pointed out in 1904, the gains of empire flow into the hands of the privileged business class while the costs are extracted from "the industry of the rest of the people."[6] The multinationals monopolize the private returns of empire while carrying little, if any, of the public cost. The expenditures needed in the way of armaments and aid to make the world safe for General Motors, General Dynamics, General Electric, and all the other generals are payed by the US government, that is, by the taxpayers.

So it was with the British empire in India, the costs of which, Marx noted a half-century before Veblen, were "paid out of the pockets of the people of England," and far exceeded what came back into the British treasury. He concluded "the advantage to Great Britain from her Indian Empire must be limited to the profits and benefits which accrue to individual British subjects. These profits and benefits, it must be confessed are very considerable."[7] The empire enriched mostly a small coterie of stockholders in the East India Company. Likewise, while the German conquest of Southwest Africa beginning in the late nineteenth century "remained a loss-making enterprise for the German taxpayer, a number of monopolists still managed to squeeze huge profits out of the colony in the closing years of German colonial domination."[8]

Consider again the question of foreign aid. It is somewhat misleading to say that the United States gives aid to this or that "country." A nation as such does not give aid to another nation. More precisely, the common citizens of our country, through their taxes, give to the privileged elites of another country. As someone once said: foreign aid is when the poor people of a rich country give money to the rich people of a poor country.

Those who think of empire solely as an expression of *national* interests rather than *class* interests are bound to misinterpret the nature of imperialism. Thus, George Kennan describes US imperialist expansion at the end of the nineteenth century as a product of popular aspiration: the American people "simply liked the smell of empire"; they "liked to see our flag flying on distant tropical islands"; and they wanted "to bask in the sunshine of recognition as one of the great imperial powers of the world."[9] In their discussion of present-day US interventionism, the liberal writers Buell and Rothschild comment that "the American psyche is pegged to being biggest, best, richest, and strongest. Just listen to the rhetoric of our politicians. . . ."[10] But does the rhetoric of our politicians really reflect the sentiments of the major portion of our people who in fact come up as decidedly noninterventionist in most opinion polls? Buell and Rothschild assert that "when a Third World nation—whether it be Cuba, Vietnam, Iran, or Nicaragua—spurns our way of doing things, our egos ache. . . ." But such countries do more than "spurn our ways," they move toward social orders that directly threaten multinational investments and capitalism as a global system. Such psychologizing about aching egos and basking in the sunshine of imperial recognition allows us to blame imperialism on the ordinary American citizens who are more the victims than the beneficiaries of empire.

In a similar fashion, the historian William Appleman Williams scolds the American people for having become addicted to the conditions of empire. It seems "we" like empire. "We" live beyond our means and need empire as part of our way of life. "We" exploit the rest of the world and don't know how to get back to a simpler life.[11] The implication is that "we" are profiting from the runaway firms that are exporting our jobs and exploiting Third World peoples. And "we" decided to send troops into Central America and Vietnam, and thought to overthrow democratic governments in a dozen or more countries around the world. And "we" urged the building of a global network of counterinsurgency, and demanded that the CIA and the US Agency for International Development (AID) train the police torturers and death squads of more than a score of countries.

In fact, ordinary Americans have seldom known about these things until after the fact, or—on the rare occasions they were informed—have opposed intervention or have not given very enthusiastic support. For Williams, imperialist policy is a product of mass thinking. In fact, mass thinking is often opposed to costly imperialist ventures. Popular support may sometimes be won for quick and easy military actions that are a balm for national pride, as with the invasion of Grenada in 1983 and the bombing of Libya in 1986, but more protracted and costly undertakings incur a general disapproval.

Pollster Louis Harris reported that, during 1982–84, by more than 3 to 1, Americans rejected increased military aid for El Salvador. Network surveys found that 80 percent opposed sending troops to that country; 67 percent were against the US mining of Nicaragua's harbors; and 2 to 1 majorities opposed aid to the contras. A 1983 *Washington Post*/ABC News poll found that, by a 6 to 1 ratio, our citizens opposed any attempt by the United States to overthrow the Nicaraguan government. A substantial majority believed that "becoming too entangled in Central American problems in an attempt to stop the spread of Communism" was "a greater danger to the United States" than the spread of Communism itself. By more than 2 to 1 the public said the greatest cause of unrest in Central America was not subversion from Cuba, Nicaragua, or the Soviet Union but "poverty and the lack of human rights in the area."[12] Far from galvanizing our leaders into overseas involvements, the American people often act as one of the few restraints. They do not usually consider such ventures to be in their interest—and they are right.

THE COSTS OF EMPIRE

Let us consider in more detail what it costs to maintain "our" military-industrial global empire. If you are an unemployed worker whose plant has just moved to South Korea or Brazil or Indonesia in pursuit of higher profits, the first thing that might come to mind is the number of jobs "our" empire has cost us. As early as 1916, Lenin pointed out that at an advanced stage capitalism would export not only its goods but its very capital, not only its products but its entire production process.[13] Today, most giant American firms do just that, exporting their capital, their technology, factories, and sales networks. It is well known that General Motors has been closing down factories in the USA; less well known is that GM has been spending billions of dollars abroad on new auto plants in countries where wages are far less than what American autoworkers are paid. This means bigger profits for GM but more unemployment for Detroit.

Over the last twenty years, American firms have tripled their total outlay in other countries, with the fastest growth rate being in the Third World. Nor is the trend likely to reverse itself. American capitalism is now *producing abroad* eight times more than it exports. Many firms have shifted *all* their manufacturing activities to foreign lands: all the cameras sold in the USA are made overseas, as are just about all the tape recorders, radios, bicycles, VCRs, typewriters, television sets, and computers.[14] One out of every three workers employed by US multinational companies are now in foreign countries. US companies continue to export US jobs to other countries at an alarming rate: 900,000 between 1980 and 1985, 250,000 of these in 1985 alone.[15] Thus do the working people of the United States pay the hidden costs of empire.

Multinationals do not have to pay US income taxes on profits made in other countries until these profits are repatriated to the USA—if ever they are. Taxes paid to the host country are treated as *tax credits* rather than mere tax deductions, that is, write-offs from the taxes that would normally have to be paid to the US Treasury rather than from the income that is taxable. The multinational can juggle the books among its various foreign subsidiaries, showing low profits in a high-tax country and high profits in a low-tax country so as to avoid paying substantial taxes anywhere.

Management's threat to relocate a plant is often sufficient to blackmail US workers into taking wage cuts, surrendering benefits, working longer hours, and even putting up money of their own for new plants and retooling—all of which represent a net transfer of income from workers to owners.

Americans are victimized by economic imperialism not only as workers but as taxpayers and consumers. The billions of tax dollars that corporations escape paying because of their overseas shelters must be made up by the rest of us. Additional billions of our tax dollars go into foreign-aid programs to governments that maintain the cheap labor markets that lure away American jobs—$13.6 billion in 1986, of which two-thirds was military aid. Our tax money also serves as hidden subsidies to the big companies when used as foreign aid to finance the kind of infrastructure (roads, plants, ports) needed to support extractive industries in the Third World.

Nor do the benefits of this empire trickle down to the American consumer in any appreciable way. Generally the big companies sell the goods made abroad at as high a price as possible on American markets. Corporations move to Asia and Africa to increase their profits, not to produce lower-priced goods that will save money for American consumers. They pay as little as they can in wages abroad but still charge as much as they can when they sell the goods at home.

From one-half to two-thirds of the major winter and early spring vegetables consumed in the United States are imported from poor countries, principally Mexico, where the land and labor cost a fraction of what they do in the USA. Yet these vegetables are not sold at cheaper prices than homegrown produce. Likewise, the General Electric household appliances made by young women in South Korea and Singapore who work for subsistence wages, and the Admiral International color television sets assembled by low-paid workers in Taiwan do not cost less than when they were made in the USA. As the president of Admiral noted, the move to Taiwan "won't affect pricing state-side but it should improve the company's profit structure, otherwise we wouldn't be making the move."[16]

We already noted how overseas investments have brought increasing misery to the Third World. Of interest here is how some of that misery comes home as a visitation upon the American people. We have heard much in our media about the "refugees from Communism"; we might think a moment about the refugees from capitalism. Driven off their lands, large numbers of impoverished Latinos and other Third Worlders have been compelled to flee into economic exile, coming to the United States, many of them illegally, to compete with American workers for entry-level jobs that are becoming increasingly scarce. Because of their illegal status and vulnerability to deportation, undocumented workers are least likely to unionize and least able to fight for improvements in work conditions. So they serve as a reserve army of labor, further depressing the wage market for American workers.

Not all immigrants are impoverished, unskilled workers. Harsh economic conditions in many nations tend to encourage the exodus of the younger and more educated without whom development is impossible. The result is "brain drain," as the rich nations siphon off the trained talent and skills of the poor nations, further adding to the differential between rich and poor countries and to the downward spiral of the Third World.

Other injustices inflicted by the empire upon poorer nations come home to take a toll upon ordinary Americans. For years now the poisonous pesticides and hazardous pharmaceuticals that were banned in this country have been sold by their producers to Third World nations where regulations are weaker or nonexistent. (In 1981, President Reagan repealed an executive order signed a half-year before by President Carter that would have forced exporters of such products to notify the recipient nation that the commodity was banned in the USA.) With an assured export market, these poisons continue to cripple workers in the American chemical plants where they are made, and then reappear on our dinner tables in the fruit, vegetables, meat, and coffee we import.[17] These products also have been poisoning people in Third World countries, creating a legacy of sickness and death that is starting to backfire on us.[18]

The absence of environmental protections throughout most of the Third World affects the health and welfare of Americans in other ways (along with the well-being of other peoples and the earth's entire ecology). The chemical toxins and other industrial effusions poured into the world's rivers, oceans, and atmosphere by fast-profit, unrestricted multinational corporations operating in Asia, Africa, and Latin America, and the devastation of Third World lands by mining and timber companies and by agribusiness, are seriously affecting the quality of the air we all breathe, the water we all drink, and the food we all eat. Ecology knows no national boundaries. The search for cheap farmland to raise cattle induces US companies to cut down rain forests throughout Central America. The nutrient-poor top soil is soon depleted and the land deteriorates from lush jungle into scraggly desert. Then the cattle-raisers move on to other forests. The tropical rain forests in Central America and the much vaster ones in the Amazon basin are being destroyed at an alarming rate and may be totally obliterated within the next two decades. Over 25 percent of our prescription drugs are derived from rain forest plants. Rain forests are the winter home for millions of migratory North

American songbirds—of which declining numbers are returning from Central America. Many of these birds are essential to pest control.[19]

The dumping of industrial effusions and radioactive wastes also may be killing our oceans. If the oceans die, so do we, since they produce most of the earth's oxygen. Over half the world's forests are gone compared to earlier centuries. The forests are nature's main means of removing carbon dioxide from the atmosphere. Today, the carbon dioxide buildup is transforming the chemical composition of the earth's atmosphere, accelerating the "greenhouse effect" by melting the earth's polar ice caps and causing a variety of other climatic destabilizations. While the imperialists are free to roam the world and plunder it at will, we are left to suffer the immediate and long-term consequences.

Additional ways that the empire strikes back home: the narcotics that victimize whole segments of our population are shipped in through secret international cartels linked to past and present CIA operatives. Large-scale drug trafficking has been associated with CIA-supported covert wars in Cuba, Southeast Asia, and Central America. As of 1988, evidence was mounting linking the US-backed Nicaraguan counterrevolutionaries to a network of narcotics smuggling that stretched "from cocaine plantations in Columbia to dirt airstrips in Costa Rica, to pseudo-seafood companies in Miami, and, finally, to the drug-ridden streets of our society."[20]

The empire victimizes its own people in other grim ways. Thousands of Army veterans exposed to nuclear tests after World War II are now dying of cancer. Vietnam veterans who came back contaminated by the tons of herbicides sprayed on Indochina are facing premature death from cancer, while their children have suffered an abnormally high rate of birth defects (in common with the children of Vietnam).[21] The US military has experimented on Americans with its chemical and bacteriological warfare methods. The Navy sprayed bacteria in San Francisco in 1950, an experiment that has since been implicated in the illness of several residents and the death of at least one person. In 1955, the CIA conducted a biological warfare test in Tampa Bay area, soon after which twelve people died in a whooping-cough epidemic. In the 1950s and 1960s, biological warfare tests were done in various cities including St. Louis and New York, using bacilli that were known to be infectious but supposedly not fatal.[22]

Empire has a great many overhead costs, especially military ones, that must be picked up by the people. The Vietnam War cost

$168.1 billion in direct expenditures for US forces and military aid to allies in Indochina. The war's indirect costs will come to well over $350 billion (for veterans benefits and hospitals, interest on the national debt, etc.). As the economist Victor Perlo pointed out, by the end of the war inflation had escalated from about 1 percent a year to 10 percent; the national debt had doubled over the 1964 level; the federal budget showed record deficits; unemployment had doubled; real wages had started on their longest decline in modern American history; interest rates rose to 10 percent and higher; the US export surplus gave way to an import surplus; and US gold and monetary reserves had been drained.[23] There were human costs: 2.5 million Americans had their lives interrupted to serve in Indochina; of these 58,156 were killed and 303,616 wounded (13,167 with a 100 percent disability); 55,000 have died since returning home because of suicides, murders, addictions, alcoholism, and accidents; 500,000 have attempted suicide since coming back to the USA. Ethnic minorities paid a disproportionate cost; thus while composing about 12 percent of the US population, Blacks accounted for 22.4 percent of all combat deaths in Vietnam in 1965. The New Mexico state legislature noted that Mexican Americans constituted only 29 percent of that state's population but 69 percent of the state's inductees and 43 percent of its Vietnam casualties in 1966.[24]

Americans pay dearly for "our" global military apparatus. The cost of building one aircraft carrier could feed several million of the poorest, hungriest children in America for ten years. Greater sums have been budgeted for the development of the Navy's submarine-rescue vehicle than for occupational safety, public libraries, and day-care centers combined. The cost of military aircraft components and ammunition kept in storage by the Pentagon is greater than the combined costs of pollution control, conservation, community development, housing, occupational safety, and mass transportation. The total expenses of the legislative and judiciary branches and all the regulatory commissions combined constitute little more than half of 1 percent of the Pentagon's yearly budget.[25]

Then there is the distortion of American science and technology as 70 percent of federal research and development (R&D) funds go to the military.[26] Contrary to Pentagon claims, what the military produces in R&D has very little spin-off for the civilian market. About one-third of all American scientists and engineers are involved in military projects, creating a serious brain drain for the civilian sector.[27] The United States is losing out in precisely those industries in which military spending is concentrated, to foreign competitors who are not burdened by heavily militarized economies. For instance, the US machine-tool industry once dominated the world market. But since so much of the industry has been absorbed by the military, foreign imports have increased six-fold and now account for more than a third of domestic civilian consumption. The same pattern has been evident in the aerospace and electronics industries, two other areas of concentrated military investment.[28]

> Benefits of military R&D to the civilian economy have been small and are declining as military technology becomes increasingly specialized and exotic. The rapid expansion of military research diverts resources from the civilian economy and retards U.S. economic growth and competitiveness in world markets. The few industries that have benefited from military research would be far better off if the money had been spent entirely on commercial research.[29]

The pattern of distortion will worsen if the Star Warriors have their way. The estimates for the Strategic Defense Initiative ("Star Wars") are stratospheric indeed, as much as several trillion dollars. The cost to the rest of the economy—as measured by the military absorption of scientific talent, the loss of export markets, and the competitive disadvantage of civilian R&D is even harder to calculate.

In his eight years in office President Reagan spent upwards of $2 *trillion* on the military. Sums of this magnitude create an enormous tax burden for the American people who, as of 1988, carried a national debt of $2.5 trillion, or *more than twice the debt of the entire Third World.* Furthermore, Americans must endure the neglect of environmental needs, the decay and financial insolvency of our cities, the deterioration of our transportation, education, and health-care systems, and the devastating effects of underemployment upon millions of households and hundreds of communities.

In addition, there are the frightful social and psychological costs, the discouragement and decline of public morale, the anger, cynicism, and suffering of the poor and the not-so-poor, the militarization and violence of popular culture and the potential application of increasingly authoritarian solutions to our social problems.

Poverty can be found in the rich industrial nations as well as the Third World. In the richest of them all, the United States, those living below the poverty level grew in the 1981–86 period from 24 million to almost 35 million, according to the government's own figures, which many consider to be underestimations—thus making the poor the fastest growing social group in the USA. In 1986, the House Select Committee on Hunger found that Kwashiorkor and marasmus diseases, caused by severe protein and calorie deficiencies and usually seen only in Third World countries, could be found in the United States, along with rising rates of infant mortality in poor areas.[30]

Those regions within the United States that serve as surplus labor reserves or "internal colonies," such as Appalachia, poor Black and Latino communities, Eskimo Alaska, and Native American Indian lands, manifest the symptoms of Third World colonization, including chronic underemployment, hunger, inadequate income, low levels of education, inferior or nonexistent human services, absentee ownership, and extraction of profits from the indigenous community. In addition, the loss of skilled, higher-paying manufacturing jobs, traditionally held by White males, has taken its toll of working-class White communities as well. So when we talk of "rich nations" and "poor nations" we must not forget that there are millions of poor in the rich nations and thousands of rich in the poor ones. As goes the verse by Bertolt Brecht:

There were conquerors and conquered.
Among the conquered the common people starved.
Among the conquerors the common people starved too.

As in Rome of old and in every empire since, the center is bled in order to fortify the periphery. The lives and treasure of the people are squandered so that patricians might pursue their far-off plunder.

Notes

1. Joseph Schumpeter, "The Sociology of Imperialism," in *Two Essays by Joseph Schumpeter* (New York: Meridian Books, 1955), p. 51.

2. Ibid., p. 53.

3. Ernst Badian, *Roman Imperialism in the Late Republic* (Ithaca, N.Y.: Cornell University Press, 1969).

4. Richard Barnet, *Roots of War* (New York: Penguin, 1973), p. 22.

5. Ibid., p. 22.

6. Thorstein Veblen, *The Theory of the Business Enterprise* (New York: Charles Scribner's Sons, 1932), p. 217.

7. Karl Marx and Frederick Engels, *On Colonialism* (selected writings), New York: International Publishers, 1972, p. 168.

8. Horst Drechsler, *Let Us Die Fighting* (Berlin: Akademie-Verlag, 1966), p. 244.

9. George Kennan, *American Diplomacy 1900–1950* (Chicago: University of Chicago Press, 1952), p. 99.

10. John Buell and Matthew Rothchild, "Behind the Nicaraguan Threat" *Progressive,* October 1984, p. 14.

11. William Appleman Williams, *Empire As a Way of Life* (New York: Oxford University Press, 1980).

12. See the discussion "Creating a Conservative Myth" in Michael Parenti, *Inventing Reality: The Politics of the Mass Media* (New York: St. Martin's Press, 1986), pp. 90–94; also Thomas Ferguson and Joel Rogers, "The Myth of America's Turn to the Right," *Atlantic Monthly,* May 1986, p. 48.

13. V. I. Lenin, *Imperialism, the Highest Stage of Capitalism* (New York: International Publishers, 1939).

14. Michel Bosquet, *Capitalism in Crisis and Everyday Life* (Sussex, England: Harvester Press, 1977), pp. 65–67.

15. C. Richard Hatch, *IPS Features* (Institute for Policy Studies, Washington, D.C., April 1986.)

16. Interview in the documentary film *Controlling Interests* (San Francisco: California Newsreel, 1978).

17. David Weir and Mark Shapiro, *Circle of Poison* (San Francisco: Institute for Food Development, 1981).

18. Ibid.

19. See the statement by the Rainforest Action Network and the Farm Animal Reform Movement in *New York Times,* January 22, 1986; also Boris Gorizontov, *Capitalism and the Ecological Crisis* (Moscow: Progress Publishers, 1982); available from Imported Publications, Chicago.

20. See "The Contra-Drug Connection," A Christic Institute Special Report, Washington D.C., November 1987; also *New York Times,* February 24 and July 16, 1987; *Washington Post,* June 30, 1987; *San Francisco Examiner,* June 23, 1986; Leslie Cockburn, *Out of Control* (New York: Atlantic Monthly Press, 1987); Alfred McCoy, *The Politics of Heroin in Southeast Asia* (New York: Harper and Row, 1973).

21. Michael Uhl and Tod Ensign, *GI Guinea Pigs* (New York: Wideview, 1980).

22. Leonard Cole "The Army's Secret Germ War Testing," *Nation,* October 23, 1982, pp. 397–99; *Guardian,* December 26, 1984.

23. Victor Perlo, "Economic Consequences of the Vietnam War," *Daily World,* April 25, 1985.

24. "The Legacy of the Vietnam War," *Indochina Newsletter,* Dorchester, Mass., November–December 1982, p. 12; Katherine Sciacchitano, "Culture Report," *National Reporter,* Spring 1987, p. 39.

25. Michael Parenti, *Democracy for the Few,* 5th ed. (New York: St. Martin's Press, 1988), p. 84.

26. James Petras in the *Guardian,* July 12, 1969; and Seymour Melman in the *New York Times,* July 26, 1981.

27. According to a study by the Center for Defense Information, *Defense Monitor,* vol. 14, 1985.

28. Ibid.

29. Ibid., p. 1.

30. *Washington Post,* May 24, 1986.

8

The Mythology of Interventionism

The substantial demands made by the US empire upon the American people have not been particularly popular. A major problem for US policymakers and corporate leaders is that the American people keep drifting off into reality, worrying about money, jobs, homes, and the quality of life in their own society. So they repeatedly must be brought back to face the harsh illusions propagated by their rulers. In pursuit of that goal, White House policymakers, corporate leaders, Pentagon propagandists, CIA opinion molders, academicians and media commentators, along with representatives from other supposedly autonomous institutions of a "pluralistic" American society, move with remarkably singleminded orchestration to justify US interventionist policy to the populace.[1] What follows are some of the basic themes of the interventionist ideology as it has developed over time.

Racism and the Subjugation of Other Peoples

Throughout history those who have hungered for land, gold, and slaves have treated colonized peoples as moral inferiors, indeed, as nonpersons. "Occasionally it is mistakenly held that Europeans enslaved Africans for racist reasons. European planters and miners enslaved Africans for *economic* reasons, so that their labor power could be exploited," noted the late Guyanese scholar, Walter Rodney. But in short time the imperialists "found it necessary to rationalize that exploitation in racist terms as well," and oppression of African people on purely racial grounds became indistinguishable from economic oppression.[2]

During the several centuries of the European conquest of North

America, the White settlers, with few exceptions, saw the Native American Indian inhabitants as "brutes" and "savages," "vermin" and "wild varmints." The land stolen from them was repeatedly described as "uninhabited." When their presence was acknowledged, they were said to "infest" the terrain. And like any infestation, they were deserving of extermination. The Puritans saw the Indians as "devils" and "devil worshipers." In the words of Roger Williams—whose vaunted tolerance and brotherly love seems to have been confined to members of his own race—Indians were "Adam's degenerate seede." While conducting the war that slaughtered the nine hundred or so men, women, and children of the Pequoit tribe in 1637, Captain John Mason exhulted that God was pleased to smite his heathen enemies and the enemies of God's people "and to give us their lands for Inheritance."[3] The choice lands went to the Endicotts, Winthrops, Underhills, Masons, and other such class leaders of the "community of Saints."

The more land the English settlers grabbed, the more racist they became in their treatment of Native Americans. They emphasized the Indian's supposedly treacherous, violent, godless nature; they prohibited the sale of guns to Indians; and forbade any fraternization that might have acknowledged the Indians' humanity. Recognition of the Native Americans' natural equality would have made it difficult to justify the theft of their lands and the systematic extermination of whole tribes. Nor did this process of extermination abate in the next two centuries. (The "father of our nation," George Washington, likened the "red savages" to wolves, "both being beasts of prey, though they differ in shape.")[4]

As with the American Indians so with the Africans who were colonized into slavery in White America. According to Chief Justice Roger Taney, in his *Dred Scott* decision (1857), Blacks were "a subordinate and inferior class of beings." Blacks were also considered children, or subhuman creatures bred for their labor and intended by Divine Providence to live in servitude. Similarly, when colonizing Southwest Africa in 1900–10, the Germans described the native peoples as "baboons" and treated them accordingly. Rudyard Kipling wrote of the Asian victims of British imperialism in his poem, *The White Man's Burden:* "Your new-caught sullen people / Half-devil, half-child. . . ." And in 1897, Winston Churchill judged Afghans to be "dangerous and as sensible as mad dogs, fit to be treated as such."[5]

So were Mexicans, Filipinos, Chinese, and more recently Viet-

namese described in ways that gave little recognition to their humanity. An American weekly magazine, the San Francisco *Argonaut*,
defended the atrocities of American troops in the Philippines in 1902
by exhulting over the enormous riches and fertility of the islands,
then noted: "But unfortunately they are infested by Filipinos. There
are many millions of them there, and it is to be feared that their
extinction will be slow. . . . Let us all be frank. WE DO NOT WANT
THE FILIPINOS. WE WANT THE PHILIPPINES."[6] As the United
States plunged into the Philippines War and other such overseas
imperialist ventures, US leaders, along with popular and scholarly
publications, propagated the view that races were distinct and separate biological entities and that the "Anglo-Saxon" race was superior
to all others, and was therefore justified in imposing its rule over
"weaker" peoples across the Pacific.[7]

The denial of the human qualities of a group, based on physical
distinctions, is the essence of racism. In this regard, the imperialists
dehumanize not only the darker races. During a visit to Ireland in
the nineteenth century, Charles Kingsley, a Cambridge historian
observed:

> I am haunted by the human chimpanzees I saw along that hundred
> miles of horrible country. I don't believe they are our fault. I believe
> there are not only many more of them than of old, but they are happier,
> better, more comfortably fed and lodged under our rule than they ever
> were. But to see white chimpanzees is dreadful; if they were black, one
> would not feel it so much, but their skins, except where tanned by
> exposure, are as white as ours.[8]

More than just an attitude, racism is a practice of subjugation
and annihilation. And while racism antedates modern imperialism,
it seems to have reached its cruelest practices with the White expansionism into Africa, the Americas, and Asia. Racism is one of the
earliest, crudest justifications for imperialism. How much easier to
play the homicidal conqueror if your victims are but subhuman
"wogs," "kaffirs," "niggers," "chinks," "greasers" "ragheads"
"slopes," and "gooks." Such defamatory terms are the vocabulary
of *imperialism* as well as racism.

Helping Inferior Peoples

When not slated for extinction as subhuman, colonized peoples
are judged to be "backward," incapable of taking care of themselves
and in need of protection and direction. Native American Indians

were deemed by Thomas Jefferson as needful of a civilizing moral uplift, the kind that would make them give up their lands and disappear beyond the Mississippi, as he wanted, or disappear into the White population—a "detribalization and incorporation" policy that is pursued to this day by the federal government. At the time of the Louisiana Purchase, President Jefferson was quick to justify American possession of that immense expanse of land by describing it as "uninhabited," the Indians being nonpersons. As for Louisiana's French and Spanish denizens, Jefferson judged them "yet incapable of self-government as children."[9]

In 1898, when pondering what to do with the Philippines (after having forcibly wrested them from the Spaniards), President William McKinley decided he "could not leave [the Filipinos] to themselves—they were unfit for self-government." McKinley tells how, after praying to "Almighty God for light and guidance," he was visited with the revelation that it would be "cowardly and dishonest" to give the Philippines back to Spain and "bad business" to turn them over to France and Germany, "our commercial rivals in the Orient," so ". . . there was nothing left for us to do but take them all, and to educate the Filipinos, and uplift and civilize and Christianize them, and by God's grace do the very best we could by them, as our fellowmen for whom Christ also died."[10] Perhaps because they had already been Christianized for several centuries by the Spaniards, the Filipinos themselves were not put to rest by McKinley's divine inspirations. Instead, as noted earlier, they valiantly resisted the US invasion at great cost to themselves.

In 1900, the irrespressible imperialist spokesman, Senator Albert Beveridge, appropriately wove together the themes of God, dollar, and sword:

> We will not renounce our part in the mission of our race, trustee under God, of the civilization of the world. . . . We will move forward to our work . . . with gratitude . . . and thanksgiving to Almighty God that He has marked us as His Chosen People, henceforth to lead in the regeneration of the world. . . .
>
> The Pacific is our ocean. . . . Where shall we turn for consumers of our surplus? . . . China is our natural customer. . . . The power that rules the Pacific is the power that rules the world. And, with the Philippines, that power is and will forever be the American Republic.[11]

It was President Woodrow Wilson who, sounding much like Jefferson, announced that "our real relationship to the rest of mankind" and "our peculiar duty" was to teach colonial peoples "order and self control" and to "import to them, if it be possible . . . the drill and habit of law and obedience which we long ago got out of . . . English history."[12] On another occasion Wilson said: "I am going to teach the South American republics to elect good men." He then proceeded to intervene violently and frequently in Latin American affairs. "We are the friends of Constitutional government in [Latin] America," he announced just before he ordered the US bombardment and occupation of Vera Cruz, a lesson in orderly constitutionalism that cost the Mexicans dearly in lives.[13]

To this day, US policymakers continue to justify the foreign aid and military assistance given to Third World countries as attempts to rescue less developed, less capable peoples from some distress (usually Communism) and bring them along the path of prosperity and self-reliance.

Protecting Our Standard of Living

On occasion, the pretense of international altruism is dropped and the interventionists talk about looking out for Number One, protecting American wealth from the incursions of a have-not world. Observe the crass utterances of President Lyndon Johnson before a cheering Junior Chamber of Commerce audience in 1966: "We own half the trucks in the world. We own almost half of the radios in the world. We own a third of all the electricity. . . ." But the rest of the world, he added, wants the same things. "Now I would like to see them enjoy the blessings that we enjoy. But don't you help them exchange places with us, because I don't want to be where they are."[14] Rather than carry the standard of democracy *into* the world, now our task was to protect our standard of living *from* the world.

Defending Democracy and Opposing Tyranny

US leaders have often claimed that their overseas efforts would bring to others the blessings of democracy. The most famous of these utterances is Woodrow Wilson's proclamation that the goal of World War I was to "make the world safe for democracy." More recently in 1964, when the democratically elected government of Brazil—headed by Joao Goulart who was instituting economic reforms and nationalizing some US business holdings—was overthrown by right-wing militarists, Secretary of State Dean Rusk told the American people that this fascist coup was a "move to ensure the continuity of constitutional government."[15] When the democratically elected government of Chile, headed by Salvador Allende, was crushed by the fascist Chilean military, defenders of that action explained that it was necessary because Allende was "endangering freedom" in Chile.

In May 1984, President Reagan defended the US-supported invasion of Nicaragua by right-wing reactionary forces (the "contras") stationed in Honduras as an effort to bring that country to elections. When the Sandinistas held elections the following November, Reagan dismissed these as fraudulent, a charge that contradicted the observations of independent teams of jurists from various Western countries.[16] Our government had voiced no urgent demand for Western-style parliamentarism during the fifty years before 1979 when the Somoza dictatorship plundered and oppressed the Nicaraguan nation. If Reagan hated tyranny enough to invade and attempt to overthrow the presumedly tyrannical Sandinistas of Nicaragua, one might wonder why he never once moved against Chile, South Africa, Indonesia, Zaire, Paraguay, Turkey, and a host of other terribly repressive regimes.

If anything, successive US administrations have worked hard to *subvert* constitutional governments, giving support to the reactionary militarists who overthrew Arbenz in Guatemala, Jagan in Guyana, Mossadegh in Iran, Bosch in the Dominican Republic, Sukarno in Indonesia, Bhutto in Pakistan, Goulart in Brazil, Allende in Chile, and democratic governments in Greece, Bolivia, Uruguay, and a number of other countries. Given this record, it is hard to believe that the CIA trained, armed, and financed an expeditionary force of right-wing counterrevolutionary mercenaries out of a newly acquired concern for human rights in Nicaragua.

In defense of the often undemocratic way the United States goes about saving democracy, our policymakers argue: "We cannot always pick and choose our allies. Sometimes we must support unsavory right-wing authoritarian regimes in order to prevent the spread of far more repressive totalitarian Communist ones." But the degree of repression cannot be the criterion guiding White House policy, for the United States has supported some of the worst butchers in the world: Batista in Cuba, Somoza in Nicaragua, the Shah in Iran,

Salazar in Portugal, Marcos in the Philippines, Pinochet in Chile, Zia in Pakistan, Evren in Turkey, and for awhile even Pol Pot in Cambodia. In the 1965 Indonesian coup, the right-wing "moderately authoritarian" military slaughtered 500,000 people, according to the Indonesian chief of security.[17] But this did not deter the US from assisting in that takeover nor from maintaining cozy relations with the same Jakarta regime that now conducts a bloody repression in East Timor.[18]

Friendly Rightists and Hostile Leftists

After World War II, the justifications for interventionism were increasingly cloaked in anticommunist terms. Our policymakers have argued that right-wing governments, for all their "deficiencies," are friendly toward us, while Communist ones are belligerent and therefore a threat to US security. But every Marxist or left-leaning country, be it a great power like the Soviet Union or small powers like Vietnam, Cuba, Angola, and Nicaragua or a mini-power like Grenada (under the New Jewel Movement), has sought friendly diplomatic and economic relations with the USA. They do so not necessarily out of love for the United States but because of a self-interested desire not to be menaced by US military power, and to enjoy the opportunities of trade that come with friendly relations. As they themselves point out, their economic development and political security would be much better served if they could improve relations with Washington. In each case, it has been the United States that has refused to establish diplomatic relations.

Take the example of Cuba: because of the American embargo, Cuba has the highest import-export tonnage costs of any country in the world, having to buy its school buses and medical supplies from Japan and other far-off countries rather than from the nearby United States. Better relations with the USA would bring the Cubans more trade, technology, and tourism, and the chance to cut their defense expenditures. Yet Havana's overtures for friendlier relations have been repeatedly rebuffed by successive administrations in Washington. Between 1981 and 1984 alone, the Reagan administration passed up at least four initiatives by the Cuban government to normalize relations.[19]

If the US government justifies its own hostility toward leftist governments on the grounds that they are hostile toward the United

States, what becomes the justification when they try to be friendly? When a newly established revolutionary regime threatens Washington with friendly relations, this does pose a problem. The solution is:

1. to heap criticism on that government for imprisoning the butchers, assassins, and torturers of the old US-backed regime,
2. denounce the new government as "totalitarian" for failing to institute Western-style, competitive electoral party politics,
3. denounce it as a threat to peace and security,
4. harass, destabilize, and impose economic sanctions,
5. attack it with surrogate forces, trained, equipped, and financed by the CIA and led by members of the former regime, or if necessary with US troops.

In other words, after denouncing the revolutionary country as a threat to peace, the counterinsurgents start a war against it.

In response, the targeted country denounces the United States' threats and hostile actions. It moves closer to other leftist nations and attempts to build up its military defenses in anticipation of a US-sponsored attack. These moves, in turn, are quickly seized upon by US officials as demonstration of the smaller country's antagonism toward us, and as justification for the policies that evoked such responses.

For example, from 1982 to 1988, the president of the United States, the secretary of state, and the secretary of defense were expressing their determination to rid "our hemisphere" of the present Nicaraguan government. Somocista-led mercenaries supported by the CIA were invading Nicaragua on two fronts, blowing up oil refineries, attacking farm cooperatives, murdering health workers and peasants, and mining Nicaragua's harbors. Yet US leaders complained repeatedly about the Sandinistas' "massive military buildup," using it as an excuse to make further moves against Managua, as if the Nicaraguans had no right to defend themselves from US threats and attacks.

It is difficult to demonstrate that small countries like Grenada (under the New Jewel) and Nicaragua (under the Sandinistas) are a threat to US security. We might recall the cry of the hawk during the Vietnam War: "If we don't fight the Viet Cong in the jungles of Indochina, we will have to fight them on the beaches of California." The image of the Vietnamese getting into their PT boats and crossing the Pacific to invade our West Coast was, as Walter Lippmann noted at the time, a grievous insult to the US Navy. The image of a minimally equipped Sandinista army of forty thousand cutting a bloody swath through Guatemala, Mexico, and across the Rio Grande, laying waste to our heartland and invading our hometowns is equally farfetched.

The truth is, the Vietnamese, Cubans, Grenadians, Nicaraguans—and for that matter, the Russians—have never invaded the United States. The United States has invaded Vietnam, Cuba, Grenada, Nicaragua, and Soviet Russia and continues to try to isolate and destabilize these countries—all of whom have made repeated overtures for friendly relations with the USA. They have nothing to lose and plenty to gain in the way of trade, tourism, securer borders, and a lighter defense burden. Life would be a lot easier for small and large socialist countries if they could enjoy normal relations with Washington. It is precisely for this reason Washington does not usually pursue such a course. The US leadership has little interest in making life easier for those who try to build an alternative social and economic order.

The Giant Red Menace

When all other interventionist arguments fail, there is always the Russian Bear. A central purpose of the interventionist mythology is to deny that a great struggle is going on between US imperialism and Third World liberation movements. Instead, US interventionism is portrayed as a defensive strategy to counter the expansionist designs of a major Communist power, usually the Soviet Union. The American people would balk at sending their sons off to die for Exxon, Chase Manhattan, and ITT. So the ruling elites tell us that we intervene to protect "US interests" or our "national security." Supposedly we are trying to prevent various Communist powers from capturing the world's resources and enslaving our allies and eventually us.

Yet it is not easy to convince the American public that a far-off country like Vietnam or a small nearby one like Nicaragua are threats to our security, so our policymakers and publicists conjure up an imagine of Moscow as the grand puppeteer. Behind the little Reds there supposedly stands the Giant Red Menace.

The Menace has not always been located in the Kremlin. In 1967, during the Vietnam War, Secretary of State Dean Rusk argued that the

Vietnamese were puppets of "Red China" and after a Communist victory in Vietnam, China would overrun all of Asia. According to Rusk, Beijing "nominated itself" to be the United States' "special enemy . . . by proclaiming a militant doctrine of the world revolution and doing something about it."[20] Vice President Hubert Humphrey voiced similar sentiments, declaring that we were fighting in Vietnam to defeat "militant, aggressive Asian Communism with its headquarters in Peking [Beijing], China."[21] Similar opinions were voiced by other officials in the Johnson and Kennedy administrations.[22]

In the mid-1970s, driven by its own conflicts with Moscow, China cultivated friendly relations with reactionary governments around the world, including many US client states. The Chinese aided anticommunist counterrevolutionaries in Southeast Asia, Africa, and elsewhere. Now US hostility focused once more on the USSR as the principle culprit behind world revolution.[23]

When the Angolan MPLA liberation forces, with the aid of Cuban troops, fought off a combined invasion by Zairian and South African forces in 1975, Senator Daniel P. Moynihan announced that the Atlantic was being turned into a "Soviet lake." When the Soviets agreed to send several flagships to assist Kuwaiti oil shipments in 1987, Moynihan warned that the Persian Gulf could become a "Soviet lake." And during the 1979–80 turmoil in the Middle East, people like Senator Henry Jackson kept warning us that the Soviet Union was the real danger behind the Palestine Liberation Front and all other stirrings in the Middle East.[24]

So in 1986 we were told that the Salvadoran rebels were puppets of the Nicaraguans who were puppets of the Cubans who were puppets of the Russians. We were asked to believe that impoverished people in El Salvador chose armed struggle—living in the jungle under the most adverse conditions and facing death and destruction delivered by the vastly superior firepower of helicopter gunships and fighter bombers—not out of hope for a better life for themselves, their families, peers, and nation, but because some ringmaster in Moscow or Beijing cracked the whip and ordered them to it. In fact, as Lenin himself put it: "Revolutions are not made to order: they cannot be timed for any particular moment: they mature in a process of historical development and break out at a moment determined by the whole complex of internal and external causes."[25] Or as the noted Chilean exile Isabel Letelier observed in a 1986 speech in

Washington: "We the people of the Third World do not need the Soviets to tell the Cubans to tell us that we are hungry."

Evidence to support the image of a Moscow-centered global menace is sometimes farfetched. President Jimmy Carter and National Security Advisor Zbigniew Brzezinski suddenly discovered a "Soviet combat brigade" in Cuba in 1979—which turned out to be a noncombat training unit that had been there since 1962. This fact did not stop President Reagan from announcing to a joint session of Congress in 1983: "Cuba is host to a Soviet combat brigade."[26] That same year, in a nationally televised speech, Reagan imaginatively transformed a Grenadian airport built to accommodate direct tourist flights, into a killer-attack Soviet forward base, and a twenty-foot deep Grenadian inlet into a potential Soviet submarine base.[27]

To justify the invasion of the tiny and relatively defenseless sovereign nation of Grenada (population 120,000), the White House depicted that country as having enormous strategic value to Cuba and the Soviet Union, an outpost from which Havana and Moscow would be able to control the crucial oil tanker lanes that came from the Atlantic through the Caribbean. Grenada supposedly was a Soviet arsenal designed to subvert and conquer other countries in the region. The weapons actually found in Grenada consisted of defensive small arms, obsolete rifles, and some artillery and vehicles, enough to equip an army of about two thousand and a militia of twice that number, hardly the stuff to dominate the Caribbean.[28]

Similarly, the portrayal of Nicaragua as an aggressive adjunct of the Soviet Union was achieved only by doing serious damage to the facts. In May 1983, the White House announced that Soviet ships were carrying heavy military equipment to Nicaragua. American reporters present at the unloading saw only field kitchens from East Germany and 1,200 tons of fertilizer. The following year, alarming reports of Soviet fighter planes being shipped to Managua proved equally false. (It was never made clear why Nicaragua did not have the right to have fighter planes as did other countries in Central America.) The State Department's own Bureau of Intelligence and Research, in a June 1984 report entitled *Soviet Attitudes Toward, Aid to, and Contacts with Central American Revolutionaries,* observed that "all too many U.S. claims proved open to question." The report characterizes Soviet military equipment in Nicaragua as "unobtrusive" and "outdated," and "the limited amounts of truly modern equipment acquired by the Sandinistas . . . came from Western Europe, not the Eastern bloc." The report concluded that "the scope and nature of the Kremlin's infusion are far short of justifying the President's exaggerated alarms."[29]

Revolutions are not push-button affairs, rather they evolve only if there exists a reservoir of hope and grievance that can be galvanized into popular action. People are inclined to endure great abuses before risking their lives in mortal combat with superior armed forces. There is no such thing as a frivolous revolution, nor one initiated and orchestrated by a manipulative cabal residing in a foreign capital. Nor is there any evidence that once the revolution succeeds, the new leaders will place the interests of their country at the disposal of Beijing or Moscow. Instead of becoming the willing puppets of "Red China," as our policymakers predicted, Vietnam soon found itself locked in combat with China. As mentioned earlier, just about every Communist country has tried to keep its options open and has sought friendly diplomatic and economic relations with the United States.

If US interventions in other countries were defensive measures against the "Soviet superpower," how do we explain the many repeated interventions, invasions, and occupations perpetrated by US rulers long before the USSR ever came into existence in 1917 or developed any substantial strength? Between 1831 and 1891, US armed forces—usually the Marines—invaded Mexico, Cuba, the Dominican Republic, Puerto Rico, Panama, Colombia, Nicaragua, Uruguay, Brazil, Haiti, Argentina, and Chile a total of thirty-one times, a fact not many of us are informed about in school. The Marines intermittantly occupied Nicaragua from 1909 to 1933, Mexico from 1914 to 1919, and Panama from 1903 to 1914. To "restore order" the Marines occupied Haiti from 1915 to 1934, killing over two thousand Haitians who resisted "pacification." The US took over customhouse control in the Dominican Republic in 1905 to protect investments and maintain debt payments, a financial supervision extending until 1941 and involving a US military invasion and occupation from 1916 to 1924.

The most dramatic interventionist testimonial was given in 1935 by the US Marine Corps Commandant, General Smedley Butler:

> I spent thirty-three years in the Marines, most of my time being a high-class muscle man for Big Business, for Wall Street and the bankers. In short, I was a racketeer for capitalism.

I helped purify Nicaragua for the international banking house of Brown Brothers in 1910–1912. I helped make Mexico and especially Tampico safe for American oil interests in 1914. I brought light to the Dominican Republic for American sugar interests in 1916. I helped make Haiti and Cuba a decent place for the National City [Bank] boys to collect revenue in. I helped in the rape of half a dozen Central American republics for the benefit of Wall Street. In China in 1927 I helped to see to it that Standard Oil went its way unmolested.

I had a swell racket. I was rewarded with honors, medals, promotions. I might have given Al Capone a few hints. The best he could do was to operate a racket in three city districts. The Marines operated on three continents.[30]

Well before there was a Soviet Union, US policymakers were responding to revolutionary movements much the way they do today. Washington refused to recognize the Haitian revolution for sixty years; suppressed popular insurgencies and assassinated their leaders—as was Sandino's fate in Nicaragua; burned villages, murdered large numbers of civilians, and set up internment camps as in the Philippines in 1899–1903 and in parts of Central America—all decades before the Bolsheviks came to power in Petrograd.

By the early 1920s, while a besieged Soviet government was grappling with civil war, blockade, embargo, and famine, President Calvin Coolidge had already learned to justify his military expeditions into other countries as safeguards against supposedly Moscow-directed uprisings, causing a skeptical Senator William Borah to comment: "The specter of Russian Bolshevist activity in Latin America was conjured but refused to walk."[31] So even before the Soviets could have been conceived as a real threat, they were conceived as an imaginary one.

The real danger was not that popular uprisings, reforms, and revolutions might serve the interests of the USSR. The real danger was—and still is—in the popular uprisings, reforms, and revolutions themselves and the threat they pose to those who own most of the world's wealth. In 1966, more than thirty years after General Smedley Butler, another former Marine Commandant, General David Sharp, offered this remarkable statement:

I believe that if we had and would keep our dirty, bloody, dollar-soaked fingers out of the business of these nations so full of depressed, exploited people, they will arrive at a solution of their own. . . . And if unfortunately their revolution must be of the violent type because the "haves" refuse to share with the "have-nots" by any peaceful method, at least what they get will be their own, and not the American style, which they don't want and above all don't want crammed down their throats by Americans.[32]

Notes

1. Michael Parenti, *Inventing Reality: The Politics of the Mass Media* (New York: St. Martin's Press, 1986), chapters 7–11.

2. Walter Rodney, *How Europe Underdeveloped Africa* (Washington, D.C.: Howard University Press, 1974), pp. 88–89.

3. The discussion on the Puritans is drawn from Richard Drinnon, *Facing West: The Metaphysics of Indian-Hating and Empire-Building* (New York: New American Library, 1980), pp. 43–46, and passim.

4. Ibid., p. 65.

5. Winston Churchill, *The Story of the Malaband Field Force,* quoted in Phillip Bonovsky, *Washington's Secret War Against Afghanistan* (New York: International Publishers, 1985), p. 13.

6. Paul Jacobs, Saul Landau, and Eve Pell, eds., *To Serve the Devil,* volume 2 (New York: Vintage, 1971), pp. 335–36.

7. C. Van Woodward, *The Strange Career of Jim Crow,* 3rd rev. ed. (New York: Oxford University Press, 1974), pp. 72–74.

8. Quoted in Michael MacDonald, *Children of Wrath* (Cambridge: Polity Press, 1986), p. 1.

9. L. W. Levy, *Jefferson and Civil Liberties, The Darker Side* (Cambridge, Mass.: Harvard University Press, 1963), pp. 81–92.

10. Thomas Bailey, *A Diplomatic History of the American People* (Englewood Cliffs, N.J.: Prentice-Hall, 1970), pp. 473–74.

11. Richard W. Van Alstyne, *The Rising American Empire* (Chicago: Quadrangle, 1965), p. 187.

12. Ibid., p. 197.

13. Albert K. Weinberg, *Manifest Destiny* (Chicago: Quadrangle, 1963), p. 435.

14. Quoted in Michael Parenti, *The Anti-Communist Impulse* (New York: Random House, 1969), p. 302.

15. Felix Green, *The Enemy* (New York: Vintage, 1971).

16. Michael Parenti, "Is Nicaragua More Democratic Than the US?" *CovertAction Information Bulletin,* no. 26, Summer 1986, pp. 48–52.

17. *New York Times,* December 21, 1977.

18. Jose Ramos-Horta, *Funu: The Unfinished Saga of East Timor* (Trenton, N.J.: Red Sea Press, 1986).

19. *Washington Post,* September 5, 1982; *New York Times,* August 5, 1984.

20. *New York Times,* October 13, 1967.

21. *New York Times,* October 14, 1967.

22. *New York Times,* July 29, 1965 and February 9, 1966.

23. On the revival of the cold war see Fred Halliday, *The Making of the Second Cold War* (London: Verso, 1983).

24. Michael Parenti, "The Mythology of U.S. Interventionism," in Leila Meo, ed., *U.S. Strategy in the Gulf* (Belmont, Mass.: Association of Arab-American University Graduates, 1981), p. 21 and passim. For Moynihan's comments on the Persian Gulf see *Washington Post,* June 2, 1987.

25. V. I. Lenin, *Collected Works,* vol. 27 (Moscow: Progress, 1965), p. 547.

26. *Washington Post,* April 28, 1983.

27. Ibid.

28. *New York Times,* November 6 and November 20, 1983; and *In These Times,* November 16, 1983.

29. Quoted in Saul Landau and Daniel Siegal, "Who Threatens the Hemisphere?" *IPS Features,* (Institute for Policy Studies, Washington, D.C., November 17, 1984.)

30. General Butler's confession has been widely quoted. The original can be found in an article by him in *Common Sense,* November 1935.

31. Quoted in Graham Stuart, *Latin America and the United States,* 4th ed. (New York: Appleton-Century-Crofts, 1943), p. 364.

32. Quoted in *In These Times,* February 25–March 10, 1987.

9

The Real Threat of Revolution

It has been noted that leftist governments do not pose a threat to US security; they cannot militarily conquer the United States, nor do they give any evidence of wanting to do so. In fact, they make repeated overtures for closer cultural, diplomatic, and economic relations with Washington. And rather than acting as puppets in a Moscow-directed conspiracy to takeover the world, they seem interested in keeping their options open with all major powers, East and West. This has been the case with Cuba, Vietnam, Mozambique, Angola, Nicaragua, and others. We also observed that US leaders have shown little dedication to democracy in the Third World and actually have helped subvert democracy in a number of nations, while cultivating close relations with some of the world's worst despots. At the same time, as noted earlier, public-opinion polls show that Americans generally oppose intervention by lopsided majorities, and millions have actively voiced their opposition to US military involvement abroad. What then motivates US interventionist policy and how can we think it is not confused and contradictory?

The answer is, Marxist and other leftist states *do* pose a real threat, not to the United States as a national entity, nor to the American people as such, but to the corporate and financial interests of our country, to Exxon and Mobil, Chase Manhattan and First National, Ford and General Motors, Anaconda and USX, to billions and billions of dollars in direct investments and loans.

But specific investments are not the only concern. US capitalists owned little of value in Grenada when the New Jewel movement took power, yet Reagan invaded that country. Similarly, the United States had relatively few investments in Indochina, most of the money there being French, yet it waged a bloody, protracted war against the revolutionary movements in that region. In such instances US interventionists are less concerned with protecting particular corporate investments than with safeguarding capitalism as a world system.

A socialist Nicaragua or socialist Grenada, as such, are hardly a threat to the survival of global capitalism. The danger is not socialism in any one country but a socialism that might spread to many countries. Multinational corporations are just that, multinational. They need the world, or a very large part of it, to exploit and expand in. There can be no such thing as "capitalism in one country." A social revolution in any part of the world may or may not hurt specific US corporations, but more than that, it becomes part of a cumulative threat to the entire global system. The domino theory (which argues that if one country in a region "falls" to Communism, others will follow like dominoes in a row) may not work as automatically as its more alarmist proponents claim, but who can deny there is a contagion, a power of example and inspiration, and sometimes even direct encouragement and assistance from one revolution to another. Henry Kissinger expressed his fear that the "contagious example" of Allende's policies in Chile might "infect" other countries in Latin America and Southern Europe.[1] At stake in Grenada, as President Reagan correctly observed, was something more than nutmeg: it was the entire Caribbean. The US invasion of that country served notice to all the other nations in the Caribbean that they were not free to chart a revolutionary course.

Those who control the lion's share of the world's riches will defend at all costs their most favored way of life. For them, freedom is experienced as a sense of well-being closely connected to their social standing and their material abundance. Revolution represents a genuine loss of that freedom: the freedom to treat their employees as they choose and make money from other people's labor, the freedom to monopolize a society's scarce resources while being unaccountable to the public interest and indifferent to the hardships thereby inflicted upon others, the freedom to control public discourse and the communication universe, and the freedom to tax poorer classes without having to pay many taxes themselves. For them, "freedom" means to be above the law in most respects, to have the government at their personal service, to live in luxury, to be waited upon by small armies of underpaid servants, to vacation in Paris and London, to enjoy a range of goods, services, and life choices that are available only to a few, and finally to see that their children enjoy all these same good things.

As the owning classes view things, revolution brings "tyranny," a world turned nightmarishly upside down, in which the ignorant masses outrageously expect to dominate the allocation of public resources at the expense of the well-bred and wellborn, even daring to occupy the very estates and offices of the rich and powerful. Thus, the privileged classes dread socialism the way the rest of us might dread poverty, hunger, and death itself. They are prepared to go to any length to defend all that they have, all that makes life worthwhile to them. History provides no examples of a dominant class voluntarily relinquishing its social position so to better the lot of the downtrodden.

These privileged interests honestly see themselves as deserving of all they have, just as they see the poor as the authors of their own miserable existence. They embrace a self-justifying class ideology. And they are readily assisted by the publicists, commentators, and academics who advance their own careers by propagating the ruling-class worldview, presenting it as a concern for security, democracy, development, and peace. These acolytes have a direct interest in seeing that their own professional and class privileges are not threatened by any alternate social order. And like the rich, they sincerely believe in the virtue of the system they defend.

The real problem for the wealthy classes is not that revolutionaries "grab" power but that they *use* power to pursue policies that are unacceptable to ruling interests in both the Western industrial world and the Third World. What bothers American political leaders (and investment bankers, corporate heads, militarists, and media moguls, and the Third World landowners, large merchants, military chieftains, usurers, sweatshop bosses, and top bureaucrats) is not the Left's supposed lack of *political* democracy but its attempt to construct *economic* democracy, to use capital and labor in a way that is inimical to the survival of the capitalist social order at home and abroad.

Sometimes US officials will say they are *for* social change just as long as it is peaceful and not violent. But judging from the way they have helped to overthrow democratic governments that were taking a nonviolent, gradualist, reformist road (such as Guatemala, Indonesia, Greece, Brazil, and Chile), it would seem they actually have a low tolerance for social changes (even peaceful, piecemeal ones) that mo-

lest the existing class structure. The admonition voiced by counterinsurgency liberals: "If *you* don't carry out basic reforms in how
the land, labor, and resources are used, then the Communists will,"
makes little sense to Third World economic elites for whom the
voluntary implementation of basic structural changes would be nothing less than an act of class suicide, as fatal to their privileged existence as any violent upheaval. It makes little difference to wealthy,
privileged interests if their favored stations in life were undone by a
peaceful transition rather than a violent one. The *means* concern
them much less than the *end* results. It is not the "violent" in violent
revolution they hate—being themselves quite able to resort to violence; it is the "revolution." (Members of the comprador class in
Third World nations seldom actually meet a violent end in revolutions; the worst of them usually manage to make it to Miami, Ma-
drid, Paris, or New York.)

Here we can appreciate the immense deceptions that underlie US
foreign policy. While professing a dedication to peaceful, nonviolent
change, US policymakers have committed themselves to a defense of
the status quo throughout the world that regularly relies on violence.
They sometimes seize upon the revolutionary ferment that might
exist in impoverished lands as an excuse for *not* making economic
changes. Not until the situation in this or that country has been
sufficiently stabilized, they say, can we venture upon reforms. Until
then, we must rely on the police and military to restore order. But
once "order" and "stability" are reimposed, that is, once the democratic agitation has been crushed or subdued, there is no longer any
felt pressure for *economic* reform.

This is not to say that imperialists are uninterested in changes
that might strengthen their hand. As already noted, they will give a
"condominiumized" independence to a client state, better to blunt
the impact of its revolutionary independence movement and cloak
the colonialist economic relationship. A particular Third World auto-
crat might prove to be so abusive and plundering as to unite the
entire country against the ruler, including propertied interests that
feel their prerogatives have been violated. In such instances the ruler
no longer serves as an instrument of stability but becomes an instiga-
tion of instability—as was the case with the Shah in Iran, Somoza in
Nicaragua, Marcos in the Philippines, Duvalier in Haiti, and ruling
military juntas in various Latin American countries.[2]

In at least some of these cases, faced by popular and potentially revolutionary agitation, the United States moves to depose the unpopular ruler and introduces a fresh face and a seemingly more democratic system, one that includes "independent" media, trade unions, student organizations, and elections between two or more (usually nonsocialist) parties. Many of these institutions, parties, and groups enjoy the largesse of CIA funding or other US aid.[3] The country will now have a parliament and a president, who engage in debates on a variety of questions, including even some essential issues like the intrusions of foreign capital, land reform, and the continued abuses committed by security forces. But little happens in the way of actual reforms.

By the late 1980s, in a number of former dictatorships of Latin America, Asia, and Africa, the United States promoted the accoutrements of political democracy without much of the substance. Elections can be regularly held in these countries, just as long as no one tampers with the class structure. The US is willing to change regimes to preserve the pro-capitalist state. Electoral contests are usually classic exercises in elite politics, as was, for instance, the Filipino election of 1987, described by one observer as "a superficial and trivial exercise" in which "no coherent program or even serious issues were placed before the people by Aquino's slate."[4] It was an election heavily weighted by patronage and personality images and tainted by a score of political assassinations, almost all of which were perpetrated by the Right.

In some of these "demonstration democracies" the situation is better than in others. In the 1980s, in the Philippines, Argentina, Uruguay, and Brazil, there was a modest decline in human-rights violations, exiles were allowed to return, and the military remained strong but had to assume a lower profile. In contrast, in places like Guatemala and El Salvador, "the return to democracy" was accompanied by a continuation of political murders and all other human-rights violations. In the several decades since the 1954 CIA coup, Guatemala has had no really effective civilian rule. The new "democratic" constitution adopted in 1986 exonerated the previous military regime for its crimes against the people, giving an ominous signal for the future. From 1978 to 1985, the Guatemalan military—trained, financed, and advised by the US military—killed or "disappeared" an estimated 50,000 to 75,000 people, mostly unarmed Indian peasants, and destroyed 440 rural villages (by the army's own count), creating 100,000 orphans, 20,000 widows, and 150,000 refugees. The new constitution also validated the military decrees that set up the rural concentration camps (the infamous "model villages") and put virtually the entire male population of the Western Highlands, some 900,000, into military-controlled compulsory "civilian patrols." Under Guatemala's new "democratic, civilian" government, the army controlled all development and social-service programs and all resources and aid throughout the countryside. The army also established numerous new outposts in the most remote villages of the highlands. In both Guatemala and El Salvador, despite the "democratic civilian" facade, the military continued to have a grip over the country, tolerating no interference from the civilian government in its affairs, and enjoying a free hand in waging counterinsurgency terror against the population.[5]

Should popular forces in these client-state "democracies" mobilize too successfully, developing political parties, labor unions, and peasant organizations that gain a real measure of power, there is a good chance that the military, funded by the United States and waiting in the wings to thwart the "Communist menace," will take over, suspend the constitution, make the necessary arrests and executions, and restore "stability." In Chile, for instance, the democratically elected Allende government was overthrown not because democracy was faltering but because it was beginning to work a bit too well, increasing production in the not-for-profit public sector, cutting down on unemployment and the cheap labor supply, reallocating the national income to favor the poorer classes, expanding human services, and nationalizing major industries.

> Had Allende been allowed to serve out his full term in office, the lesson of Chile might have been that socialists and communists *can* play by the electoral rules of democracy and that profound changes *can* be accomplished peacefully rather than violently. Instead, the lesson of the Chilean experience is . . . that it was our government, not Allende's Popular Unity, that promoted military violence and the demise of constitutional rule.[6]

When the people of any particular country are successful in seizing state power and begin to change the socio-economic order, this becomes a cause for alarm among the ruling circles in the US. A *New York Times* editorial referred to "the undesirable and offensive Managua regime" in Nicaragua and the danger of seeing "Marxist power ensconsed in Managua."[7] But what specifically is so dangerous about "Marxist power"? What is undesirable and offensive about the Managua government? What has it done to the United States or to its own people? Is it the literacy campaign? The health-care and housing programs? The agricultural cooperatives? The attempt at increasing production and achieving a more equitable distribution of food, goods, and services for all? In large part, yes. Such reforms, even if not openly denounced by the US government, make a country suspect because they are symptomatic of an effort to erect a new and potentially competing economic order in which the prerogatives of private investment are no longer secure.

Consider the counterinsurgency study conducted by the Thai government in 1976, which recommended the following indicators for determining whether an area should come under suspicion as an insurgent stronghold: "The sudden disappearance of drug addiction; increased demand for books, paper, and pencils; improvement in public sanitation; and a great improvement in the internal cleanliness and order of the villages."[8] Reactionary governments like that in Thailand are not only indifferent to the welfare of their people, they are hostile toward signs of betterment—if these be indicative of a revolutionary liberation that might eventually threaten the existing class system.

Supporters of the counterrevolutionary effort against Nicaragua claim they are concerned about bringing democracy to that country and keeping Nicaragua independent of "Soviet influence." They come closer to their true complaint when they condemn the Sandinistas for interfering with the private-profit sector. Similarly, Henry Kissinger came close to the truth when he defended the fascist overthrow of the democratic government in Chile by noting that when forced to choose between saving the economy or saving democracy, we must save the economy. Had Kissinger said we must save the *capitalist* economy, it would have been the whole truth. For under Allende, as already noted, the danger was not that the economy was collapsing but that it was changing—in a socialist direction.

In sum, the US will replace autocracies with pseudo-democracies if that helps secure the existing economic system. Or it will overthrow democracies and promote autocracies when that is the necessary thing to do. In some instances, US policymakers are not able to do what they want or are not sure what to do. Thus by the late 1980s in Chile, General Pinochet was becoming a liability, another Somoza or Marcos, the focal point of an increasingly active mass opposition. The obvious solution would have been for the United States to de-

pose the dictator and institute a government that was more democratic in form, thereby forstalling a militant revolutionary development. The trouble was that in Chile, unlike some other countries, the
masses are highly politicized, and despite all the repression, the Left
is large and effectively organized. A democratic government might
work too well; it might bring some kind of leftist, strongly reformist
coalition back into power, creating the same problems for the mon-
eyed interests as existed under Allende. So US policy toward Chile
consisted of criticizing the dictator for his "excesses" but doing nothing to unseat him, hoping in the meantime that the US-financed
repressive forces in Chile might better immobilize and crush the militant Left.

Am I arguing that US leaders are insincere when they say they
want to advance the cause of democracy in other lands? Do they not
believe what they are saying? Whether US interventionists believe
their own arguments is not the key question. Sometimes they do,
sometimes they don't. Sometimes Ronald Reagan was doing his Hollywood best, as when his voice quavered with hypocritical compas-
sion for the Miskito Indians in Nicaragua, and sometimes he was
sincere, as when he spoke of his long-standing loathing for Communism. We need not ponder the question of whether US leaders are
motivated by their class interests or by a genuine commitment to
anticommunist ideology—as if these two things were in competition
with each other instead of being two sides of the same coin. The
arguments our leaders proffer may be self-serving and fabricated, yet
also sincerely embraced. It is a creed's congruity with one's material
self-interest that often makes it all the more compelling. In any case,
much of politics is the rational use of irrational symbols. The arguments in support of interventionism may sound irrational and non-
sensical, but they serve a rational purpose.

Can it be that US corporate investors and political leaders derive
some satisfaction from seeing millions of human beings in the Third
World suffer from poverty and political repression? Can we really
believe that each day they contrive new ways of contributing to the
misery of Third World peoples? No, but each day they ponder how
best to maintain their profitable holdings, and secure an "investment
climate" that allows the capital accumulation process to do its thing.
They do not particularly want to see people suffer. Generally they are
indifferent or removed from the miseries of the poor, both in the
Third World and in their own countries. If pressed on the point they

will insist that their investments lessen misery by developing the economies of countries inhabited by people who are presumed incapable of developing themselves. And, in any case, they see even the worst of the repressive right-wing regimes as far better than the dread scourge of class revolution.

US policymakers say they cannot afford to pick and choose the governments they support, but that is exactly what they do. As detailed earlier, the United States generally sides with those governments that are receptive to capitalist investment, while opposing those that seem to be moving in a socialist direction. This holds true regardless of whether the governments are autocratic or democratic in form. (Occasionally, friendly relations are cultivated with noncapitalist nations like Yugoslavia and China if these show themselves to be in useful opposition to other socialist nations or open to capital penetration.)

Once we grasp this point, we can move from a liberal complaint to a radical analysis. We can spend less time criticizing the "foolishness" of US policy and more time understanding its underlying interests. Those who do not see the defense of imperialism as a major component of American foreign policy are understandably at a loss to explain why a government such as ours, so professedly dedicated to democracy, comes down so often on the side of corrupt and brutal despots. Because these liberal critics are confused about what policymakers are doing, they assume that the policymakers themselves are confused.

Thus, a former CIA officer describes the US overthrow of the democratically elected government in Guatemala in 1954 (an undertaking in which he had participated) as "a tragic error . . . an error being repeated today [in Nicaragua] . . . It is painful," he continues, "to look on as my government repeats the mistake in which it engaged me thirty-two years ago."[9] The writer William Shirer is quoted as saying that for "the last fifty years we've been supporting right-wing governments, and that is a puzzlement to me. . . I don't understand what there is in the American character . . . that almost automatically, even when we have a liberal President, we support fascist dictatorships or are tolerant towards them."[10] The liberal columnist Richard Cohen is similarly befuddled:

> I dream that someday the United States will be on the side of the peasants in some civil war. I dream that we will be the ones who will help the poor overthrow the rich, who will talk about land reform and

education and health facilities for everyone, and that when the Red Cross or Amnesty International comes to count the bodies and take the testimony of women raped, that our side won't be the heavies.[11]

Why are we always on the wrong side? asks Cohen. It is a good question; too bad liberal critics never get around to answering it. It is not enough to complain about how bad things are, we must also explain *why* such things persist. A half-century ago, President Franklin Roosevelt attempted a partial answer when justifying US support of Nicaragua's dictator, Anastasio Somoza: "He may be a son-of-a-bitch, but at least he's our son-of-a-bitch."[12] But what exactly is the community of interest between US leaders and right-wing dictatorships that make them "ours" as opposed to the left-wing governments that also want to maintain friendly relations with us? Is there just some strange contest between two indistinguishable global cults, one that calls itself "the Left" and the other "the Right"? Or is there not a social content to the labels?

As already noted, people such as Somoza are "ours" because they open their countries to capital investment on the most favorable terms for the investor (and for themselves); they are essential cogs in the struggle to make the world safe for capitalism. For this reason they are called "rightists" and "anticommunists" and "staunch allies." And when reformists come to power, with the intent of using the resources and labor of the country for the collective benefit of the people, they are called "leftists," "Marxists," and "Communists," whether they think of themselves that way or not.

During the 1980s, liberal critics complained of a lack of coherence in US policy. They pointed to the "inconsistency" in the Reagan administration's policy of (1) imposing trade embargoes on Nicaragua in order to pressure that nation into becoming more "democratic" and more "cooperative," while (2) refusing to apply sanctions against South Africa, claiming such measures would retard the development of democracy in that country. But if we understand the class content of that policy, it comes out to be quite consistent. Its purpose was to punish leftist anti-imperialist governments and not punish rightist ones that are a part of global capitalism.

The Reagan-appointed Assistant Secretary of State for Inter-American Affairs Elliott Abrams argued in 1984 that El Salvador's right-wing regime could not be expected to institute a democracy while in the midst of a civil war. He noted that popular government could not be implanted overnight, that it took a hundred years for democracy to develop in the West, and that we cannot expect to impose our standards on a Latin American country.[13] Yet he and the administration he served demanded nothing less than a perfect democracy from Nicaragua, while that country was immersed in a violent war promoted by the United States.

These kinds of polemical inconsistencies should be exposed and rebutted. But, again, just because the arguments constructed to defend a policy are false and contradictory does not mean the policy itself is senseless. One should not confuse techniques with substantive goals. The US government is usually on the wrong side, against the poor and downtrodden, because the wrong side is the right side, given the class interests upon which the policy is fixed.

There are those who say we must learn from the Communists, copy their techniques, and thus win the battle for the hearts and minds of the people, as if "Communist techniques" were mysterious diabolic ploys. In fact, Communist methods are well known, but can we imagine the ruling interests of the United States applying them? Drive out the latifundia owners and sweatshop bosses and confiscate their property; imprison the militarists and torturers; kick out the plundering corporations and nationalize their holdings; redistribute the land and develop agricultural cooperatives; take the print and broadcast media out of the hands of the rich few and put them under public ownership; propagate a dedication to the egalitarian goals of the revolution; install a national health program; construct schools, hospitals, and clinics; mobilize the population for literacy campaigns and for work in publicly owned enterprises; initiate food and fuel rationing systems that benefit the very poorest sectors of the population.

If US leaders did all this, they would do more than defeat the "Marxist revolutionaries," they would have carried out their revolutionary programs; they would have become like the Marxists. For it is what Communists do that makes them what they are. US leaders would have prevented Marxist revolution only by bringing about its effects—thereby defeating the very goals of US policy.

The former CIA operative cited earlier observed that though he had been told he was battling Communism in Guatemala, in truth "Communism was not the threat we were fighting. The threat was land reform."[14] But land reform is much of what Communism is about in the Third World, taking the land from the rich and using it for social production and common needs. That is what the big landowners hate about Communists—or about any other reformers, even those who do not consider themselves Marxists. Adlai Stevenson once commented: "We know . . . how easy it is to mistake genuine local revolt for Communist subversion."[15] It is easy to mistake the two because they are one and the same. Certainly for the industrialists and financiers, it makes little difference whether their holdings are confiscated by "genuine local" rebels or "Communist subversives." That the owning classes hate Communism and fear its presence everywhere, does not make the hatred irrational, even if their fears are often exaggerated. They hate the economic changes that might obliterate their class existence and so they label such changes "Communist"—which they sometimes are and sometimes are not.

At this point others might respond that the Communists do something else besides give land to the poor: "They build armies and secret police. They seize monopoly control of the media. They impose one-party rule, and they deny people their freedoms of speech and religion." In responding to these assertions, we face the considerable task of separating fact from anticommunist fantasy. (At the same time we should keep in mind that not every criticism of socialist revolution or existing Communist societies is an unfounded fantasy.)

In order to survive, a social revolution—be it in Russia in 1917 or South Yemen in 1967 or Nicaragua in the 1980s—must do two things fairly early in its existence. First, it must build some kind of defense against the counterrevolutionary onslaught soon to come both from within and from capitalist countries. Second, the revolution must also break the power of the previously dominant class, and this means getting a thorough grip on state power, the security forces, courts, and bureaucracy. The revolution also must destroy both the economic base of that class and the influence it might still wield over social institutions and over certain sectors of the population.

Individual members of the privileged class may flee into exile, engage in counterrevolutionary efforts, or in some cases, switch sides and join the revolutionary cause. But the class itself must eventually cease to exist as a social formation in order for the revolution to develop in its own right. Just as the power of the feudal aristocracy had to be broken in order for capitalism to emerge fully, so must imperialism and capitalism in Third World nations be overcome if a new system is to prevail.

In the brief history of the United States, the forces of revolution and civil war broke the power of two dominant classes. During and after the American Revolution, the Tories had their lands, homes, and printing presses confiscated, and they were jailed, forced into exile, or executed. Then, after the Civil War, the slavocracy in the South had hundreds of millions of dollars in human "property" taken away. Although slavery was replaced by a lynch-law sharecropper system, social relations between the races in the South were never again what they had been during antebellum days. Both these historic upheavals represent important democratic gains for our nation and both were accompanied by much violence and coercion.[16] So today, revolutions often have to use coercive means to vanquish class oppression and privilege, depriving the propertied elites of their class-based "freedom" and of their existence as a social entity.

What is significant is not that *we* find revolutionary practices undesirable but that the people who live under these new social systems find much that is preferable to the old regimes, much they are prepared to defend. The CIA-sponsored Bay of Pigs invasion of Cuba in 1961 was a fiasco not because of "insufficient air coverage," as some of the invaders claimed, but because the Cuban people, instead of rising to join the counterrevolutionary expeditionary force as anticipated by the CIA, closed ranks behind their revolution. Among the invaders taken prisoner were men who between them had previously owned in Cuba 914,859 acres of land, 9,666 houses, 70 factories, 5 mines, 2 banks, and 10 sugar mills.[17]

Another "captive people," the North Vietnamese, acted equally strangely during the dreadful aerial war conducted against their country by the Nixon administration. Rather than treating the severe destruction caused by the US bombings as a golden opportunity to overthrow "Hanoi's yoke," they rallied to the support of their beleaguered government.

Revealing explanations as to why people side with the Communist revolutionaries come from some rather unexpected sources. During the Vietnam War, the US ambassador to South Vietnam, Henry Cabot Lodge, admitted: "For years now in Southeast Asia, the only people who have been doing anything for the little man—to lift him up—have been the Communists."[18] Similarly, the *New York Times* columnist James Reston wrote, "Even Premier Ky [the US-backed ruler of South Vietnam] told this reporter today that the Communists were closer to the peoples' yearnings for social justice and an independent life than his own government."[19]

To applaud social revolutions (even ones labeled "Marxist") is not to oppose political freedom. To the extent that social revolutionary governments lift their people from the worst miseries of the old order, they increase human options and freedom. There is no such thing as freedom in the abstract; there is freedoom to speak as one chooses, freedom to get an education and be able to find a job, freedom from want and hunger, freedom to worship or not worship, and so forth. Social revolutionary governments extend a number of these freedoms without destroying those that never existed for the populace.

Consider Cuba, a country portrayed in the USA as a totalitarian menace. Before the socialist revolution in 1959, there was chronic underemployment in Cuba and massive unattended social needs; there was much work that needed to be done and many underemployed people willing to do it, but little was done because the land, labor, and capital of the nation were used for the extraction of lucrative export crops such as sugar, tobacco, rum and other such corporate enterprises. After the revolution, however, there was suddenly a labor shortage instead of a labor surplus. People were urged to volunteer for work teams on their days off. There was more than enough work because now the resources of the country were being dedicated to the backlog of social needs created by centuries of maldevelopment.

When Cuba nationalized the holdings of US companies, the United States retaliated with an economic boycott—demonstrating one of the ways US foreign policy dedicates itself to the interests of corporate investors. Before the embargo, the United States absorbed more than half of Cuba's exports and supplied nearly three-quarters of Cuba's imported goods. Deprived of US markets and industrial goods, the Cuban revolutionary government—in order to survive—turned to existing socialist countries, especially the Soviet Union, for trade and aid in the 1960s (as did Nicaragua in the 1980s). Over the years, the Cubans have repeatedly sought to improve relations with the United States in order to benefit from American trade, technology, and tourism. They would "prefer not to be spending so much time and energy on national defense," as even the *New York Times* noted.[20]

Still beset by many economic problems, Cuba is no paradise on earth; but it stands in marked contrast to the rest of Latin America. Cuban life expectancy rose from fifty-five years in 1959 to seventy-three years by 1984. Infant mortality has dropped to the lowest in Latin America, on a par with developed countries. Cuba's per capita food consumption is the second highest in Latin America. It has a free public-health system (something Americans still do not have). The literacy rate is over 95 percent, the highest in Latin America and higher than in the USA; almost all children under sixteen are attending school.[21] In Cuba, the paint may be peeling off some of the buildings, but unlike so many other Latin American countries, there are no hungry children begging in the streets. And this is why many progressive people look positively upon social revolutions. The children are fed and the people are far better off than in nonrevolutionary Third World countries.

But what about individual rights and liberties? The standard anticommunist axiom is: "Any revolutionary victory for Communism anywhere represents a diminution of freedom in the world." The concern for freedom is admirable but the assertion is false. The Chinese revolution did not crush democracy; there was none to crush under the prerevolutionary, reactionary, US-supported Kuomintang regime. The Cuban revolution did not destroy freedom; it destroyed a hateful police state. The Algerian, Vietnamese, and Angolan revolutions did not abolish national liberties; none existed under European colonialism. The Sandinista revolution did not take away the freedom of the Nicaraguan people; there was precious little freedom under Somoza.

Nor is it true that leftist governments are more repressive than right-wing fascist ones. The political repression today in Nicaragua and Cuba is mild compared to the butchery perpetrated by the prerevolutionary regimes in those countries. The revolutionary governments in Angola and Mozambique treat their people a lot more gently than did the Portuguese colonizers. There is a good deal of free speech and public debate in social revolutionary countries—within the parameters of socialism—which means that no one is free to advocate openly a return to capitalism and imperialism. Nor can people organize against the revolution, although they usually can criticize particular government policies. Yet there is certainly room for an expansion of public debate and criticism in socialist countries, as a Communist leader like Mikhail Gorbachev has admitted.

Also contrary to the mythology propagated in the West: in all existing Marxist-oriented nations, be it Cuba, the Soviet Union, Nicaragua, Vietnam, or Ethiopia, the people enjoy freedom of religion. However, there is evidence that certain sects like the Seventh Day Adventists occasionally have been harassed in some socialist countries (for instance, Cuba) because of their right-wing political ideology and their unwillingness to affirm allegiance to the state, as have the right-wing members of the Catholic church hierarchy (in Nicaragua) because of their commitment to the counterrevolution. And some practitioners of Judaism in the USSR have run into trouble, not because of their religious practices as such but because they have sought to emigrate to the West and are seen by officials as having adopted an anti-Soviet "pro-Zionist" stance. Most Jews in the USSR seem content with their lives and careers; those who are not, should be allowed to leave.[22]

Leftist hostility toward established religions has centered less on theological questions (most leftists being indifferent to such things) than on the church's long-standing readiness to support the dominant capitalist classes. Religionists such as the liberation theologists, who have aligned themselves with the poor, have won the open admiration and cooperation of Communists and others on the revolutionary Left.

Most socialist countries hold regular elections and some have multiparty representation in their national legislatures. But neither under socialism nor capitalism is electoral competition a sure test of democracy. In Western capitalist nations, some two-party or multi-party systems are so thoroughly controlled by well-financed elites that capitalist interests predominate no matter who is elected. In contrast, a one-party system, especially in a newly emerging social revolutionary country, might actually provide *more* democracy—that is, more popular participation, more policy debate within the party, and more accountability and responsiveness to the people than occurs between the elite-dominated parties in the other systems. Thus in 1987, the Communist party of the People's Republic of Vietnam underwent a "grassroots criticism" directed against corruption and parasitism in party ranks, leading to the dismissal of three members of the top leadership and a revamping of various party organizations—a process that sharply conflicts with the image propagated in the West of a muted subservient Communist rank and file run by an unresponsive totalitarian leadership.[23]

Aside from participation and debate, there is the question of what kind of life the political order produces for its people. What class of people benefits from the way the politico-economic system uses and regulates the land, labor, resources, and capital of the society? Human rights encompass human needs as well as personal liberties. Hungry, destitute people have little occasion to enjoy political liberties. Not surprisingly, given the harsh material realities they face, there are many societies that emphasize group identity, communal betterment, and the struggle against poverty rather than the pursuit of individual gain. Even a *New York Times* editorial allowed that: "There are nations such as Tanzania with a single political party, a controlled press and yet a generally humane attitude by rulers toward ruled, with a real commitment to alleviating the misery of the poorest citizens."[24] How a political system measures up to the standards of democracy should be judged not only by its ability to hold elections but by its ability to serve democratic ends, not only by its formal procedures but its substantive outputs, the way its policies actually serve the needs of its people rather than the greed of a coterie of domestic compradors and foreign investors.

Notes

1. Seymour Hersh, "Kissinger Called Chile Strategist," *New York Times*, September 11, 1974.

2. For a detailed account of Marcos in the Philippines, see Raymond Bonner, *Waltzing with a Dictator* (New York: Times Books, 1987).

3. Jeff Gerth, "CIA Has Long Sought To Sway Foreign Voters," *New York Times*, May 13, 1984.

4. Bruce Occena, "Philippine Elections: Elite Democracy Consolidates Power," *Frontline*, May 25, 1987, p. 11. On similar elections in the Dominican Republic, Vietnam, and El Salvador see Edward Herman and Frank Brodhead, *Demonstration Elections* (Boston: South End Press, 1984).

5. Stephen Kinzer and Stephen Schlesinger, *Bitter Fruit: The Untold Story of the American Coup in Guatemala* (Garden City, N.Y.: Doubleday, 1982); William Branigin, "Issue of Disappearances Still Gnaws at Guatemala's Civilian Government," *Washington Post*, June 18, 1987; Nancy Lorence, "Guatemala's History Augurs Ill for Democracy," *New York Times*, December 5, 1985; John Fried, Marvin Gettleman, Deborah Levenson, and Nancy Peckenham, eds., *Guatemala in Rebellion* (New York: Grove Press, 1983).

6. Saul Landau and Peter Kornbluh, "Chile: The Ambassador Has Forgotten What Happened," *Washington Post*, October 1, 1983.

7. *New York Times*, March 30, 1983.

8. Preston Wood, "Thais Uniting Against U.S.-backed Junta," *Workers World*, December 31, 1976.

9. Philip Roettinger, "The Company, Then and Now," *Progressive*, July 1986, p. 50.

10. Shirer quoted in M. R. Montgomery, "The Press and Adolph Hitler," *Boston Globe Magazine*, January 30, 1983, p. 11.

11. Richard Cohen's column, *Washington Post*, March 14, 1982.

12. An oft-cited statement by Roosevelt, most recently quoted in Bonner, *Waltzing With a Dictator*.

13. Abrams interviewed on the MacNeil/Lehrer NewsHour, January 17, 1984.

14. Roettinger, "The Company . . ."

15. Quoted in *In These Times,* June 11, 1985.

16. See Herbert Aptheker, *The American Revolution 1763–1783* (New York: International Publishers, 1960); and James S. Allen *Reconstruction: The Battle for Democracy 1865–1876* (New York: International Publishers, 1937).

17. Newsletter, Center for Cuban Studies, 3, Winter 1976, p. 28.

18. Quoted in *New York Times,* February 27, 1966.

19. *New York Times,* September 1, 1965.

20. *New York Times,* August 5, 1984.

21. See "Why Cuba Scares Reagan," *Guardian,* January 11, 1984; also Maurice Zeitlin, *Revolutionary Politics and the Cuban Working Class* (New York: Harper Torchbooks, 1970).

22. For a treatment of human rights in the USSR see Albert Szymansky, *Human Rights in the Soviet Union* (London: Zed, 1984). According to a study of Soviet Jews now living in the USA, the most common reason given for coming to the US was a desire to be reunited with relatives. A less common reason offered was a desire for economic betterment. Very few respondents cited religious freedom as a reason for leaving: see Soviet Interview Project, University of Illinois, 1986–87. For a view of Soviet Jews other than the one given us by the US media see Avtandil Ruckhadze, *Jews in the USSR* (Moscow: Novosti Press, 1984); David Dragunsky, *What Letters Tell* (Moscow: Novosti Press, 1984). Both titles are available from Imported Publications, Chicago.

23. Report on National Public Radio, February 5, 1987; for examples of grass roots democracy in Nicaragua, see Gary Ruchwarger *People in Power, Forging a Grassroots Democracy in Nicaragua* (So. Hadley, Mass.: Bergin and Garvey, 1987); Peter Rosset and John Vandermeer, eds., *Nicaragua: Unfinished Revolution* (New York: Grove Press, 1987).

24. *New York Times* editorial, January 11, 1977.

10

The Costs of Counterrevolution

If we grant that revolutions improve the lot of the common people, we still might wonder whether the gain is worth all the pain. When pondering this question, we seldom measure the costs of revolution against the misery and starvation suffered under older regimes through all the centuries before. Mark Twain compared the "two Reigns of Terror," that of the revolution and that of the regime that preceded it:

> The one lasted mere months, the other had lasted a thousand years; the one inflicted death upon ten thousand persons, the other upon a hundred millions; but our shudders are all for the "horrors" of the minor Terror, the momentary Terror, so to speak. . . . A city cemetery could contain the coffins filled by that brief Terror which we have all been so diligently taught to shiver at and mourn over; but all France could hardly contain the coffins filled by that older and real Terror—that unspeakably bitter and awful Terror which none of us has been taught to see in its vastness or pity as it deserves.[1]

Robert Heilbroner addressed himself to the same question: "The way in which we ordinarily keep the books of history is wrong." We make no tally of the generations claimed by that combination of neglect and exploitation so characteristic of old regimes, the hapless victims of flood and famine in the Yangtze valley of yesterday, the child prostitutes found dead in the back alleys of old Shanghai, the nameless muzhiks stricken by cold and starvation across the bleak plains of Czarist Russia. And today, "no one is now totaling up the balance of the wretches who starve in India, or the peasants of North-eastern Brazil who live in swamps on crabs, or the undernourished and permanently stunted children of Indonesia or Honduras. Their sufferings go unrecorded and are not present to counterbalance the

scales when the furies of revolution strike."[2] Even if we were successful in repressing all popular revolts today and forever, the everyday
violence against humanity that is the common condition of status
quo reactionism, described in earlier chapters, would still be with us.

In any case, most of the violence in revolutionary struggles can be
attributed to the counterrevolutionary forces that seek to turn the
popular tide. The Russian Revolution was not a very bloody affair
compared to the years of repression that preceded it. Both the czarist
and the bourgeois Kerensky government that briefly replaced it fell
apart with relatively little resistance. The real carnage came with the
intervention by Western capitalist nations and the Western-supported
White Guard armies that burned and pillaged the countryside in a
protracted war of attrition and atrocity.[3] A more recent example:
almost all the killing that occurred during the Sandinista rebellion in
Nicaragua was perpetrated by the US-trained and equipped Somocista
National Guard.[4]

Upon coming to power, the revolution encounters many formidable hurdles: a crippled economy and a plundered ecology, shortages of essential materials, an enormous national debt that must be
honored lest international credit and trade be withdrawn, and a
staggering legacy of poverty and disease. The professional classes, a
highly privileged minority usually hostile to the new egalitarian policies, are likely to depart in substantial numbers, creating a still
greater scarcity of trained personnel in technology, medicine, and
administration.

The revolution's leaders are targeted for assassination by its
enemies. Western powers impose embargoes designed to strangle the
economy which—because of past colonial dominance—is heavily dependent on the former imperialists for materials and spare parts.
Widespread counterrevolutionary sabotage and armed attacks destroy whole villages and food supplies, causing serious economic
dislocation and even famine. These attacks are usually directly supported by the former colonial powers and in the postwar era by the
CIA. Meanwhile, US opinion manufacturers point to the hardships
endured by the people in revolutionary countries as proof that the
new leaders are making a mess of things and socialism cannot work.

Throughout the 1980s, the counterrevolutionary mercenaries
who have waged war against such countries as Nicaragua, Angola,
and Mozambique, were described as "guerrillas." In fact, they won
little support from the people of those countries, which explains why

they remained so utterly dependent upon aid from the United States and South Africa. In an attempt to destroy the revolutionary economy and thus increase popular distress and discontent, these counter-revolutionaries attacked farms, health workers, technicians, schools, and civilians. Unlike a guerrilla army that works with and draws support from the people, the counterrevolutionary mercenaries kidnap, rape, kill and in other ways terrorize the civilian population. These tactics have been termed "self-defeating," but they have a logic symptomatic of the underlying class politics. Since the intent of the counterrevoluionaries is to destroy the revolution, and since the bulk of the people support the revolution, then the mercenaries target the people.

In Mozambique, for example, over a period of eight years the South African–financed rebels laid waste to croplands, reducing the nation's cereal production enough to put almost 4 million people in danger of starvation. The rebels destroyed factories, rail and road links, and marketing posts, causing a sharp drop in Mozambique's production and exports. They destroyed 40 percent of the rural schools and over 500 of the 1,222 rural health clinics built by the Marxist government. And they killed hundreds of unarmed men, women, and children. But they set up no "liberated" areas and introduced no program for the country; nor did they purport to have any ideology or social goals.[5]

Likewise, the mercenary rebel force in Angola, financially supported throughout the 1980s by the apartheid regime in South Africa and looked favorably upon by the Reagan administration, devastated much of the Angolan economy, kidnapping and killing innocent civilians, displacing about 600,000 persons and causing widespread hunger and malnutrition. Assisted by White South African troops, the rebels destroyed at least half of Angola's hospitals and clinics. White South African military forces, aided by jet fighters, engaged in direct combat on the side of the counterrevolutionaries. The rebel leader, Jonas Savimbi, offered no social program for Angola but was lavish in his praise of the apartheid rulers in Pretoria and critical of Black South African leaders.[6]

So with the contra forces that repeatedly attacked Nicaragua from Honduras for some seven years. In all that time they were unable to secure a "liberated" zone nor any substantial support from the people. They represented a mercenary army that amounted to nothing much without US money—and nothing much with it, having failed to launch a significant military offensive for years at a time. Like other counterrevolutionary "guerrillas" they were quite good at trying to destabilize the existing system by hitting soft targets like schools and farm cooperatives and killing large numbers of civilians, including children.[7] (While the US news media unfailingly reported that the Nicaraguans or Cubans had "Soviet-made weapons," they said nothing about the American, British, and Israeli arms used by counterrevolutionaries to kill Angolans, Namibians, Black South Africans, Western Saharans, Nicaraguans, Guatemalans, and Salvadorans.)

Like counterrevolutionaries in other countries, the Nicaraguan contras put forth no economic innovations or social programs other than some vague slogans. As the *New York Times* reported, when asked about "the importance of political action in the insurgency" the contra leaders "did not seem to assign this element of revolutionary warfare a high priority."[8] They did not because they were not waging a "revolution" but a counterrevolution. What kind of a program can counterrevolutionaries present? If they publicize their real agenda, which is to open the country once more to the domination of foreign investors and rich owners, they would reveal their imperialist hand. But if they put forth a progressive social program, they would be duplicating what was being done by the revolutionary government. One then would question why they were going through such trouble to destroy a government that was already doing what they themselves supposedly wanted; and this in turn would call into question either their veracity or their sanity.

At a meeting of the National Lawyers Guild in Washington, D.C., May 24, 1987, which I attended, the former contra leader Edgar Chamorro related how, when recruited by the CIA to form a political front for the contras, he was told by his CIA advisors that in his public pronouncements he should not mention his desire to restore private property to the owning class; he should say he was for the revolution and that he just wanted to put it back on the right track toward democracy. The CIA advisors found nothing wrong with his desire to reestablish the powers of the owning class; they just did not want Chamorro saying it in public.

Many of the problems faced by fledgling revolutions can be traced to their enemies. After the 1979 revolution in Nicaragua, the Sandinista government launched nationwide public-health campaigns that virtually eliminated polio (something the previous Somocista regime could not get around to doing in thirty years), and increased the average life expectancy by three years.[9] Yet the health programs continued to be hamstrung by the shortage of doctors (half of whom fled the country after the revolution) and by the US embargo and the contra attacks which frequently targeted clinics and medical personnel.

Like most of the Third World, Nicaragua during the Somoza dictatorship was one of imperialism's ecological disasters, with its unrestricted industrial and agribusiness pollution and deforestation. Upon coming to power, the Sandinistas initiated rain forest and wildlife conservation measures and alternative energy programs. The new government also adopted methods of cutting pesticides to a minimum, prohibiting the use of the deadlier organochlorides commonly applied in other countries. Nicaragua's environmental efforts stand in marked contrast to its neighboring states. But throughout the 1980s, the program was severely hampered by contra attacks that killed more than thirty employees of Nicaragua's environmental and state forestry agencies, and destroyed agricultural centers and reclamation projects.[10]

No socialist revolution has had the luxury of an unhampered development. All are put under seige by the imperialist nations for many years after coming to power, some for their entire history. To survive and protect the well-being of its people, the revolution must destroy the class freedom of privileged exploiters and other enemies. The revolutionary party must mobilize the mass of the people around the task of national reconstruction, exhorting them to make new sacrifices and maintain their vigilance against the counterrevolutionaries. As bad as conditions get during the terrible days of counterrevolutionary attrition, the ordinary poor experience a better, more hopeful life under the new revolutionary government. For the people who had known only the misery that came with the free-market rationing of the previous regime, standing on line for a modest ration of flour and beans, which they are now able to buy at government subsidized prices, is indeed worth the pain, as they testify. For the poor who saw their children die of hunger and disease under the old regime, the food allotments and medical vaccinations are more than just modest gains; they are the difference between life and death. For them there is no going back, no matter what the costs.[11]

Not all the population, however, is prepared to face the struggle and sacrifices demanded by the revolution. It has been claimed that a third of the people supported the American Revolution, a third opposed it, and a third were undecided or neutral. Yet today few Americans would argue that our nation's struggle for independence lacked legitimacy because a majority of our compatriots reportedly failed to support it. In present-day social revolutions there may be sectors of the population that are indifferent or unfriendly towards the revolutionary struggle, or just frightened by the dangers. Many people soon tire of the sacrifices and try to leave. Security measures taken by the new government to prevent desertions from the battle for production or from the military struggle against foreign intervention are readily publicized in the West as evidence of the regime's unpopularity and even of its totalitarianism.

The *New York Times* quoted one Nicaraguan peasant as saying, "Many have benefited from the revolution and they support the Sandinistas" but "there are many who oppose the revolution because of the crisis we live in."[12] Observing that the contras are a well-equipped army, some peasants are reportedly reluctant to cast their lot with either side because they do not know who will win. Some send their sons off into the mountains to avoid being drafted into the Sandinista army. Some dislike the Sandinistas for allegedly being atheistic Marxists and for limiting their freedom to maintain independent farms and for pressuring them to join state cooperatives and carry guns to protect the cooperatives from contra attack. Those who refuse are treated as suspect and denied credit and state assistance.[13]

So every revolution makes enemies even among some of the people it is trying to help. But again most of this should be tallied as the costs of counterrevolution, not revolution. If the US-financed contra mercenaries were not waging murderous attacks against the Nicaraguan populace, there would be no need for a conscription army and no resentful peasants who would send their sons away to avoid the draft. If there had been no landowners and disdainful professionals, no class of blackmarketeers, pimps, profiteering merchants, police thugs, functionaries, collaborators, torturers, and assassins making the world safe for the old regime in the service of imperialism, and no embargoes and aggressions from abroad designed to make the revolutionary economy scream, the revolution would have little need for a secret police and people's militia; it would produce few if any political prisoners, fleeing émigrés, and "boat people," seeking to make it to America.

The US government is ready to accept just about anyone who emigrates from a Communist country. In contrast, the hundreds of millions of Third World *refugees from capitalism,* who would like to come to this country because the conditions of their lives are so hopeless, are not allowed in, so they do not even attempt to apply (although hundreds of thousands have entered illegally). If given a chance, many people from poor countries, including revolutionary ones, would flee to a rich country.

There are critics, including some who identify themselves as on the Left, who treat it as an historical betrayal that a revolution fighting for its life, facing attack and encirclement from without and sabotage and subversion from within, might set up security forces of its own and take other strong measures to defend itself. They are shocked that the revolution might make terrible mistakes and commit abuses and crimes against suspected individuals or even sectors of the population, developing an internal security system that devolves into an autocracy of its own. The critics argue: "If revolutions are for the people, why do they mimic the governments they replaced by having armies, secret police, and a censored press? If we cannot have freedom and cannot dance, we won't be part of your revolution, as the anarchist Emma Goldman said. If the new government is so popular among the masses, then it would not need political jails. Did not Lenin say that the goal of socialism was disarmament?"

Yes, but Lenin never said that the goal of socialism was suicidal unilateral disarmament. A socialist revolution without security forces would have to be a revolution without powerful enemies. Those who seem primarily concerned with being able to dance after the revolution have not told us what to do about the grimmer realities. As a matter of fact, most revolutions do promote a growth in cultural activities, in an attempt to make art a vital experience for the many instead of an elite diversion for the few.[14] But the revolution must also deal with the counterrevolutionary bombings and assassinations, the massacre of village populations, and the destruction of production facilities and food supplies. If the revolution is under serious attack, its supporters are not likely to take a mellow approach to things. They are not apt to encourage a pluralistic diffusion of power and a wide-open ideological diversity. Instead, their inclination will be to demand a militant lockstep unity and an unwavering loyalty to the cause.

Any nation at war or under seige might do the same. During the Civil War, President Lincoln suspended the writ of habeas corpus, jailed thousands of antiwar dissenters without charge or trial, censored news dispatches, suppressed such publications as the *Chicago*

Times, and put Baltimore under martial law. During World War I, the US government suppressed publications and sentenced thousands of people to long prison terms for merely criticizing our participation in the war. During World War II, there was stringent press censorship; no one would think of publishing a pro-Nazi newspaper; the poet Ezra Pound was prosecuted for anti-American statements; all persons of Japanese ancestry on the West Coast were imprisoned in concentration camps, though there was not a shred of evidence suggesting they were agents of Japan. All these repressive measures were taken even though the enemy never came close to invading the United States. It is a rare country, if any, that would tolerate a full panoply of liberties, including publications by enemy sympathizers, during times of war and foreign invasion.

Yet the critics of revolution are quick to attack a country like Nicaragua for closing down *La Prensa* in 1986. No longer the newspaper that had stood up to the Somoza dictatorship, *La Prensa* now had a right-wing publisher and staff. Its new editors openly supported the contra war against their own country, a war that had brought 16,000 deaths as of 1987. One coeditor, Pedero Joaquin Chamorro, Jr., was actually on the board of directors of UNO, the contras political front. One of the paper's directors, Jaime Chamorro, publicly appealed to the US Congress to continue supporting the war against Nicaragua. *La Prensa,* itself, received substantial funding from the National Endowment for Democracy, a corporation established and funded by the US Congress.[15]

If freedom of speech and other civil liberties are the real concern of US policymakers, then they should try treating revolutionary governments with more friendship and less belligerency, fostering the kind of normality and security that would encourage the widest range of freedoms in these otherwise beleaguered countries. In any case, Communist countries already are more accessible to Western media than we are to their media. In countries like the Soviet Union, Poland, Hungary, and Cuba, US television programs, movies, books, and magazines are in relative abundance compared to the almost nonexistent supply of films and publications from these countries in the United States. (Gorbachev himself pointed out this discrepancy to President Reagan at their first meeting in Geneva in 1985. He offered to stop jamming Voice of America broadcasts to the USSR if Washington would allow normal frequency transmission of Radio Moscow to the USA, an offer the US government let pass.)

Cuba is bombarded with American broadcasting, including Spanish-language stations from Miami and a US government propaganda station called "Radio Marti." Rather than interfering with US stations, Havana has asked that Cuba be allowed a frequency for Cuban use in the United States, something Washington has refused to do. In response to those who attack the lack of dissent in the Cuban media, Fidel Castro promised to open up the Cuban press to all opponents of the revolution on the day he saw American Communists enjoying regular access to the US major media.[16]

Critics have argued that revolutions often create something worse than the thing they replace, especially when the crazies take power, hence, the mass murders of the Pol Pot regime in Kampuchea (Cambodia), the fanatically repressive theocracy in Iran under the mullahs, and the "madman rule" of Colonel Qaddafi in Libya. But an endorsement of socialist revolution does not extend to every upheaval that occurs in the world. Pol Pot's Khmer Rouge in Kampuchea instituted an atavistic, xenophobic order, a harsh agrarian collectivism that reduced its people to the status of helots, ruled over by a youthful, fanatical military caste. This social order bore a stronger resemblance to ancient Sparta than to Marxist-Leninist socialism. It should be noted that many—but certainly not all—of the grotesque distortions of Khmer Rouge rule have their roots in the US-sponsored war that came before. The savage US bombings intentionally depopulated the food-growing areas of Cambodia and forced masses of people into the cities. The subsequent hunger endured by displaced rural people when the war ended was one of the causes for the forced deurbanization imposed by the Khmer Rouge and many of the ensuing outrages.[17]

Iran under the Ayatollah Khomeini is another tragic case. The mullahs who rule are a religiously fanatical, xenophobic, petty bourgeois coterie, hostile to both the US and the USSR. After years in power they have done little to improve the lot of their people, instead pursuing a senseless and bloody war against Iraq long after Iraq sued for peace. When the mullahs took over US oil reserves, Iran was targeted by US policymakers and the media as a major menace. But when they began pursuing a counterrevolutionary course, offering no socialist reforms, exterminating the Iranian Communist Tudeh party, and showing themselves friendly to private capital, Washington softened its approach, unfroze the overseas Iranian assets it had seized, and even engaged in a secret arms-for-hostages deal with Teheran.

Unlike Kampuchea and Iran, Libya's Colonel Qaddafi took a

different course. From 1981 to 1987, he was relentlessly dipicted by US policymakers and the US media as a mentally unhinged despot bent upon terrorizing Americans for the sheer diabolic fun of it. In truth, however, while the Reagan administration cultivated hostile confrontations with Libya and even bombed that country in an attempt to kill its leader, Qaddafi repeatedly called for talks to resolve any differences between Tripoli and Washington. His overtures were summarily rejected by US leaders and ignored or downplayed by the US press. The administration's concerted propaganda campaign against Libya, dutifully projected by the business-owned media, actually had many Americans convinced that this country of 3 million people with a ragtag army of 55,000 was a mortal threat to the United States.

The real threat Libya posed was not to the United States but to multinational capitalism. After Qaddafi seized power in the 1969 colonels' revolt, he and his followers took a country that had resembled Saudi Arabia in its political repression and its elite wealth and mass poverty, and transformed it into a much more egalitarian society. Qaddafi's big sin was that he nationalized the oil industry and began using the nation's capital and labor for public needs rather than multinational corporate gain. The revolutionary Libyan government drove out the old rich ruling class, built hundreds of thousands of free housing units, instituted free education and free medical care, planted millions of trees, and encouraged women to go to school. The government lifted the per capita income and overall living standards of the people to the highest in the Arab world. It was these socialistic economic changes that caused US leaders to single out Qaddafi as a "fanatical Muslim terrorist," an image unfortunately not discouraged by his own penchant for grandiose posturing and intemperate pronouncements. The Qaddafi threat was the same as the Sandinista and the Cuban threats: he was changing the existing social order in a noncapitalist direction.[18] In the world of imperialism, the characters may change, but the script remains rather consistent.

Notes

1. Maxwell Geismar, ed., *Mark Twain and the Three R's* (New York: Bobbs-Merrill, 1973), p. 178. The selection is originally from Twain's *Connecticut Yankee in King Arthur's Court* (1889).

2. Robert Heilbroner, "Counterrevolutionary America," *Commentary*, April 1967, p. 34.

3. For accounts and further documentation of these atrocities see Michael Sayers and Albert Kahn, *The Great Conspiracy, The Secret War Against Soviet Russia* (San Francisco: Proletarian Publishers, 1946).

4. This mode of terrorist warfare was continued in Nicaragua by the US-funded contra forces for years after the Sandinista victory, as we shall see; also note Dieter Eich and Catlos Rincon, *The Contras, Interviews with Anti-Sandinistas* (So. Hadley, Mass.: Bergin and Garvey, 1987).

5. Sheila Rule, "A War and Drought Extend the Famine in Mozambique," *New York Times,* November 9, 1986; Augustus Richard Norton, "The Renamo Menace: Hunger and Carnage in Mozambique," *New Leader,* November 16, 1987, pp. 5–8; also *New York Times,* November 1 and June 22, 1987; *Washington Post,* December 11, 1986.

6. Sheila Rule, "As War Takes Its Toll, the Angolan Mire Deepens," *New York Times,* September 19, 1986; John Battersby, "Angolan Rebel Commends Botha," *New York Times,* June 7, 1987; *Washington Post,* December 11, 1986 and August 23, 1987; also William Pomeroy, *Apartheid, Imperialism and African Freedom* (New York: International Publishers, 1986); John Stockwell, *In Search of Enemies: A CIA Story* (New York: W. W. Norton, 1978).

7. Julia Preston, "Rebels Kill Youngsters On Farm," *Washington Post,* July 1, 1986; William Branigin, "Nicaraguan Rebels' Tactics Assailed," *Washington Post,* May 17, 1987; Stephen Kinzer, "Rebels Need a Victory on Battlefield in Nicaragua" *New York Times,* March 15, 1987; Joel Brinkley, "Nicaraguan Rebel Tells of Killing As Device for Forced Recruitment," *New York Times,* September 12, 1985; Eich and Rincon, *The Contras.*

8. *New York Times,* June 16, 1986.

9. Julia Preston, "Nicaraguan Medical Care Crimped by Shortages," *Washington Post,* January 27, 1987.

10. Len Harris, "Agricultural Advances in Nicaragua," *Daily World,* May 28, 1986; Joshua Karliner, "Nicaragua: An Environmentalist's Perspective," *IPS Features* (Institute for Policy Studies, Washington, D.C. May 1986).

11. Alvin Levie, *Nicaragua, the People Speak* (So. Hadley, Mass.: Bergin and Garvey, 1987).

12. *New York Times,* June 3, 1987.

13. Ibid.

14. For example, note the cultural developments in Cuba as discussed in the various reports by Anna Veltfort, Carol Benglesdorf, Michael Myerson, and Andrea Hernandez in *Cuban Resource Center Newsletter* (New York), October 1973; on cultural achievements in the USSR see various issues of *Soviet Life* published in the United States.

15. David Kairys, "Nicaragua Isn't the First Government to Censor," *Washington Post,* June 7, 1986; "La Prensa: Post Mortem of a Suicide," *Democratic Journalist,* December 1986, pp. 13–14; also letters in *New York Times,* August 3, 1986, and *Washington Post,* April 6 1987.

16. Fidel Castro interviewed in the PBS documentary *Shadow of a Doubt,* shown in October 1986.

17. On Cambodia see Noam Chomsky and Edward Herman, *After the Cataclysm* (Boston: South End Press, 1979), pp. 135–294.

18. Tom Foley, "US Fears Libya's Anti-imperialism," *Daily World,* January 15, 1986; *Peace and Solidarity* (Oakland, Calif.: May 1986), p. 1; Alexander Cockburn's column in *Wall Street Journal,* April 17, 1986.

11

Other Variables—or Must We Ignore Imperialism?

At this point, if not sooner, someone will complain that my analysis is "simplistic," and that it ascribes all international events to purely economic and class motives and ignores other variables like geopolitics, culture, ethnicity, nationalism, ideology, and morality. The world is much more complex than the "reductionist Marxist materialist view" allows, it is said. But I have not argued that the struggle between global capitalism and revolutionary change explains everything about current world politics nor even everything about US foreign policy. However, it explains quite a lot; so isn't it time we investigate it? If mainstream opinion makers really want to portray political life in all its manifold complexities, then why are they so reticent about the immense realities of imperialism? To be able to write whole volumes about American foreign policy and never treat the policy imperatives relating to US overseas capital investment is both a remarkable and a common omission.

The existence of other variables does not demonstrate the nonexistence or unimportance of capitalist interests. No social action is "solely" or "merely" or "only" motivated by one force, even those as encompassing as capitalism and imperialism. But the presence of other motivations does not compel us to dismiss economic realities, nor to treat these other variables as exclusive of class interests. One can have both a moralistic or geopolitical intent and an economic interest, and rather than canceling each other out, they can be mutually reinforcing. As noted earlier, one of our most moralistic presidents, Woodrow Wilson, talked about bringing to Latin America the blessings of not only constitutionalism and Christianity but of capitalism too. He saw all three as integral components of the same marvelous order. Indeed, for all his moralizing, Wilson understood something about imperialism when he wrote in 1907:

> Since trade ignores national boundaries and the manufacturer insists on having the world as a market, the flag of his nation must follow him, and the doors of the nations which are closed against him must be battered down. Concessions obtained by financiers must be safeguarded by ministers of state, *even if the sovereignty of unwilling nations be outraged in the process.* Colonies must be obtained or planted, in order that no useful corner of the world may be overlooked or left unused.[1]

As one historian noted: "Wilson's moralism did not exclude an early, persistent, and hard-headed concern for America's overseas economic expansion."[2] Wilson's secretary of state, Robert Lansing, advised him that US policy should see to it that no other countries interfered with any American commercial expansion and that overseas colonies be available to absorb both an excess of population and "an accumulation of capital desiring investment. . . ." As president of the United States, Wilson himself noted that the United States was involved in a struggle to "command the economic fortunes of the world."[3]

Mainstream scholars usually confine their attention to Wilson's idealism and say nothing about his commitment to capitalism at home and abroad; they then condemn as "reductionist" and "one-sided" those who dare explore this neglected side of Wilson's policy.

In their eagerness to dismiss class considerations, the anti-Marxist critics overlook the fact that US policymakers themselves voice a commitment to US economic interests abroad. After World War II, according to one historian who made a thorough examination of the question, Secretary of War Henry Stimson and other top policymakers agreed that "long-term American prosperity required open markets, unhindered access to raw materials, and the rehabilitation of much—if not all—of Eurasia along liberal capitalist lines."[4] In his 1953 State of the Union message President Eisenhower observed: "A serious and explicit purpose of our foreign policy [is] the encouragement of a hospitable climate for investment in foreign nations." Nothing ambiguous about those statements. In 1979, in what became known as the Carter Doctrine, President Carter proclaimed, in so many words, a readiness to go to war with anyone who tampered with US-owned oil in the Middle East.

In 1982, Vice President George Bush observed: "We want to

maintain a favorable climate for foreign investment in the Caribbean region, not merely to protect the existing U.S. investment there, but to encourage new investment opportunities in stable, democratic, free-market–oriented countries close to our shores."[5] It should be noted that Bush considered the Marcos dictatorship in the Philippines to have been a government that adhered to "democratic principles and to the democratic process."[6] President Reagan indicated in unequivocal terms what he was trying to defend: "What I want to see above all else is that this country remains a country where someone can always be rich. That's the thing we have that must be preserved."[7] It is not too much to note that this lofty goal, the freedom to be rich, necessitates preserving the existing system of capital accumulation at home and abroad.

This is not to discount other motives such as nationalism, militarism, the search for national security, the pursuit of power, and the need to be "number one"—expressions of which can be found in many right-wing organizations, in Hollywood and television shows, and in the minds of policymakers and military leaders themselves. Sometimes these concerns take on a momentum of their own. McMahan puts it well:

> U.S. reasons for wanting to control the third world are to some extent circular. Thus third world resources are required in part to guarantee military production, and increased military production is required in part to maintain and expand U.S. control over third world resources. . . . Instrumental goals eventually come to be seen as ends in themselves. Initially the pursuit of overseas bases is justified by the need to maintain stability, defend friendly countries from communist aggression, and so on—in other words, to subjugate and control the third world; but eventually the need to establish and maintain overseas bases becomes one of the *reasons* for wanting to subjugate and control the third world.[8]

The tendency to see the world as a Manichean contest between American democracy and the evil empire of the Soviet Union, the tendency to celebrate American military power and American victories as ends in themselves—such attitudes indeed may both feed upon and bolster interventionist policy and are encouraged by political leaders, but usually they do not of themselves explain the political direction the policy takes. It is not militarism that creates US policy but US policy that generates militarism—which is not to deny that militarism may then have a feedback effect of its own, but *it will be in directions that do not conflict in any essential way with the interests of global capitalism.*

One observer maintains that "in our culture, war is a deep-down, bone-marrow part of the common-sense view of the nature of things."[9] Others have argued that warlike impulses afflict the male gender in particular. But if the American populace—especially its male portion—is so possessed by macho, nationalistic, militaristic propensities, why does the state find it necessary to conscript men into military service, threatening them with imprisonment if they fail to comply? Why do opinion polls show that most Americans (males included) are opposed to peacetime draft, and favor negotiated arms reductions, peaceful settlement of disputes with the Soviets, and disengagement from Third World conflicts? Wars—and cold wars—between nations are created and pursued by complex social organizations, not by individual aggression or some other personal behavior (although wars can then serve as outlets of individual aggression for those unusual persons who thrive on combat).

Again, if nationalistic, macho aggrandizement has such a grip on our foreign policy, why is it expressed in such selective ways—toward Cuba, Nicaragua, Angola, Libya, and other socialist-oriented countries? And why are US leaders so *un*macho at other times, showing such accommodating, passive, gentle, supportive tolerance toward South Africa, Paraguay, Zaire, El Salvador, Indonesia, and other tyrannical countries of the free-market world?

In 1987, President Reagan said that the goal of his bloody little war against Nicaragua was to force the Sandinistas to carry out their program. Since he had originally opposed the Sandinistas' accession to power, it was not clear why he now would go to such violent lengths to see their program put into effect. Maybe Reagan was just being an irrational big-power bully; but then why did he not show the same bullying intrusiveness and aggression toward the undemocratic and repressive Chun government of South Korea? Throughout 1986–87, the South Korean people engaged in intensive protests and struggles for a democratic constitution, yet a State Department official said it "would be wrong to talk about our launching any initiatives" because the turmoil is "an internal Korean matter."[10] While playing the bully who could tell the Nicaraguans how to run their country, the United States dared not interfere in the internal affairs of South Korea. (Washington belatedly began to urge liberalization in

Korea as the rioting grew to seemingly dangerous levels of intensity in 1987.)

Barnet and Kornbluh argue that President Reagan's aggressive behavior toward Nicaragua was "motivated by a 'control mentality' which has dominated the history of US relations with Latin American revolutions."[11] They go on to quote Henry Kissinger, who once said in regard to Chile: "We set the limits of diversity." But what political interests determine "the limits"? Kissinger himself revealed where the line is drawn, when he said on June 27, 1970, in anticipation of the fascist coup he helped promote in Chile: "I don't see why we need to stand by and watch a country go Communist because of the irresponsibility of its own people." If US policy in Latin America arises from some "control mentality," that mentality also has a consistent and specific political *content,* and is directed toward selective goals. The need to play the policeman of the world and try to control the destinies of other countries may be a compelling one for policymakers, but it operates selectively in a direction that is compatable with the interests of global capitalism and inimical to socialist revolution.

Millions of people, including rich and poor, can get swept up in a nationalistic fervor over one or another issue. But in the case of the owning class, this ardor is sustained, rather than contradicted, by its material interests. Much of what passes for "patriotism" in American society is usually defined from the perspective of a capitalist social order, one that measures our nation's worth more by its military might than by the justice of its social policies. The corporate class's love of America has not prevented it from repeatedly abandoning American communities for cheaper labor markets and bigger profits abroad. This is not to say that US expansionism has been impelled by the profit motive alone but that various other considerations—such as national security and patriotism—have been defined in ways that are congruent with the interests of a particular class. These other attitudes and interests usually do not compete against economic class motives but dovetail with them.

It is certainly not true that [imperialist] governments went into Africa or Asia *simply* to serve powerful economic interests. Nor did they embark upon imperialist expansion *simply* because they were "compelled" to do so by such interests. Vast historical movements of this kind cannot be reduced to these simplicities. But here too the many other purposes which governments have wished to serve in quest for

empire have involved, preeminently, the furtherance of private economic interests. They may *really* have been concerned with national
security, the strengthening of the economic and social fabric, the shoul-
dering of the white man's burden, the fulfillment of their national destiny and so forth. But these purposes required, as they saw it, the
security by conquest of lands which were already or which could become zones of exploitation for their national capital interests, whose
implantation and expansion were thus guaranteed by the power of the
state. In this case too the fact that political officeholders were seeking to
achieve many other purposes should not obscure the fact that, *in the
service of these purposes,* they became the dedicated servants of their
business and investing classes.[12]

The point is not that nations act imperialistically for "purely"
material motives but that the ideological and cultural motives,
though perhaps embraced with varying degrees of intensity by various sectors of the population, serve the material interests of a particular class, at a cost to the rest of the populace.

There are those who assert that the central motivating force
behind US foreign policy is not the need to maintain domination of
world finances and world resources, not the need to protect global
capitalism, but a rabid, obsessional anticommunism. Anticommunists see Communists—and their allies and "dupes" in various
countries—as working in concert to crush freedom and take over the
entire world. Anticommunism is certainly a real force. It is even
embraced by many people who might otherwise benefit from a class
revolution and who cannot explain what Communism is. This mind-
set is a tribute to the efficacy of a ruling-class propaganda that has
been disseminated for more than a century in this and other capitalist
nations.[13] Yet, despite the relentless anticommunist pounding to
which the American public has been subjected, support for anticommunist interventionist policies remains weak, while the public's desire for peaceful relations with the Soviets remains strong.[14]

Anticommunism is not an alternative or competing explanation
of US policy but a complementary one. We need to ask, why do our
economic and political elites have such a fear and loathing of Communism and try so persistently to instill the same sentiments in the
populace? Here we return to the arguments offered in earlier chapters. It cannot be that rulers abhor Communism because it is des-
potic; they get along quite well with despots of all kinds as long as
these autocrats do not tamper with private investments and know
how to keep their people in line. Communism is hated because it is a

class enemy. We need not ponder the question of whether our leaders are motivated by their class interests or by a genuine commitment to anticommunist ideology—as if these two things were in competition with each other instead of being mutually reinforcing.

This is not to say that there may not be ideological, religious, nationalistic, ethnic, and tribal conflicts in many parts of the world—be it Northern Ireland, Spain, Corsica, Nigeria, Uganda, Lebanon, or India—that are self-generating and seem to have little to do with class and economic considerations. Though on closer examination, we discover that, even behind many of these conflicts, economic issues play a major part, involving struggles over land or the resistance by one group to the exploitation imposed by another. For instance, the religious and tribal violence in Nigeria is also a conflict between the northern Muslim region, which is less developed and poorer, and the southern Christian-dominated region, which is more prosperous.

In some cases, imperialism enlists these conflicts to its own cause. Thus, the CIA aided and encouraged the Meo and Mung tribesmen in Indochina and separatist elements in Angola and Ethiopia to fight against the social revolutions in those respective places. In so doing, the CIA played upon long-standing grievances that these ethnic minorities had against the majority populace dating back to prerevolutionary days. The CIA did the same thing with the Miskito Indians in the Atlantic region of Nicaragua, supplying separatist groups with guns and supplies in an effort to destabilize Sandinista rule.[15]

There is one very important argument that has not been dealt with; it has to do with the Soviet Union and it goes something like this: "The United States intervenes throughout the world for geopolitical reasons, in order to defend itself against Soviet aggrandizement. Moscow's goal is world domination and we are the only country strong enough to prevent that from happening. We must make sure that other countries remain in our camp in order to prevent them from falling into the Soviet orbit. If we defend only the United States, the day will come when we will have only the United States to defend. Ronald Reagan said 'Let's not delude ourselves. The Soviet Union underlies all the unrest that is going on . . . in the world.'[16] While that may be an overstatement, the question of Soviet global military power and Soviet imperialist expansionism cannot be ignored. Did not Khrushchev say, 'We will bury you'?" So the argument goes. We will examine it in the pages ahead.

134   THE SWORD AND THE DOLLAR

Notes

1. Quoted in Lloyd Gardner, *Safe for Democracy* (New York: Oxford University Press, 1984), p. 41. Emphasis added.

2. William Appleman Williams, "American Intervention in Russia: 1917–1920," in David Horowitz, ed., *Containment and Revolution* (Boston: Beacon Press, 1967), p. 28.

3. Ibid.

4. Melvin Leffler, "The American Conception of National Security and the Beginning of the Cold War, 1945–48," *American Historical Review*, 90, February 1985, p. 358.

5. Quoted in Jeff McMahan, *Reagan and the World* (New York: Monthly Review Press, 1985), p. 18.

6. Ibid., p. 23.

7. Ibid., p. 24.

8. Ibid., p. 16.

9. John Alexis Crane, "Does War Make Sense?" *The Churchman,* November 1981.

10. Quoted in *Washington Post,* June 28, 1987.

11. Richard Barnet and Peter Kornbluh, "Contradictions in Nicaragua," *Sojourners,* May 8, 1984, p. 10.

12. Ralph Miliband, *The State in Capitalist Society* (New York: Basic Books, 1969), p. 84.

13. See Michael Parenti, *Inventing Reality: The Politics of the Mass Media* (New York: St. Martin's Press, 1986), especially chapters 7, 8, and 9.

14. See opinion survey results and discussion in Chapter 15.

15. William Blum, *The CIA, A Forgotten History* (London: Zed, 1986).

16. *Wall Street Journal,* June 3, 1980.

12

The Cold War
Is an Old War

The conventional view is that the rivalry between the United States and the Soviet Union, known as the "cold war," began soon after World War II. Both nations had been allies in the struggle against the Axis powers, but in short time Soviet expansionism supposedly forced an otherwise friendly Washington to adopt a "containment policy," countering Moscow's thrusts and military buildups.

In fact, the capitalist nations, including the United States, had treated Soviet Russia as a threat virtually from the first days of its existence. The cold war that surfaced after World War II was really a continuation of an antagonism prevailing from the time of the Bolshevik Revolution in Russia in 1917—long before the Soviets could ever have been a military threat to the West. Most Americans remain unfamiliar with this history. Let us give it some attention here, for it reveals patterns that are still very much with us.

Ruling-class hostility toward socialism existed generations before any socialist nation came into existence. The endless stream of antiradical imagery issuing from press and pulpit, the bourgeois orthodoxy enforced within professions and schools, the use of police and courts as instruments of political oppression, in short, all the means whereby a dominant class wages war against heretical notions, have been utilized for over a century by the dominant institutions of capitalist nations—and nowhere more effectively than in the United States.[1] Long before the Russian Revolution, ruling groups in the United States railed against the "perfidious" syndicalists, anarchists, socialists, and Communists for seeking to "reduce all economic classes to one dismal level." On his American tour in 1882, the prominent laissez-faire theorist Herbert Spencer warned: "We are on the highway to Communism, and I see no likelihood that the movement in that direction will be arrested."[2] The leaders of society equated socialism with anarchy and the dissolution of civilization; they equated the end of their *capitalist* order with the breakdown of *all* social order.

When the workers, under the leadership of Lenin's Bolshevik party, seized power in Russia in 1917, the working people of America expressed neither fright nor hysteria; indeed, many worker organizations offered expressions of solidarity.[3] But the fear was palpable among the owning classes of this and other capitalist nations. The fabric of bourgeois history had been torn. The worst nightmare was coming true: a successful socialist revolution by the unlettered masses against the capitalist system. Might not other countries follow suit unless drastic measures were taken?

Beginning in August 1918, fourteen nations, including the United States, Great Britain, France, and Japan invaded Soviet Russia in an attempt to overthrow the Bolshevik government. In addition to using their own troops, they provided aid to the reactionary pro-czarist White Guard generals. Apologists for this action have given various reasons why the intervention took place. Supposedly it was an attempt to keep Russia in the war against Germany; but this cover story did not explain why the allied invasion and blockade continued for two years *after* the war against Germany had ended in November 1918.[4] Supposedly the Western allies were concerned about rescuing Czech prisoners-of-war who were engaged in skirmishes with the Reds inside Russia; but this issue arose well after the decision to intervene had been contemplated and was seized upon more as an excuse than as a sufficient cause for a massive multinational invasion.

In fact, the allied leaders intervened in Russia for the same reason ruling classes have intervened in revolutionary conflicts before and since: to protect the status quo, to contain and reverse class revolution. Consider the capacity for collusive interventionism manifested by European monarchs against the French Revolution at the end of the eighteenth century. All the bitter rivalries that had plagued the courts of Europe weighed less than the aristocracy's own instinct for class survival. Recall how in 1871 Bismarck hastened to mobilize the same French army he had just defeated so that it might be used by the French ruling class against the revolutionary uprising of French workers. Bismarck feared "the impact the [Paris] Commune might have upon his archenemies at home, the German Socialists. . . ."[5]

Likewise, after the 1918 armistice ending World War I, the victorious Western allies allowed the German militarists to retain 5,000 machine guns to be used against German workers "infected with Bolshevism." France, Great Britain, and the United States made it clear that they would not tolerate a socialist government in Germany nor even permit normal relations between Berlin and the Soviet government. "Wilson had once wanted a revolution in Germany to eliminate the military class; now he feared it like the plague."[6]

To say that various "nations" intervened in Russia in 1918–20 is to overlook the fact that the respective voices of these nations spoke in distinctly upper-class accents. The Western rulers dreaded the class nature of the Bolshevik Revolution and said so repeatedly. Secretary of State Lansing noted that the Bolsheviks represented "a despotism of the proletariat" and sought "to make the ignorant and incapable mass of humanity dominant on the earth." They appealed "to a class which does not have property but hopes to obtain a share by process of government rather than by individual enterprise. This is of course a direct threat at existing social order in all countries." The danger, Lansing went on, was that it "may well appeal to the average man, who will not perceive the fundamental errors." The Bolsheviks appealed "to the proletariat of all countries . . . to the ignorant and mentally deficient, who by their numbers are urged to become masters." Furthermore, rather than just talking about the "abolition of the institution of private property," the Bolsheviks had actually "confiscated private property" in Russia. "Here seems to me," Lansing concluded, "to lie a very real danger in view of the present social unrest throughout the world." For the property-loving Lansing, Bolshevism was understandably the "most hideous and monstrous thing that the human mind has ever conceived."[7]

Others shared Lansing's sentiments. The British ambassador in Russia, Sir George Buchanan, complained: "The Socialists [in Russia] would prefer to run a class war rather than the national war. . . ." General Alfred Knox, chief British military advisor in Russia, warned: "Distribute the land in Russia today, and in two years we'll be doing it in England." US ambassador to Russia, David Francis, urged armed intervention because the socialist elements organized into councils (or Soviets) "composed of workingmen and soldiers . . . are advocating abolition of classes and the right of soldiers to disobey their officers." Francis vowed that he would never "talk to a damned Bolshevik."[8]

Concerned that the invasion of Russia would be ineffective, Woodrow Wilson was more hesitant to intervene than some other leaders. But he never made secret his distaste for the Bolsheviks and never offered friendly relations to them. As he wrote to a US senator: "I don't think you need fear of any consequences of our dealings with the Bolsheviki because we do not intend to deal with them." And as he told British leaders, he supported intervention even "against the wishes of the Russian people knowing it was eventually for their good. . . ."[9] Like other members of his class, Wilson was horrified by the dangers of class equality posed by the Russian Revolution and the effect it might have on social relations in other countries, including Germany and the United States. Some of his observations were recorded by his physician:

> [President Wilson was concerned] that if the present government of Germany is recognizing the soldiers and workers councils, it is delivering itself into the hands of bolshevists. He said the American negro returning from abroad would be our greatest medium in conveying bolshevism to America. For example, a friend recently related the experience of a lady friend wanting to employ a negro laundress offering to pay the usual wage in that community. The negress demanded that she be given more money than was offered for the reason that "money is as much mine as it is yours."[10]

Wilson also feared that Bolshevism would affect the way business in America was conducted; business leaders might have to accede to having workers on their boards of directors.[11]

The class nature of the invasion became apparent also to some of its participants. Members of the allied expedition to Archangel (in Northwestern Russia) observed that the cheering crowds greeting the British and American troops "consisted entirely of the bourgeoisie and that there was not a workman to be seen."[12] A British colonel stationed in a Siberian urban center angrily observed:

> The bourgeoisie makes one almost a Bolshevik oneself. Here is a rich town, full of quite rich people; the ordinary population is short of everything including food . . . the army lacks everything . . . the hospital . . . crammed with wounded but with . . . no beds, shirts, mattresses, towels, bandages, swabs, surgical instruments, anaesthetics, medicines. . . . Yet not one . . . of the bourgeoisie even goes near the hospital or dreams of sparing just an hour or even so much as meeting the train loads of wounded and offering them a cup of tea. . . . The bourgeoisie goes nightly to the opera and then on to dance or what not until four or five even.[13]

An American sergeant in Murmansk registered his sympathy for the people against whom he was fighting:

> ... the way these kids and women dress would make you laugh if you saw it on the stage. But to see it here only prompts sympathy ... and loathing for a clique of blood-sucking, power-loving, capitalistic, lying, thieving, murdering, tsarist army officials who keep their people in this ignorance and poverty. ... After being up here fighting these people I will be ashamed to look a union man in the face. ... The majority of the people here are in sympathy with the Bolo [Bolsheviks] and I don't blame them.[14]

Even the British prime minister, Lloyd George, observed the Bolsheviks had "the only army that believed that it has any cause to fight for."[15]

The allied intervention involved hundreds of thousands of military personnel and lasted over two years. The US role was more than just token. US troops in Siberia and in Archangel and Murmansk conservatively estimated at 40,000, not counting naval forces, engaged in extensive hostilities and suffered several thousand casualties, including 436 who perished in combat or from disease. American and other allied troops participated regularly in atrocities. Widespread pillaging and killing of civilians were carried out by the reactionary White armies led by Generals Kolchak, Denikin, and Yudenitch. In one series of pogroms, Denikin slaughtered 100,000 Jews. The White armies were assisted by a German expeditionary force under General Von der Goltz, who, after the armistice and with US and British funding, joined his former adversaries against the common class enemy. Von der Goltz executed 3,000 persons in Riga alone.[16]

By 1919, the White Guard armies were wholly dependent on American and British aid, amounting to hundreds of millions of dollars. In a report to Congress in January 1921, Herbert Hoover admitted that the humanitarian relief funds voted by Congress had been used by him to supply these counterrevolutionary armies. Hoover also withheld aid intended for Hungary until the short-lived revolutionary Bela Kun government was overthrown and the reactionary Admiral Horthy was installed, backed by the bayonets of a Rumanian army that executed hundreds of revolutionaries and Hungarian Jews. Hoover also placed large sums at the disposal of the rightist Polish militarists during their invasion of Soviet Russia in April 1920.[17]

The Western capitalists had possessed substantial holdings in czarist Russia that were now jeopardized by socialist revolution. Hoover, alone, had secured a major interest in no less than eleven Russian oil corporations. When the allied armies entered Soviet Russia, they were followed by business people, bankers, and government officials. Coal, grain, timber, ores, furs, gold, oil, and machinery were extracted from the occupied areas and shipped to the USA and other capitalist countries.[18] Russia's immense natural wealth was very much on the minds of Western leaders.

During the 1980s, millions of Americans were treated to movies like *Red Dawn* and *Invasion USA* and television series like ABC's "Amerika," which portrayed imaginary Soviet invasions of the United States. Most Americans would probably be surprised to hear that in real life the reverse had happened. Even some of our presidents seem unaware of the real history. Appearing on Soviet television while on a visit to the USSR in 1972, President Nixon announced: "Most important of all, we have never fought one another in war." Referring to the United States and the Soviet Union in his 1984 State of the Union message, President Reagan said: "Our sons and daughters have never fought each other in war."[19]

The Soviets know otherwise. They remember what most of us have forgotten or never knew. In the United States there are relatively few historians critical of the West's invasion of revolutionary Russia, little mention of it in our textbooks, and no network documentaries or movies about this extraordinary episode. Can you imagine the treatment had it happened the other way around? Suppose that in 1920 or so, after general strikes and armed uprisings by workers in various sectors of the USA, the young Soviet government had sent an expeditionary force through Alaska into Seattle, Portland, and down the coast of California, in support of American strikers and rebels, and had engaged in pitched battles, killing many thousands of our more affluent citizens and destroying properties and homes for two years before being forced to retreat back to Russia. We would still be hearing about it in books, movies, and documentaries. Network news commentators would warningly refer to it whenever the Soviets proposed an arms reduction. Politicians would treat it as everlasting proof that Moscow was out to get us. And it would remain a subject of lively study in American schools from the first grade up through the graduate level.

The antagonism that Western capitalist leaders felt toward the Soviet Union did not end with the allied intervention against revolutionary Russia but persisted throughout the next two decades right up to World War II. The cold war is an old war; its roots go back to the time when capitalism's global monopoly was broken. After the Russian Revolution, the world would never be the same.

BETWEEN TWO WARS
AND TWO WORLDS

In the twenty years after the Western intervention in Russia, right up until the Second World War, both the United States and Great Britain refused to enter into any mutual defense pacts or other cooperative endeavors with the USSR; the USA even withheld diplomatic recognition of the Communist government until 1933.

In contrast to the hostility felt toward the Soviet Union, presidents, prime ministers, plutocrats, and popes displayed a remarkable forbearance and even admiration for the fascists in Italy and the Nazis in Germany, seeing them as bulwarks against Communism.[20] When Hitler remilitarized the Rhineland in 1936, England and France did not move to stop him, even though they had a combined military superiority over Germany. While Hitler and Mussolini sent troops and armaments to help the fascist General Franco crush the Spanish Republic in 1936–39, the United States, Great Britain, and France maintained an embargo against that beleaguered democracy, effectively contributing to its defeat. The Soviet Union and Mexico were the only nations to aid the Republic. Soviet shipments had to run a gauntlet of German and Italian submarines, with a loss of tons of munitions and arms, while the French government blocked Soviet overland deliveries into Spain. But fuel supplies from US companies continued to flow to Franco's invading army.[21] The Republic was defended mostly by the workers and peasants of Spain, including anarchist and Communist forces, along with Communist-led international contingents. Western leaders preferred to see Franco's dictatorship installed with the assistance of fascist guns, rather than risk the survival of a democratic republic that might go too far to the left. After the fascist victory in Spain in 1939, Great Britain, France, and the United States quickly extended diplomatic recognition to the Franco dictatorship.

When Hitler annexed Austria in 1938, the Western leaders acted as if nothing too terrible had happened. With the active cooperation of the US government, American corporations continued to expand their investments in German heavy industry, including German arms production.[22] That same year, when Hitler laid claim to the Sudentenland (the heavily industrialized western portion of Czechoslovakia that contained a large German population), British and French leaders hurried to Munich and conceded to another Nazi annexation. Less than half a year after the Munich concessions, Hitler marched his troops into all of Czechoslovakia.

Some Western leaders had thought to appease the Nazi leader, satisfying his appetite for expansion by throwing him a few weaker nations. They also hoped to channelize German expansionism in an eastward direction against the Soviet state, using fascism to obliterate socialism. With a few exceptions like Winston Churchill, Western leaders were more concerned with the Bolshevik specter than the fascist reality. They feared Hitler's emergent power but they did not look upon fascism with the same loathing they did Communism. Unlike the Communists, the fascists were not a threat to private enterprise; if anything, they had crushed socialist organizations in Germany and Italy and had made those countries safer for private capital.

Nevertheless, fascist powers did pose a problem for the Western nations. As latecomers, the German and Italian (and Japanese) capitalists were competing for markets, colonies, and investments against the Western capitalist nations. They were "expansionist" in that they challenged a status quo long dominated by the western imperialists. Yet most members of the ruling circles in the West were willing to give Hitler a good deal of room, if only because they saw him as a bulwark against Communism in Europe and in Germany in particular. Their tolerance of Hitler has since been condemned as "appeasement." More accurately it was a kind of complicity born of a mutual class hatred for revolutionary socialism. To be sure, Chamberlain and his associates were eager to avoid war, but much of that eagerness arose not from a newly found pacifism but from a willingness to strike the kind of bargain with the Nazi leader they would never dream of entering into with the Soviets. As the historian Geoffrey Barraclough argued:

> Hitler's successes in foreign policy were due less to German rearmament, the deficiencies and limitations of which were known in competent military circles, than to the tacit alliance of powerful reactionary elements in England and France which, although loathe to see a reasser-

tion of German equality, were still more unwilling to check it by military alliance with Soviet Russia or to run the risk of social revolution [in Germany] as a result of Hitler's fall.[23]

For Western leaders who had never quite reconciled themselves to the existence of a socialist Russia and who at the same time feared Germany's growing strength, the desired strategy was to turn Hitler's aggression against the USSR. This was not an altogether unrealistic plan, given the rabid anticommunism and anti-Sovietism professed by the Nazi leaders. In his memoirs, the Commander in Chief of the French armed forces, General Gamelin wrote that one of the aims of the Anglo-French alliance was to bring about a clash between German and Soviet interests.[24] The diplomatic historian Thomas Bailey observes: "There had been much loose talk in the Western democracies of egging Hitler on Stalin so that the twin menaces would bleed each other white in the vastnesses of Russia. . . ."[25]

In Asia, the United States and Great Britain did little to deter Japanese aggressions in Manchuria and China. Here too the anticipation was that the Japanese might move against the USSR—which indeed happened. In 1938, the Japanese militarists entered an alliance with Germany and Italy (the Anti-Comintern Pact), avowing a joint struggle against world Communism. The Japanese then attacked the USSR near the Outer Mongolian area, leading to a full-scale war that ended with Japan's suffering 18,000 casualties and military defeat.

Repeated overtures by the Soviet Union to conclude collective security pacts with the United States and Great Britain in order to contain both German and Japanese aggression were ignored or rebuffed, including the Soviet attempts to render armed assistance to Czechoslovakia. As the American historian George Vernadsky wrote: "Soviet leaders lost what little confidence they had had in the sincerity and ultimate purposes of the democracies. It was evident that had Hitler at that time struck directly at Russia he would have encountered little if any opposition from France or Britain. . . ."[26] Similarly, the anticommunist Foster Rhea Dulles noted:

[The US government's] attitude had done nothing to free the Soviet Union of its fear that the Western democracies would encourage Hitler to launch a crusade against Communism as a means of saving their own skins. . . . If it was impossible to crush [Nazi] aggression by a united front, Stalin felt the next best thing for Russia was to attempt to divert any immediate German attack from the Soviet Union.[27]

Isolated by the West, frustrated in its last minute attempts to form an anti-Nazi alliance with Great Britain and France, and believing that it was being set up as a target for Hitler's aggression, the Soviet Union signed an eleventh-hour nonaggression treaty with Hitler in 1939. To this day, cold warriors parade the Hitler-Stalin pact as proof of Moscow's diabolic affinity for Nazism and its willingness to cooperate with Hitler in the dismemberment of Poland. Thus, conservative news columnist George Will wrote in 1987: "The 1939 Nazi-Soviet pact truly was a joining of kindred spirits." On another occasion, Will described the Soviet Union as a regime that was "once allied with Hitler."[28] The pact was a treaty but not an alliance. It no more denoted an alliance with Nazism than would a nonaggression treaty between the United States and the Soviets denote a US alliance with Communism. On this point, conservative English historian A. J. P. Taylor is worth quoting at length:

> It was no doubt disgraceful that Soviet Russia should make any agreement with the leading Fascist state; but this reproach came ill from the statesmen who went to Munich. . . . [The Hitler-Stalin] pact contained none of the fulsome expressions of friendship which Chamberlain had put into the Anglo-German declaration on the day after the Munich conference. Indeed Stalin rejected any such expressions: "the Soviet Government could not suddenly present to the public German-Soviet assurances of friendship after they had been covered with buckets of filth by the Nazi Government for six years."
>
> The pact was neither an alliance nor an agreement for the partition of Poland. Munich had been a true alliance for partition: the British and French dictated partition to the Czechs. The Soviet government undertook no such action against the Poles. They merely promised to remain neutral, which is what the Poles had always asked them to do and which Western policy implied also. More than this, the aggreement was in the last resort anti-German: it limited the German advance eastwards in case of war, as Winston Churchill emphasized. . . . [With the pact, the Soviets hoped to ward] off what they had most dreaded—a united capitalist attack on Soviet Russia. . . . It is difficult to see what other course Soviet Russia could have followed.[29]

When Hitler attacked Poland, the Soviets moved into Latvia, Lithuania, and Estonia, the Baltic territories that had been taken from them by Germany, Britain, and Poland in 1919. They overthrew the right-wing dictatorships that the Western counterrevolutionaries had installed in the Baltic states and incorporated them as three republics into the USSR. The Soviets also took back Western Byelorussia, the Western Ukraine, and other areas seized from them and incorporated into the Polish rightist dictatorship in 1921 under the Treaty of Riga. This has been portrayed as proof that they colluded with the Nazis to gobble up Poland, but the Soviets reoccupied only the area that had been taken from them twenty years before. History offers few if any examples of a nation refusing the opportunity to regain territory that had been seized from it. In any case, as Taylor notes, by reclaiming their old boundaries, the Soviets drew a line on the Nazi advance—which was more than what Great Britain and France seemed willing to do.

When Hitler subsequently attacked both France and the Soviet Union, he forged in war the East-West alliance that London and Washington had repeatedly rejected and Moscow had repeatedly sought. But even before hostilities ceased, well before the Soviets could be accused of betraying the Potsdam agreements by setting up their own *cordon sanitaire* of socialist states in Eastern Europe and well before the Red Army could be accused of threatening the security of Western Europe, the West was preparing to resume the crusade to make Eurasia safe for capitalism. As Kim Philby, the British agent who defected to the USSR, writes:

> Between the wars, the greater part of [the British intelligence] service's resources had been devoted to the penetration of the Soviet Union and to the defense of Britain against what was known generically as Bolshevism. . . . When the defeat of the Axis was in sight, SIS [British intelligence] thinking reverted to its old and congenial channels.[30]

An Associated Press report, dated December 21, 1970, begins:

> Ten months before D-Day, military strategists discussed the possibility of repelling the Russians if they suddenly began overrunning Nazi Germany.
>
> Gen. George C. Marshall, World War II U.S. chief of staff, asked his British counterpart in August 1943, if he thought Germany would help allied troops enter Europe "to repel the Russians."
>
> The quotation came from official minutes of the Combined Chiefs of Staff which were made public today in London and Washington.
>
> Sir Alan Brooke, British chief of staff, told Marshall he had been thinking along similar lines.[31]

On the eve of the first atomic test—before Potsdam and long before the Soviet "threats" that supposedly led to the cold war—President Truman's first thoughts were of the Russians: "If [the atomic bomb] explodes, as I think it will, I'll certainly have a hammer on those boys." According to one visitor, Truman asserted that "the

Russians would soon be put in their places" and that the United States would then "take the lead in running the world in the way that the world ought to be run."[32] This might explain Truman's eagerness to demonstrate the destructive effects of the atom bomb before the war ended. General Groves, the head of the Manhattan Project that developed the bomb, testified: "There was never—from about two weeks from the time I took charge of the project—any illusion on my part but that Russia was the enemy and that the project was conducted on that basis. . . . Of course, that was reported to the President."[33] Thus, a monster bomb, developed by European refugees to defeat Hitler, was dropped by Americans on the Japanese mostly in order to intimidate the Russians.

Supposedly devoid of any hostile intent of its own and hoping to build friendly relations with the USSR, the United States suffered a rude awakening and was reluctantly obliged to assume world leadership in response to "the Soviet Challenge." This scenario, as we have just seen, does not describe the mind-set of the Truman administration in the closing days of World War II. Yet it remains the conventional explanation of how the cold war began. As described by Mose Harvey, a member of the State Department's Policy Planning Council: "The Soviets had chosen to, as it were, declare war on us—much to our surprise. We had little choice but to concentrate on the various threats thrusted before us."[34]

Of the "various threats," the most menacing was said to be the Soviet army itself. Poised across Central Europe in massive array at the end of World War II, the Red Army supposedly had been deterred from invading Western Europe only by US possession of the atomic bomb. As Winston Churchill asserted at the time: "Nothing preserves Europe from an overwhelming military attack except the devastating resources of the United States in this awful weapon."[35] While the United States engaged in large-scale demobilization after the war, the Soviets purportedly retained their forces at full strength. The political scientists Arora and Lasswell claim: "There was, in fact, a period of such rapid withdrawal of American forces abroad that communist forces were given a new lease on life in many countries."[36]

It is not clear where the rapid US withdrawal took place: certainly not from West Germany, France, Italy, Austria, Korea, or Japan, nor from the hundreds of US military bases that were being set up around the world, nor from the seas and oceans patrolled by US fleets. It is true that Western armies were not kept anywhere at wartime strength but the same holds for the Red Army. After the war, it was the Soviets who withdrew their troops from Manchuria, Korea, Norway, Denmark, Austria, and elsewhere. The Soviets supported the idea of a unified, neutral, demilitarized Germany—free of all foreign troops—until 1954, when a militarized West Germany was made a part of NATO. By 1948, the USSR had demobilized its forces from 11.3 million to 2.8 million. Most Western observers now agree that these numbers were accurate and that the Red Army's strength was "considerably exaggerated in the West during the early postwar years."[37] Soviet divisions were (and still are) much smaller and lacked the extensive logistical supports of Western divisions. Nor did Soviet occupation forces in postwar Europe have the 3 to 1 numerical superiority considered necessary by military commanders for a successful attack. Also, a large portion of the Red Army was composed of noncombat units engaged in mending the extensive damage wreaked by war, rebuilding industries and housing complexes and working on collective farms.[38]

The Soviets had lost more than 20 million citizens in World War II; fifteen large cities were either completely or substantially ruined; 6 million buildings were obliterated, depriving 25 million people of shelter. Some 31,000 industrial enterprises, 65,000 kilometers of railway, 56,000 miles of main highway, and thousands of bridges, power stations, oil wells, schools, and libraries were destroyed; tens of thousands of collective farms were sacked and millions of livestock slaughtered.[39] Following a trip to the USSR in 1947, British Field Marshal Montgomery wrote to General Eisenhower: "The Soviet Union is very, very tired. Devastation in Russia is appalling and the country is in no fit state to go to war."[40]

It is highly unlikely that a war-torn, exhausted Soviet Union, whose population longed passionately for peace, was deterred from launching World War III only by the atom bomb. Even without the bomb, the United States possessed 67 percent of the world's industrial capacity within its own boundaries, and had 400 long-range bomber bases in addition to forward-attack naval-carrier forces around the Eurasian perimeter. In contrast the Soviets had no strategic air force, meager air defenses, and a navy that was considered ineffective except for its submarines.

In 1949, while US cold warriors took steps to remilitarize Germany and form a military defense pact of Western nations (NATO), a CIA report stated: "There is no conclusive evidence of Soviet preparation for direct military aggression during 1949."[41] Yet the threat was, and still is, repeatedly conjured up to justify US military build-ups in Europe and elsewhere. As recently as 1987, *New York Times* columnist William Safire could write that "NATO successfully deterred the Russians for two generations. . . ."[42]

Recent research indicates that top US defense officials in the postwar era did not expect a Soviet military attack. Their real fear was that they would lose control of Europe and Asia to revolutions caused by widespread poverty and economic instability.[43] While they talked of saving noncommunist states from a Soviet takeover, their primary purpose seemed to be the reverse: using the "Soviet threat" as an excuse to intervene in other countries in Europe and elsewhere. As is still the case today, the "Giant Red Menace" was conjured up to win public support for military and economic counterrevolutionary aid to European and Asian capitalist-dominated nations. While protecting the West from an impending but nonexistent Soviet invasion, US forces and US aid bolstered conservative political rule within Greece, Turkey, Egypt, and Kuomintang China.

In Greece, during the civil war of 1945–48, it was the British army, financed and assisted by the United States, that fulfilled this counterrevolutionary role. Working with Greek right-wing forces, the British imposed a terror that included the incarceration of 13,000 citizens without trial or habeas corpus, the wholesale takeover of administrative and police functions by royalists and ex-Nazi collaborators, the purging of elected labor-union leaders, the destruction of forty-eight liberal and leftist printing presses, and the political murder of thousands of opponents of the Voulgaris regime. The *New York Herald Tribune* of September 17, 1946, reported "a pitiless war on scores of thousands of women and children in a desperate effort to halt growing rebellion and wipe out not only communists, but all democratic, liberal and republican elements." The United States's insistence that Stalin introduce Western-style democracy into Eastern Europe was accompanied by no compelling urge to practice the same in Greece where US-supported British troops reestablished a proto-fascist monarchist regime, committing far more acts of violence and political suppression than were perpetrated by the Communists in postwar Poland.

As in Greece, so in North Africa, Turkey, the Philippines, and South Korea, the United States supported the rule of fascist collaborators and other reactionaries and helped destroy resistance organizations. These interventions were designed not to thwart "Soviet power" but to prevent an indigenous social revolution from taking place. If our policymakers were capable of lying about Soviet intentions and capabilities in order to justify their counterrevolutionary policies during the postwar era, it is not unreasonable to entertain the possibility that they are doing the same today.

Notes

1. William Preston, Jr., *Aliens and Dissenters* (Cambridge, Mass.: Harvard University Press, 1963); Sidney Fine, *Laissez-Faire and the General Welfare State* (Ann Arbor: University of Michigan Press, 1956); David Caute, *The Great Fear* (New York: Simon & Schuster, 1978); Michael Parenti, *Inventing Reality: The Politics of the Mass Media* (New York: St. Martin's Press, 1986).

2. Spencer quoted in Max Lerner, "The Triumph of Laissez-Faire," in Arthur Schlesinger, Jr. and Morton White, eds., *Paths of American Thought* (Boston: Houghton-Mifflin, 1963).

3. Richard Boyer and Herbert Morais, *Labor's Untold Story* (New York: United Electrical, 1972), pp. 202, 215.

4. Lloyd Gardner, *Safe For Democracy, The Anglo-American Response to Revolution, 1913–1923* (New York: Oxford University Press, 1984), pp. 170, 180; William Appleman Williams, "American Intervention in Russia: 1917–1920," in David Horowitz, ed., *Containment and Revolution* (Boston: Beacon Press, 1967), p. 62.

5. Allistair Horne, *The Fall of Paris* (Garden City, N.Y.: Doubleday, 1967), p. 344. This book avoids any class analysis of the Paris Commune, which explains why it is one of the few on this subject that is in print and available in paperback.

6. Gardner, *Safe For Democracy,* pp. 198–200.

7. Williams, "American Intervention . . ." pp. 38, 42–43, 61; Gardner, *Safe For Democracy,* p. 161.

8. The quotations in that paragraph come from Gardner, *Safe For Democracy,* pp. 133, 148, 134, and 151 respectively.

9. Both quotations are from Williams, "American Intervention," pp. 61 and 57 respectively.

10. Cary Grayson's diary, quoted in Gardner, *Safe For Democracy,* p. 242.

11. Ibid.

12. Christopher Dobson and John Miller, *The Day They Almost Bombed Moscow* (New York: Atheneum, 1986), p. 64.

13. Ibid., pp. 239–40.

14. Ibid., pp. 189–90.

15. Quoted in Gardner, *Safe For Democracy,* p. 243.

16. Michael Sayers and Albert Kahn, *The Great Conspiracy, The Secret War Against the Soviet Union* (San Francisco: Proletarian Publishers, 1946), chapters 6, 7, 8 and passim; Dobson and Miller, *The Day They Almost . . .,* pp. 23, 248, 270. For a more complete account of White Army atrocities see George Stewart, *The White Armies of Russia* (New York: MacMillan, 1933).

17. W. W. Liggett, *The Rise of Herbert Hoover* (New York: H.K. Fly, 1932), pp. 255, 260–67; also B. M. Weissman, *Herbert Hoover and Famine Relief to Soviet Russia* (Stanford, Calif.: Hoover Institution Press, 1974), pp. 34, 37, 215.

18. John Hamill, *The Stange Career of Herbert Hoover Under Two Flags* (New York: William Faro, 1931), pp. 298–300; Albert Sirotkin, "A Bitter Memory in the Soviet Union," Novosti Press Agency (Moscow) reprinted in *People's Daily World,* March 25, 1987.

19. Dobson and Miller, *The Day They Almost . . .,* p. 200 for the Nixon and Reagan statements.

20. On how US leaders and the business-owned press looked kindly upon Mussolini and Hitler, see Michael Parenti, *Inventing Reality; The Politics of the Mass Media* (New York: St. Martin's Press, 1986), pp. 115–16; John Diggins, *Mussolini and Fascism: The View from America* (Princeton, N.J.: Princeton University Press, 1972).

21. Leonard Levenson, "US Communists in Spain" *Political Affairs,* August 1986, p. 23; Arthur Landis, *Spain, The Unfinished Revolution* (New York: International Publishers, 1975).

22. Charles Higham, *Trading with the Enemy: An Expose of the Nazi-American Money Plot, 1933–1939* (New York: Dell, 1983).

23. Geoffrey Barraclough, *The Origins of Modern Germany* (New York: G.P. Putnam's Sons, 1979), p. 453.

24. Maurice Gamelin, *Servir: La Guerre,* quoted in Oleg Rzheshevsky, *World War II: Myths and the Realities* (Moscow: Progress Publishers, 1984), p. 83; available from Imported Publications, Chicago.

25. Thomas A. Baily, *A Diplomatic History of the American People,* 10th ed. (Englewood Cliffs, N.J.: Prentice-Hall, 1980), p. 709. See then-Senator Harry Truman's comments to that effect: *New York Times,* June 24, 1941.

26. George Vernadsky, *A History of Russia,* vol. 3 (New Haven, Conn.: Yale University Press, 1969), p. 391. For a good study of Soviet efforts to form an alliance with the West against Hitler, see Pavel Sevostyanov, *Before the Nazi Invasion* (Moscow: Progress Publishers, 1981).

27. Foster Rhea Dulles, *The Road to Teheran* (Princeton, N.J.: Princeton University Press, 1944) pp. 201–03; also Joseph Brandt, "The Soviet-German Nonaggression Pact," *Political Affairs,* August 1986, pp. 37–40.

28. The two quotations are from Will's columns in the *Washington Post,* May 21, 1987 and November 16, 1986, respectively.

29. A. J. P. Taylor, *The Origins of the Second World War* (London: Hamilton, 1961), p. 262.

30. Kim Philby, *My Silent War* (New York: Ballantine Books, 1968), p. 101.

31. The AP report is reproduced in S. W. Gerson, "The Cold War Story the *New York Times* Suppressed," *Daily World,* December 29, 1970.

32. William Appleman Williams, *The Tragedy of American Diplomacy* (Cleveland: World Publishing, 1959), p. 168–69. On how Truman reneged on the Yalta agreements, see Diana Shaver Clemens, *Yalta* (New York: Oxford, 1971).

33. Quoted in Bert Cochran, *The War System* (New York: Macmillan, 1965), pp. 42–43.

34. Mose Harvey, "Focus on the Soviet Challenge," lecture recording, Westinghouse Broadcasting Co., 1964.

35. Churchill quoted in Matthew Evangelista, "Stalin's Postwar Army Reappraised," *International Security,* 7, Winter 1982–83, p. 110.

36. Satish Arora and Harold Lasswell, *Political Communication: The Public Language of Political Elites in India and the United States* (New York: Holt, Rinehart & Winston, 1969).

37. Evangelista, "Stalin's Postwar Army . . . ," p. 115 and the official US reports cited therein.

38. Ibid., pp. 117–19, 125.

39. D. F. Fleming, *The Cold War and Its Origins* (Garden City, N.Y.: Doubleday, 1961).

40. Evangelista, "Stalin's Postwar Army . . . ," p. 134.

41. Ibid.

42. *New York Times,* June 22, 1987.

43. Melvin Leffler, "The American Conception of National Security and the Beginnings of the Cold War, 1945–48," *American Historical Review,* 90, February 1985, pp. 363–64.

13

The Arms Chase

The Soviets may have been in no condition to invade Western Europe in the 1940s but, argue the cold warriors: "Today they are a major industrial power with a nuclear force that can destroy us. Lest we invite aggression as did the appeasers at Munich, we had better maintain a strong defense to discourage the Kremlin from attacking us or using their military superiority to dictate to us." The image is of an American leadership compelled to engage in an endless arms race in order to prevail against a persistently imposing Soviet power.

The reality is something else. For one thing, there never has been an arms race as such. The model of a race is of two opponents seeking to move as far ahead of each other as possible. But actually there is an arms *chase*, with one side, the United States, consistently and unilaterally deploying new and more deadly weapons, and the other side, the USSR, playing catch-up, being anywhere from two to eleven years behind the US. This was true of the atomic bomb, the hydrogen bomb, long-range bombers, medium-range missiles, tactical nuclear weapons, intercontinental ballistic missiles (ICBMs), submarine-launched ballistic missiles, multiple warhead missiles, and multiple individually targetable re-entry vehicles (MIRVs). Thus the United States introduced nuclear-armed submarines in 1959, the Soviets in 1968. The US had MIRVs in 1970, the Soviets in 1975. As of 1988, the US had built cruise missiles and manuverable re-entry vehicles (MARVs), while the Soviets had yet to develop such weapons. When the US announced its plans to build a neutron bomb in 1981, the Soviets publicly urged that the weapon not be built, saying in so many words: if you build it, then we will have to.

For decades, contrary to the above facts, US cold warriors and militarists have made it appear that the United States lagged dangerously behind the Russians. Only by exaggerating Soviet capabilities could they justify the gargantuan spending that gave perpetual impetus to their own arms buildup. In 1954, the US Air Force alerted us to an imaginary "bomber gap," predicting that the Soviets would deploy 1,400 long-range jet bombers by 1959. (By 1962, they had fewer than 200.) This was followed in 1960 by Pentagon warnings of a "missile gap" and predictions that the Kremlin would have up to 1,000 ICBMs by 1961. (In fact, the Kremlin had about 4 by 1962). Likewise in 1967–69 there was supposedly an "antiballistic missile gap" and in 1975, we were said to be falling dangerously behind the Russians in the development of MIRVs. In each instance, it was discovered—only after Congress had allocated billions of dollars—that no such gap existed and that US arms were superior in number.[1]

In 1987, the Department of Defense reported that the "relative technology level" of nuclear warheads was "changing significantly" in favor of the USSR—during the very time the Soviets had observed a unilateral eighteen-month moratorium on nuclear testing. This prompted Rep. Edward Markey (D-Mass.) to ask the Joint Chiefs of Staff, how could the Soviets make such dramatic technological gains without testing? To which the chiefs responded: "As a result of your inquiry, a review was made" of the claim and "no substantive reason could be identified to justify" it.[2]

In the 1980s, the goal pronounced by President Reagan was "to close the gap with the Soviets, and ultimately reach the position of military superiority. . . ."[3] In eight years, his administration spent about *two trillion* (two thousand billion) dollars on defense, more than the combined defense expenditures of the Truman, Eisenhower, Kennedy, Johnson, Nixon, Ford, and Carter administrations. Yet in a June 1986 press conference, President Reagan claimed that the United States was still militarily inferior to the Soviet Union—leaving some observers to wonder how so much money could buy so little security.[4]

Even before Reagan's massive escalation in defense appropriations the United States already spent more on arms than did the Kremlin. To justify devouring so much of the public treasure, the military-industrial establishment must continually convince Congress and the American people of two somewhat contradictory things: (1) that our money is well-spent and we are maintaining the best defense system in the world: and (2) that we desperately need to increase our defense budget because we remain militarily inferior to the Soviets and vulnerable to attack. If all these years we have been sitting ducks in a "window of vulnerability," literally inviting Soviet aggression, as the Reaganites maintained, and if the Soviets are indeed an "evil empire" so diabolic as to seize upon any advantage in order to obliterate us and impose their rule upon the world, then we might wonder why they have not already attacked us.

It is often pointed out that the Soviets spend a higher portion of their GNP on defense than does the United States. What is left unsaid is that they have a much smaller industrial base than we; so they are actually spending less than the US in absolute amounts. Furthermore, US estimates of Soviet military spending is calculated at American pay and upkeep scales. Thus, every time the US military gets a pay raise, Soviets spending is tabulated as going up and the "gap" increases in their favor—since they have more soldiers. When such calculations are made on the huge Chinese army, the bizzare mathematical result is that Chinese defense spending "equals" ours.[5]

Throughout the 1970s and 1980s, the United States had fewer "strategic" missiles than the USSR but almost 3,000 more nuclear warheads on them. (A "strategic" weapon is of intercontinental range or long enough range to hit an adversary's soil.) By the mid-1980s, the US had 11,000 strategic warheads compared to 8,250 for the Soviets. While 75 percent of the Soviet ICBMs were land-based and readily targeted by US forces, about half of the American strategic arsenal was deployed in invulnerable submarines. Scare propagandists have made much of the fact that Soviet missiles are larger and hoist more megatonnage, but they never mention that US missiles are more accurate. As Tom Gervasi noted, if we wanted to, we could have built larger missiles with warheads of greater explosive force. But we chose not to. Because of superior accuracy, US warheads threaten far greater damage on targets in the Soviet Union—with a fraction of the explosive power of Soviet missiles.[6]

In addition, there is no ring of Soviet bomber bases surrounding the United States, but there are over 300 US bases, many of them with nuclear arms, surrounding the Soviet Union and the Warsaw Pact nations. So who should feel threatened by whom?

It is frequently argued that we must maintain a nuclear superiority to compensate for the overwhelming advantage in conventional forces enjoyed by the Soviets. NATO's 44 divisions, it is said, are no match for 211 Soviet divisions. But 87 of the Red Army divisions are in Soviet Asia, and only about a third of all Soviet divisions are at full strength. Many would take months to mobilize. Even at full strength, a Soviet division is one-third the size of a US division and one-half as large as a Western European division; it is not as well logistically supported and lacks the sophisticated precision-guided armaments of Western divisions.[7] The truth is NATO and Warsaw Pact forces are about equal in numbers. General Frederick Kroesen, commander of the US Army in Europe, noted: "It disappoints me to hear people talk about the overwhelming Soviet conventional military strength. We can defend the borders of Western Europe with what we have. I've never asked for a larger force."[8] General David Jones, erstwhile chairman of the Joint Chiefs of Staff, observed: "I would not swap our present military capability with that of the Soviet Union. . . ." Similar sentiments were expressed by former Secretary of Defense Harold Brown and another former chairman of the Joint Chiefs of Staff, General Maxwell Taylor.[9]

In the air, the Soviets have a larger number of short-range interceptors for air defense but NATO has more long-range fighter-bombers and more combat aircraft and helicopters. On the seas, the Warsaw Pact countries have more ships than NATO (1,800 to 1,500), but as the Pentagon itself notes: "Gross numerical comparisons are misleading since they do not account for size or capability. . . . Our navy remains the best in the world."[10] NATO's ships are larger, with more firepower, and—unlike the Soviet fleet—designed to operate far from home for extended periods, with eighteen large-deck aircraft carrier groups capable of attacking sea and land targets. In contrast, the Soviet surface fleet has only two full-sized carriers and lacks the global port system and mobility of the US fleet.[11]

The above statistics do not support the alarmist view propagated by Reagan that the USSR "has conducted the greatest military buildup in the history of man." In 1973–77, the Soviet land-based ICBM force declined by seventy missiles, and again by seventy-nine in 1978–82. The CIA estimated that from 1976 to 1983, the annual growth rate of Soviet military spending sunk to 2 percent or even lower.[12]

In the face of these facts, scare propagandists maintain the myth of Soviet superiority only by a dishonest process of selective counting. Thus John Corry, a conservative writer for the *New York Times*, following a practice regularly indulged in by White House and Pentagon officials, reports: "The Soviet Union has 5,000 ICBM warheads; the United States has 1,054 missile silos."[13] By comparing Soviet warheads to US missiles—without noting that US missiles also have multiple warheads—Corry leaves a false impression of overwhelming

Soviet superiority. Calculations of land-based ICBMs also fail to take into account the great superiority enjoyed by the United States in strategic missiles on submarines and bombers. Our leaders and our media do not count the forward-based, highly accurate tactical missiles we have on ships and planes around Europe that can hit Soviet soil and therefore are of strategic effect. Nor do they count the French and British intermediate-range land-based missiles that are aimed only at the USSR. (If the Czechs and Bulgarians had such missiles, US leaders would insist they be counted as part of the East's arsenal.)

Regarding conventional forces, the cold warriors count *unarmed* Soviet construction brigades as combat units because they are uniformed. Because French forces were withdrawn from NATO command, they are no longer counted; yet France remains in NATO and has over 50,000 combat troops positioned in West Germany. US officials count all the tanks the Warsaw Pact nations have produced, including ones exported, or stored, or placed in reserve, or stationed in the Far East. But they count only NATO tanks deployed in active units, excluding tanks in reserve units and they say nothing of NATO's superior antitank firepower.[14]

While the United States has been the main impetus in the arms chase, the Soviets cannot be dismissed as a purely dependent variable. Not long after the Cuban missile crisis of 1963, when it appeared to them (and others) that they had come close to being nuked by the United States, the Soviets substantially increased their military spending in an attempt to achieve something close to parity with the United States. This striving for parity was treated by US leaders as evidence of Soviet belligerency and served as a feedback impetus for US arms escalation, thereby creating a self-fulfilling dynamic. We escalate, claiming it is only in self-defense; they escalate in an attempt to catch up, thus lending confirmation to the alarm that motivated our initial efforts, and justifying further escalations by us.

Yet the two major powers are not simply caught in a mindless cycle of arms buildup. As already noted, the United States has been the first to develop almost every new major weapons system and has striven for a superiority that threatens to destabilize the military balance between East and West. Previously the US had been publicly committed to a policy called "mutually assured destruction," known by the appropriate acronym, MAD. With MAD, each side had sufficient retaliatory force aimed at the other's population centers, thereby staying the hand of a would-be aggressor by threatening an unacceptable retribution of death and destruction. While this policy of deterrence was little more than a balance of terror, it possessed the considerable virtue of making nuclear war seem unwinnable and too horrible to chance.

In actuality, though MAD was the announced policy, it was neither a technological reality nor a policy commitment. For decades, US political and military leaders had been preoccupied with developing a counterforce capability, that is, the kind of striking power that would bring nuclear victory by destroying not the enemy's cities but its nuclear defenses. So along with targeting cities, US attack plans took aim at Soviet missiles, bombers, and submarine tenders. By the late 1980s, the United States was close to building a first-strike capacity.[15] "First strike" is not simply first use of nuclear arms but the ability to destroy another nation's strategic arsenal with one blow. The targeting of another nation's missiles, rather than its cities, is inherently aggressive rather than defensive, for it is intended not as a deterrence but as a way to destroy the other side's ability to retaliate. The US would not hit the Soviets' silos *after* they had fired their missiles since there is no sense in destroying empty silos. First-strike deployment is seriously destabilizing; it undermines deterrence by introducing the capacity to destroy the opponent's ability to deter. Several things are needed for a "successful" first strike:

Numerical Superiority

In order to wipe out all or almost all of an enemy's strategic force with one attack and still have enough missiles left to hit its cities in a second strike (should the enemy refuse to surrender), it helps to have a numerical superiority in, or at least an abundance of, warheads. The United States has an advantage in strategic warheads and in tactical missiles that have strategic capability because they are forward based and within easy striking distance of the USSR. None of the Soviet medium-range missiles is forward based; none of them can hit our American-based strategic missiles or our cities. Just one Trident submarine carries enough warheads to wipe out almost all of the USSR's major urban areas. If the goal is not merely to maintain a credible deterrence but to develop a first-strike capacity that can hit the tens of thousands of silos, bases, depots, ports, and command centers in the opposing nation, then the overkill in weapons, the ability to obliterate an opponent "a hundred times over," suddenly begins to make sense—to the extent that anything about nuclear war makes sense.

Accuracy

With the deterrence offered by MAD, one need only have the ability to strike at an opponent's cities; accuracy can be measured in hundreds of feet or even a mile or two. With first strike, one must hit the enemy's missiles, which are much smaller targets than cities. In the most ambitious nuclear-arms buildup in US history, the Reagan administration began deploying MX multiple warhead missiles with sufficient power and precision to destroy Soviet land-based ICBMs in hardened underground silos. Likewise, the new D-5 nuclear missiles put in the Trident II giant submarines are powerful and accurate enough to destroy Soviet ICBMs in their silos, making them first-strike weapons. Three thousand Trident missiles can knock out all Soviet land-based missiles. (One Trident II submarine carries a total destructive power of about fifteen to twenty megatons. The combined megatonage of US bombs dropped on Europe and Japan during World War II was about two megatons.)

Shortened Delivery Time

If it takes an hour for our missiles to reach them and an hour for their missiles to reach us, then if we let ours fly at them, they have an hour in which to detect the incoming missiles and let theirs fly at us. This would deter us (or them) from launching a first strike. But we now have D-5 missiles on Trident II submarines, forward-based missiles on planes, and sea-launched cruises missiles on suface warships and submarines that are so close to the Soviet coastline as to give virtually no warning of an attack. The more we shorten delivery time, the more deterrence breaks down. This is why the Soviets felt so threatened during the 1980s by the Pershing II and cruise missiles that the United States placed in Western Europe.

Elimination of Retaliatory Capacity

Both the USA and the USSR signed an antiballistics missile (ABM) treaty in 1972 because they recognized that ABMs could thwart each other's retaliatory capacity and undermine deterrence. Anything that weakens the deterrence of one or the other side is dangerously destabilizing. Yet beginning in the late 1970s and continuing throughout the 1980s, the US worked hard at neutralizing the Soviet retaliatory capacity. As already noted, by targeting Soviet land-based ICBMs, the US was potentially in a position to destroy 75 percent of the USSR's strategic nuclear force with a first strike. (A first strike by the Soviets against the US land-based ICBMs would take out only 25 percent of the US strategic force.) The relatively small number of Soviet nuclear-armed submarines and bombers could also be eliminated in a first strike. The US has deployed more effective long-range, early-warning radar installations to help in the interception of Soviet bombers. These bombers make up only about 5 percent of the Soviet strategic system and must fly over vast stretches of sea and land controlled by the United States and its allies, making their interception and destruction relatively easy.

The Pentagon has put great effort into the development of antisubmarine warfare and is now quite adept at tracking Soviet submarines not only off our coastal waters but around the globe. Soviet submarines have access to the oceans only by passing through the Danish Straits, the Turkish Straits, and straits close to Japan and South Korea, all of which are narrow, mineable, and heavily monitored and dominated by US and allied navies. At any one time, the Soviets are able to maintain only about four nuclear-armed submarines at sea. Soviet surface fleets face the same bottleneck access to the oceans as do their submarines, and have few friendly bases and facilities around the world to allow them to deploy an antisubmarine force. In any case, the Soviet navy has not been successful at tracking US nuclear-powered submarines.[16]

The US is also developing a counterforce, or "decapitation" strike, designed to destroy Soviet command and control centers. The Reagan administration's "Defense Guidance" plan says that these strikes will "render ineffective the total Soviet (and Soviet allied) military and political power structure," thus paralyzing the Soviet retaliatory capacity.[17] The US also has a variety of space satellites that can intercept Soviet radio and radar signals and an antisatellite weapon that eventually might be capable of destroying Soviet communications and surveillance satellites. All this can be considered part of the US first-strike arsenal.

The Backup "Shield"

Even the best first strike would probably not be able to knock out all Soviet missiles. So the Reagan administration started developing an antimissile system in outerspace, the so-called Strategic Defense Initiative (SDI), more popularly known as "Star Wars." Critics of the program point out that 80 percent of the physicists, chemists, engineers, and mathematicians in the National Academy of Sciences oppose SDI; only 10 percent favor it. Most scientists doubt it is a workable defense system, one that could never be of any real military value. They observe that it could never be tested in advance as a full system, so the United States would never know if it would work until it is too late; it must be able to detect, attack, and destroy enemy missiles almost instantly after they go into boost-phase; undetected flaws in the computer software might cause all or part of the system to malfunction in a crisis; the estimated cost of SDI is a trillion dollars and the final figure may be several times higher; and while the system is horrendously expensive, the Soviets could easily damage, destroy, deflect, or elude it at a fraction of the cost.

Critics note that SDI must work faultlessly the first time or else the missiles that get through, even if only 5 percent of the many thousands sent our way, would be enough to destroy our entire society. But this criticism is relevant only if we assume that SDI is intended as a defensive shield against a Soviet first strike—which it is not. As various scientists have noted, Star Wars makes more sense as a *backup shield to a US first strike,* designed to ward off the relatively few remaining Soviet missiles that might compose a feeble retaliation. As has been said, a leaky umbrella offers no protection in a downpour, but is useful in a drizzle.

Critics also observe that SDI has an offensive potential; weapons in space vehicles would allow no warning time, sending down a blast at the speed of light from just eighty miles above in outerspace, destroying vast areas and paralyzing the Soviet command. Lasers on space vehicles can produce firestorms at industrial sites, perhaps making SDI a more efficient instrument of destruction than the missiles it supposedly would intercept.[18]

In response, the Soviets have been upgrading the accuracy of their ICBMs, to make them capable of hitting US land-based missiles. Unfortunately, this expediency does nothing to restore deterrence. A Soviet first-strike weapon does not cancel out or deter a US first-strike capacity. If anything, any first-strike capacity undermines deterrence, making a preemptive attack that much more fearfully compelling for the other side. Yet we should not conclude that the upgraded Soviet ICBMs are comparable to an entire first-strike counterforce. A suit of clothes does not make an entire wardrobe. The USSR does not have the ability to stop massive retaliation by US bombers and submarines. Geography is not on their side. Their air and sea mobility is limited and vulnerable. Their attack time is much longer and susceptible to detection. Even the Scowcroft Commission—established by the Reagan administration itself—concluded that the Soviet Union had no first-strike capability to speak of.

Supporters of SDI argue both sides of the street, now claiming that it is a purely defensive weapon (hence, the deceptively appealing metaphor of a "shield"), now demanding that we develop our space weaponry in order to maintain strategic superiority. In order to get Star Wars funded by Congress, President Reagan argued that it was needed as a bargaining chip in arms-control negotiations. Then he refused to put it on the bargaining table at Reykjavik in 1986, and announced again in October 1987 that it could not be treated as a bargaining chip. He repeatedly claimed he would share SDI with the Soviets once it was completed. But if willing to neutralize its effects by sharing it with Moscow, why was Reagan unwilling to just drop the whole project and cooperate with the Russians in a reduction of strategic weapons, thus making SDI unnecessary? When Gorbachev asked him this at Reykjavik, he responded unconvincingly that a "madman" might in the meantime get hold of nuclear weapons and SDI would be the only global defense. As for Reagan's promise to share SDI, Gorbachev said, "I don't believe you," pointing out that in the past, the United States had been unwilling to share even its dairy technology.

The push for a *final* superiority rests on the assumption that this time the Soviets would never be unable to achieve parity. But if the US does deploy a Star Wars system, the Soviets are likely to augment their offensive arsenal in order to assure their ability to penetrate it and thereby maintain some deterrence. Furthermore, they may well attempt an outerspace antimissile system of their own (along with an expanded land-based ABM system) causing the US to expand *its* offensive arsenal. As Defense Secretary Caspar Weinberger said, a Soviet SDI would present "one of the most frightening prospects I could imagine" and would require "immediate additions" to our offensive arsenal.[19] Apparently we have every reason to be frightened by their "defensive shield" but they have no cause to be frightened by ours. What the late Soviet leader Yuri Andropov predicted about SDI is likely to come true: "It would open the floodgates to a runaway race of all types, both offensive and defensive."[20]

Rather than making us stronger and safer, the quest for military superiority and first strike creates a more hairtriggered nuclear stand-off. "Mutually assured destruction" or MAD has been replaced by what I would call "instant nuclear strategic annihilation of nearly everyone" or INSANE. Some of us can be forgiven if we doubt that the shift from MAD to INSANE represents a move toward a more secure world. If anything, the world is more under the gun than ever before. Yet, as we shall see in the pages ahead, there are policymakers in Washington who are not at all opposed to putting the world under the gun, especially since they believe they can keep their finger on the trigger and point it where they like.

Notes

1. On the general tendency of US officials to exaggerate Soviet military strength see Tom Gervasi, *The Myth of Soviet Military Superiority* (New York: Harper & Row, 1986); George Kistiakowsky, "Hazards of Soviet Scare Stories," *Christian Science Monitor*, January 17, 1977; Tom Wicker, "Beware of Gaposis," *New York Times*, January 9, 1981.

2. *Washington Post*, March 27, 1987.

3. Quoted in Fred Halliday, *The Making of the Second Cold War* (London: Verso, 1983), p. 48.

4. As late as February 1987, former member of the Reagan administration Eugene Rostow wrote that "the Soviet Union is a stronger military power than the United States and . . . its military strength is growing more rapidly than ours." *Washington Post*, February 20, 1987.

5. Richard Stubbing, "The Imaginary Defense Gap: We Already Outspend Them," *Washington Post*, February 14, 1982; Franklin Holzman, "A Gap? Another?" *New York Times*, March 9, 1983; Arthur Macy Cox, "The CIA's Tragic Error," in Gary Olson, ed., *How the World Works* (Glenview, Ill.: Scott, Foresman, 1984), pp. 252–57.

6. Gervasi, *The Myth of Soviet Military Superiority*, chapter one; Halliday, *The Making of the Second Cold War*, pp. 55–59; and the special issue of *Economic Notes*, January 1983. On the numbers of nuclear warheads possessed by each side see estimates by various defense study groups and agencies reported in *Washington Post*, May 16, 1984.

7. Andrew Cockburn, *The Threat: Inside the Soviet Military Machine* (New York: Vintage, 1984); also information prepared by the US Defense Intelligence Agency and Rep. Lee Aspin (D.–Wisc.) in *New York Times*, April 24, 1976; estimates by Gordon Adams of the Center of Budget and Policy Priorities, *New York Times*,

January 10, 1984; and by defense analysts Barry Posen, Fen Hampson, and John Mearsheimer in *International Security* (Summer 1982, Winter 1983–84, and Winter 1984–85, respectively), who conclude that NATO provides a formidable deterrence; also the book by the former NATO general, Nino Pasti, *Euromissiles and the Balance of Forces* (Helsinki: World Peace Council, 1983), pp. 42–47; Alain Enthoven and K. Wayne Smith, *How Much Is Enough? Shaping the Defense Program, 1961–1969* (New York: Harper & Row, 1971), especially chapter four.

8. Quoted in *New York Times*, November 18, 1985.

9. Jones, Brown, and Taylor quoted in Clayton Fritchey, "Military Inferiority Complex," *Washington Post*, August 1, 1980.

10. *Department of Defense Annual Report FY 1982* (Washington, D.C.), p. 77.

11. "The Soviet Navy: Still Second Best," *Defense Monitor* (publication of the Center for Defense Information, Washington, D.C.), vol. 14, no. 7, 1985.

12. *New York Times*, January 23, 1985; Robert Kaiser, "The Mythology that Confuses Our Arms Debate," *Washington Post*, January 13, 1985.

13. *New York Times*, November 20, 1983; see Fred Kaplan, *Dubious Spector: A Skeptical Look at the Soviet Nuclear Threat* (Washington, D.C.: Institute for Policy Studies, 1980).

14. Gervasi, *The Myth of Soviet Military Supremacy*, pp. 185–203.

15. It is thought that the move toward a first strike began with Jimmy Carter's Presidential Directive 59 in 1980, but our military and political leaders had long considered Soviet bomber and missile bases as prime targets: see Robert Aldridge, *First Strike! The Pentagon's Strategy for Nuclear War* (Boston: South End Press, 1983), pp. 22–40; Tony Palomba, "First-Strike: Shield for Intervention," in Joseph Gerson, ed., *The Deadly Connection* (Philadelphia: New Society Publishers, 1986).

16. See Aldridge, *First Strike!;* and Michio Kaku and Daniel Axelrod, *To Win a Nuclear War: The Pentagon's Secret War Plans* (Boston: South End Press, 1987); Gervasi, *The Myth of Soviet Military Superiority*, pp. 10, 203–204.

17. *New York Times*, May 30, 1981.

18. William Broad, *Star Warriors* (New York: Simon & Schuster, 1985); also Broad's article in *New York Times*, August 13, 1987; Philip Boffey, "Physicists Express 'Star Wars' Doubt; Long Delays Seen," *New York Times*, April 23, 1987; survey of National Academy of Sciences conducted by Cornell Institute for Social and Economic Research, released October 30, 1986; also *New York Times*, September 16, 1986 and February 11, 1987; Norman Cousins, "The Saga of SDI," *Christian Science Monitor*, January 27, 1987; Yevgeni Velikov, ed., *Weaponry in Space* (Moscow: Progress Publishers, 1985); available from Imported Publications, Chicago.

19. Weinberger quoted by Townsend Hoopes in a letter to the *Washington Post*, March 22, 1987.

20. Andropov quoted in *New York Times*, March 6, 1985; also William Colby and Robert English, "Star Wars May Destroy Strategic Defenses," *New York Times*, February 15, 1987.

14

"Rational" Nuclearism

It should be clear by now that every attempt to gain military superiority has fostered only a more costly, more dangerous arms escalation. Nuclear weapons make us "stronger" yet less secure. The more quickly weapons can reach their targets, the less chance is there to guard against mishap and miscalculation. The more weapons there are, the more possibilities for accidental war. Witness the following:

Radar and computer malfunctions at the North American Air Defense (NORAD) set off unclear warnings "probably dozens of times over the last 10 years," according to one specialist speaking in 1982.[1] In 1980, a malfunctioning forty-seven-cent computer chip reported that the Soviets had launched a massive attack against the United States. In all, from 1977 through 1984, the US early warning system produced 20,784 false indications of incoming missile attacks. More than a thousand of these were serious enough to require a concerned second look.[2] Inside Cheyenne Mountain, a nuclear-attack warning post, 147 alerts were recorded between January 1979 and May 1980. Most of these were quickly identified as false alarms, but at least a half dozen took American military authorities to second and third levels of alert.[3]

US nuclear-weapon storage sites located near communities in our own nation pose an additional hazard, as do the 30,000 US warheads, any number of which are being transported on any one day by plane, train, and truck across the USA. Aside from "minor" radiation leaks and spills, the Pentagon admits to thirty-two serious nuclear-arms mishaps between 1950 and 1980. Well-placed sources put the figure at four times that number.[4] To mention a few instances: In 1966 a B-52 accidentally dropped four nuclear bombs over Spanish territory; two of which burst on impact, scattering radioactive debris over a wide area. On January 24, 1961, a crashing B-52 bomber jettisoned two nuclear bombs over North Carolina;

one broke on impact; the other was prevented from exploding only because one of six safety switches held up. If the sixth had failed, a detonation 1,800 times stronger than the Hiroshima blast would have destroyed North Carolinia and endangered much of the Eastern seaboard. Radioactive plutonium from the accident was never recovered. In 1980, a Titan II missile exploded in Arkansas; its nuclear warhead did not go off but the explosion killed two mechanics, injured twenty-one other people, and hurled the nine-megaton warhead 200 yards away.[5]

US nuclear weapons are loaded with safety devices, but since safeguards cannot be so elaborate as to interfere with a missile's firing, there is a limit to the safety they provide. No doubt the Soviets also have had their share of false alarms, computer breakdowns, and near disasters. The danger exists on both sides, for both sides. During a US–Soviet crisis, when tensions run high, a false warning or a serious accident could trigger the opening of a nuclear war. The advantage in first strike may become so overwhelming as to make it a grimly tempting choice. Gervasi offers this scenario:

> In the judgment of the leaders of both nations, advances in weapons technology may [give] them too much to lose if they wait for an attack. When striking first seems to offer the only chance of surviving a nuclear war, they will certainly feel they have no other choice. When the damage they hope to avoid seems so much greater than the retaliatory damage they know must follow, they will accept retaliation. Then retaliation, hitherto unacceptable, will no longer deter them. This is how deterrence can collapse.
>
> In a crisis, normal safeguards on the use of nuclear weapons will be rapidly removed. . . . Each nation's preparations will be scrutinized by the other. Defensive preparations may be misread as offensive preparations. Prudence may no longer dictate restraint. It may demand that each nation assume the worst. . . . This mutually reinforcing pattern of misinterpretation and overreaction may be impossible to break before it ends in war.[6]

Given the nature of nuclear war, what does it mean to have "superiority" or an "advantage" in striking power? The vocabulary of war used for centuries by militarists made sense only when wars lasted more than an hour and our planet itself was not put at risk. Today's nuclear calculations leave out the most essential considerations regarding the destruction of the earth's fragile ecosystems. Assuming we launched a first strike and wiped out all of the Soviet nuclear force, thereby winning the war, what would we have won?

The compound effects of a major strike have never been measured and can only be imagined. We have never exploded even two ten-megaton bombs simultaneously, let alone a thousand. The scientific forecast is frightful.

Even in a "limited" nuclear war, scientists say, large quantities of nitrogen oxides would be injected into the stratosphere, causing extensive damage to the ozone layer. The National Academy of Sciences estimates that if the two nations used only 10 percent of their nuclear arsenals they would destroy 80 percent of the ozone in the Northern Hemisphere and 30 to 40 percent in the Southern Hemisphere. A severely damaged ozone would allow excessive ultraviolet radiation from the sun, producing serious flesh burns and scorching the earth's surface. The destruction of only 20 percent of the ozone layer would blind every organism on earth, including humans and the insects needed for pollinating vegetative life. Toxic fumes like cyanide and chloride, produced by the fires in cities, would poison the atmosphere. Massive amounts of fallout radiation, deposited in the troposphere and stratosphere, would return to earth over periods of weeks and years, entering our water and food supplies. After a US first strike, not only the few surviving Russians but all of us would absorb damaging amounts of radioactive iodine and strontium.

Even in areas well removed from the attack, cancer deaths would multiply dramatically. We might expect numerous human, animal, insect, and plant mutations and other genetic distortions of an enduring nature. The millions of sickened people and unburied corpses could lead to typhoid plagues and other diseases that would infect surviving populations all over Eurasia and beyond. The explosions from US missiles could generate a firestorm over the Russian land mass that might burn out the earth's atmosphere, ending all life on the planet. Or the explosions might raise the earth's temperature a few degrees, enough to melt the arctic icecaps and flood the Northern Hemisphere.[7]

Studies conducted independently of each other by American and Soviet scientists concluded that a nuclear war would create a climatic catastrophe known as "nuclear winter." Even with 80 percent of the bombs targeted at military sites rather than cities, the explosions and ensuing fires would cause massive amounts of smoke, chemicals, radioactive dust, and fine particles of debris to rise to the troposphere and stratosphere, blocking out the sun and causing a sudden drop in the earth's temperature. A drop in only 15° C is enough to eliminate

grain production in the Northern Hemisphere. Subfreezing tempera-
tures would last for months, killing all vegetation, making water
unavailable, leaving no human survivors in the Northern Hemisphere and effecting drastic changes in the Southern Hemisphere.
Countries such as Nigeria, India, and Brazil might well be destroyed
without a single bomb being dropped on their territory, or at best
they would be reduced to prehistoric population levels and horrible
survival conditions.[8]

In sum, a "successful" first strike against an adversary, even if it
could achieve the nearly impossible goal of eliminating all retaliation,
would be an attack on everyone else. The complex, fragile interrela-
tions of the earth's ecosystems are still not fully understood, but we
do know that nature observes no political boundaries. No nation is
an island unto itself. Hence, no nation can "win" a nuclear war
without inflicting doom upon most of the earth's inhabitants, including its own.

A greater scientific understanding of the doomsday quality of
nuclear war has been developing in recent years, revealing the awe-
some ignorance in which our leaders and strategists have hitherto
been operating, an ignorance that has allowed them to contemplate
and even threaten nuclear attacks without having to consider the
dreadful consequences. We should put to rest the view that our policymakers know things we do not and hence they know best. In fact,
they sometimes manifest a dangerous lack of information about technological realities. During the Cuban missile crisis, for instance, President John Kennedy feared that the Soviets might try to sneak missiles
into Cuba in submarines. None of his advisors pointed out that the
Soviets had no such capacity (in 1962). President Reagan once expressed the incorrect notion that Trident missiles could always be
recalled after being launched—this from the person empowered to
launch them.[9] Neither our presidents nor their advisers have had
anything to say about nuclear-induced fire storms, atmospheric
burn-out, hemispheric floods, ozone disaster, or nuclear winter. They
choose to remain silent about these things. They wield the power of
gods while themselves being either willfully deceptive or dangerously
ignorant.

Instead of stressing the doomsday nature of nuclear conflict, our
leaders cast about for arguments to justify the endless augmentation of
their dreadful arsenal. They propagate myths not only about the De-
mon Soviets but about nuclear war itself. In 1982, the *Washington*

Post noted that President Reagan and other high administrative figures were reportedly of the opinion that with sufficient advance preparation an all-out nuclear exchange could be survivable.[10] In 1981, asked by Senator Claiborne Pell whether he envisioned either the US or the USSR surviving a nuclear exchange, Eugene Rostow, then-director of the Arms Control and Disarmament Agency (ACDA) answered: "The human race is very resilient, Senator Pell." Rostow explained further: "Japan afterall not only survived but flourished after the nuclear attack. . . . Depending upon certain assumptions, some estimates predict 10 million [dead] on one side and 100 million on the other but that is not the whole population."[11] Zbigniew Brzezinski, President Carter's national security advisor, made a similar point: "Of course it's horrendous to contemplate, but in strictly statistical terms, if the United States used all of its arsenal in the Soviet Union and the Soviet Union used all of its against the United States, it would not be the end of humanity. That's egocentric. There are other people on the earth."[12] In other words, since not *everyone* in the world will perish (itself a debatable assertion), why make such a self-centered fuss about the hundreds of millions of us who will?

According to President Reagan's Deputy Under-Secretary of Defense T. K. Jones: "Everybody's going to make it if there are enough shovels to go around. Dig a hole, cover it with a couple of doors and then throw three feet of dirt on top. It's the dirt that does it."[13] No simple task for urban apartment dwellers. Asked to envision a post-nuclear society, federal emergency coordinator William Alcorn said: "I think to a certain extent we may have to start from scratch. But I think nowadays there's a natural tendency on the part of Americans to try to go back to their roots. To go back to original pioneer days."[14] While serving as director of our civil-defense program, Louis Guiffrida reassured us: "Nuclear war would be a terrible mess, but it wouldn't be unmanageable."[15] One of America's authentic Dr. Strangeloves, RAND corporation strategist Herman Kahn, asserted that nuclear war would not effect the nation's economic momentum. It would increase the number of children born with genetic defects but many children already are born defective; thus, Kahn reasoned, "War is a terrible thing, but so is peace. The difference seems in some respects to be a quantitative one of degree and standards."[16]

Once we embrace the macabre notion that nuclear war is not all that bad, we are not far from the delusion that it is winnable. While campaigning for the Republican presidential nomination in 1980,

George Bush in an interview with reporter Robert Scheer said he did not accept the doctrine that a nuclear war is unwinnable. It is possible, he reasoned, to knock out all or most of the Soviet delivery system in a first strike and force them to a quick surrender while sustaining casualties that would leave most of our population and industry intact. How many Americans would survive? Five percent? Bush responded: "More than that." Though he seemed not to know the exact number, the losses were acceptable to him.[17] State Department consultant Colin Gray, a dedicated nuclearist, plots a winning course for our side:

> The United States should plan to defeat the Soviet Union and to do so at a cost that would not prohibit U.S. recovery.... A combination of counterforce offensive targeting, civil defense, and ballistic missile and air defense should hold U.S. casualties to approximately 20 million, which should render U.S. strategic threats more credible.[18]

In 1982, the Pentagon issued a Defense Guidance, approved by Secretary Weinberger, which read in part: "Should deterrence fail and strategic nuclear war with the U.S.S.R. occur, the United States must prevail and must be able to force the Soviet Union to seek earliest termination of hostilities on terms favorable to the United States."[19]

In April 1981, the Reagan administration made public the novel view that a war between the two nations could very well be limited, nonnuclear, of protracted duration, and fought in several parts of the world simultaneously. It would not be catastrophic; it would be a nice, old-fashioned war. Seven months later, Reagan allowed that there could be a limited *nuclear* war between the two countries, involving "the exchange of tactical weapons," confined to the European theater. The Soviets responded that a limited nuclear exchange was not possible and would inevitably assume a worldwide character, leaving no one safe.[20]

No doubt, when saddled with leaders who are inclined to see the brighter side of nuclear conflict, we need repeatedly emphasize that such a war is unwinnable and that *both sides* would be destroyed. Yet this view contains the unintentional but stunning implication that the only thing, or most important thing, keeping us from incinerating millions of human beings in the USSR is that we too would be obliterated. It implies that if the destruction were not mutual, then a nuclear attack might well be an acceptable option at some future time. To be sure, there are strategists in high places who have drawn this very conclusion. Let us assume they are right, that the United States could win a nuclear war without sustaining millions of American casualties and without destroying most of our planet's life support systems. What exactly would such a victory bring? We are told that the Soviet people are the innocent captives of the Soviet system. But to vanquish that system by nuclear arms we would have to slaughter millions upon millions of unoffending men, women, and children, obliterate their cities and farmlands, and contaminate over one-sixth of the earth's surface. There is no moral justification for an act of that ferocity and genocidal magnitude—not even a guarantee that it could succeed without much damage to us.

A policy that entertains the possibility of nuclear victory is not only insane, it is profoundly evil. We often hear the advocates of *realpolitik* warn us that in a world such as this we cannot afford to give much weight to moral questions. Quite the contrary: in a world such as this, morality is our first—and perhaps last—line of defense, the force that must move us in strong opposition to the strategems of heartless "realists."

If nuclear war is unwinnable in any sense, then nuclear weapons are unusable. So why do we keep building them? Again, we must remember that "we," the American people, aren't doing any such thing. In nuclear freeze referenda throughout the nation and in successive opinion polls and massive demonstrations, the American people have put themselves on record as being strongly opposed to nuclear buildups and in favor of a bilateral nuclear freeze. It is not "we" who push for more arms but our leaders. But it is not enough to criticize leaders who promote notions about the manageability of a nuclear war; we also must ask why they continue to maintain such views. They do so not because they are hopelessly deluded but because nuclear weaponry and astronomical defense budgets serve their interests in real ways.

One obvious impetus to military escalation is corporate America itself, especially the defense industry. Military spending is a titanic pork barrel, a WPA project for the giant corporations, their single most important source of investment and profit. Along with the corporations, there exists a whole subsidiary network of subcontractors and politicians, strategists and military bureaucrats, researchers and technicians who are part of the permanent war economy, getting their fix from the multibillion-dollar Pentagon connection. Beset by recession, overcapitalization, declining investment opportunities, and the ever-present threat of a falling rate of profit, postwar American capitalism turned to military Keynesianism to bolster its earnings. SDI is only the latest and potentially biggest program in this process. As the *Wall Street Journal* itself observed:

> For defense contractors across America, President Reagan's Star Wars Program is more than a new strategy for national defense. It is the business opportunity of a generation, a chance to cash in on billions of dollars of federal contracts. . . . And the industry is starting to mobilize its fabled lobbying apparatus to build political support for what critics charge could become the greatest federal pork-barrel project in history.[21]

The defense industry's financial rewards are breathtaking. American taxpayers cover the industry's costs and assume most of its financial risks. Almost all defense contracts are awarded without competitive bidding and with little or no subsequent supervision, allowing for outrageous profiteering. Weapons systems have a built-in obsolescence and a high replacement rate. Military spending is readily expandable, there being no public criteria for what might be "enough." Defense appropriations do not compete with private demand but create an investment area that brings in the very highest profits.[22] (In contrast, federal human services expand the nonprofit sector, redistribute income, create alternative sources of income that help working people resist the downward pressure on wages, and put government in direct competition with business.)

Whether we are fighting a major war or not, whether the international climate is one of détente or cold war, the US military budget climbs ever upward, increasing by over 200 percent between 1977 and 1987. As George Kennan observed: "Were the Soviet Union to sink tomorrow under . . . the ocean, the American military-industrial complex would have to go on, substantially unchanged, until some other adversary could be invented."[23]

All the arguments made against runaway military spending—that it is socially wasteful, that it creates fewer jobs per dollar than almost any nonmilitary expenditure, that it produces scarcity and poverty in the civilian sector, that it is the single greatest consumer of taxes and a major consumer of precious minerals, fuel, metals, land, and water—are all true but they are largely irrelevant to the powerful interests that feed at the public trough. For them the danger is not hostile Russians but friendly ones, not arms escalation but arms reduction.

There is another reason US leaders endlessly pursue military buildup. Nuclear weapons are an integral part of the US effort to maintain a global influence. With nuclear supremacy, the United States presumably (1) would be able to dictate terms to the Soviets in any confrontation between the two powers and (2) would use its superiority "as a shield to allow it to intervene in Third World nations with little or no fear of the Kremlin countering its moves."[24] The United States could take whatever measures necessary to suppress revolutionary upheavals in other countries—maybe even undoing existing socialist governments.

Our leaders would have us believe that our weapons are intended for defending us and Europe against Soviet aggression. Yet much of our military capacity is composed of aircraft carriers, destroyers, battleships, amphibious assault ships, fighter bombers, short-range missiles, rapid deployment troop units, and the like, most of which would be of little value in an all-out war with the USSR. But these forces are very useful for establishing a US global presence and an ability to intervene unilaterally in "troublespots" throughout the Third World. Though it is rarely mentioned in public forums or in the news media, *much of our military is intended for intervention, not for defense.*[25]

Enjoying nuclear dominance, US leaders could retain a better grip on things. They say so themselves. Explaining why the Carter administration was engaging in a massive buildup of nuclear and conventional forces, then-Secretary of Defense Harold Brown pointed to "the growth in international turbulence . . . in the Caribbean, Southeast Asia, Korea, Afghanistan and Iran. . . . Our strategic [nuclear] capabilities provide the foundation on which our security rests. . . . With them, our other forces become meaningful instruments of military and political power."[26] While serving as director of the Arms Control and Disarmament Agency, Eugene Rostow observed:

> [T]he nuclear weapon is a persuasive influence in all aspects of diplomacy and of conventional war, and in [a] crisis we could go forward in planning the use of our conventional forces with great freedom precisely because we knew the Soviet Union could not escalate beyond the local level. . . . [However] as our lead in nuclear power diminished, our capacity to control the escalation of crises diminished correspondingly. So did our capacity to use conventional forces or credibly threaten their use.[27]

A top Defense Department representative during the Reagan administration, Richard Perle, said:

I've always worried less about what would happen in an actual nuclear exchange than *the effect that the nuclear balance has on our willingness to take risks in local situations*. It is not that I am worried about the Soviets attacking the United States with nuclear weapons. . . . It is that I worry about an American president feeling that he cannot afford to take action in a crisis because Soviet nuclear forces are such that, if escalation took place, they are better posed than we are to move up the escalation ladder.[28]

So it is not quite true that nuclear weapons are unusable. They are being used all the time, as resources of power, brandished to let others know who is boss. What is the use of having nuclear weapons if you cannot threaten someone with them? And what is the use of threatening others unless the threat is credible, unless they think you mean it? And they are more likely to think you mean it if you develop an overwhelmingly unanswerable superiority that can be used with near impunity. As the disarmament activist Tony Palomba put it: "The capability of launching a first strike is a nation's 'trump card' " in the game of international politics. To wield a nuclear power so preponderant that victory is assured—whether the weapons are used or not—is a desire "as old as the weapons themselves."[29]

And wield that power our leaders do. Were the Soviets to threaten anyone with their missiles, they would be denounced for practicing "nuclear blackmail"; but just about every American president since the atom bomb was invented has contemplated the "nuclear option" or has actually threatened to use nuclear arms, sometimes against nonnuclear countries and sometimes against the USSR. Here is a partial listing: Truman threatened the Soviets with the atom bomb when they were slow in withdrawing their troops from Iran immediately after World War II. In 1950, he publicly warned that nuclear weapons were under consideration in the Korean War. In 1953, during that same war, Eisenhower made secret nuclear threats against China and North Korea. In 1954, Secretary of State Dulles actually offered tactical nuclear weapons to the French during their final losing battle in Vietnam, but Paris declined the offer. Johnson considered nuclear weapons in Vietnam in 1968. Nixon contemplated using nuclear bombs against North Vietnam on a number of occasions from 1969 to 1972. In 1973, he also thought of using them when it was feared that the Soviets might intervene in the Middle East. On two other occasions, anticipating aggression by Moscow against the Chinese during a border dispute and possible Soviet intervention in the 1971 India-Pakistan war, Nixon toyed with the nuclear option. The "this-might-mean-world-war threat" was applied by Carter in 1980 and reiterated by Reagan in 1981 in response to what both presidents imagined would be a Soviet thrust into northern Iran and other parts of the Middle East.[30] The first two years of the Reagan administration seemed to offer nothing but chilling pronouncements from Alexander Haig, Caspar Weinberger, and other officials regarding the possibility of a violent collision with Moscow.

Not yet mentioned were the two occasions when President Kennedy contemplated using nuclear weapons: during the Berlin crisis of 1961 and the Cuban missile crisis of 1962. In both instances, his planners had reported "ideal" conditions: the United States would be able to destroy the Soviet war-making capacity. The Soviets had at most a dozen ICBMs, of which but one or two might get through. According to Kennedy aides, during the Cuban missile crisis the odds were one-third to one-half that the US would launch a nuclear attack. But the policymakers' nuclear ardor cooled when they realized that even one or two Soviet retaliatory missiles landing on American soil might cause "minimal" casualties of 3 to 15 million Americans.[31] Both Kennedy and his advisors were dangerously ignorant about atmospheric burnout, ozone destruction, arctic floods, or nuclear winter. The few Soviet missiles that deterred them may have saved us all.

In sum, the arms buildup continues because there is a "rational" dimension to nuclearism. It is thought to be essential for maintaining what former Reagan-administration official Eugene Rostow called "a progressive and integrated capitalist world economy. . . ."[32] Nuclear weapons are a part of the arsenal of imperialism. The Soviets have to be put under the gun because—as stated way back in 1946 by top policy planners in the Truman administration—"the ultimate aim of Soviet foreign policy seems to be the dominance of Soviet influence throughout the world" and "the final aim . . . is the destruction of the capitalist system."[33] The concern about capitalism is a genuine one, though seldom so candidly expressed. The characterization about Soviet foreign policy, however, is open to serious challenge.

Notes

1. *New York Times,* June 24, 1982.
2. "Accidental Nuclear War," *The Defense Monitor,* (Center for Defense Information, Washington, D.C.), 15, no. 7, 1986. Lloyd Dumas, "Human Fallibility and

Weapons," *Bulletin of the Atomic Scientists,* November 1980, pp. 15–20; Louis Rene Beres, *Apocalypse* (Chicago: University of Chicago Press, 1980); Arthur Macy Cox, *Russian Roulette* (New York: Times Books, 1982).

3. Bill Prochnau, "The Third World War and a Trip Through the Looking Glass," *Washington Post,* April 30, 1982.

4. Jack Anderson, "Are We Safe From Our Own Nuclear Weapons?" *Parade,* October 18, 1981, pp. 12–15.

5. See the citations in note 2; also Anderson, "Are We Safe . . . ," and Peter Lewis, "Risks Are Growing in A-War Systems," *New York Times,* May 3, 1987.

6. Tom Gervasi, *The Myth of Soviet Military Superiority* (New York: Harper and Row, 1986), pp. 36–37.

7. On the effects of nuclear war see Arthur Katz, *Life After Nuclear War* (Cambridge, Mass.: Ballinger, 1982); Y. Velikov, ed., *The Night After: Climatic and Biological Consequences of a Nuclear War* (Moscow: Progress Publishers, 1985), available from Imported Publications, Chicago. Ruth Adams and Susan Cullen, eds., *The Final Epidemic* (Chicago: Educational Foundation for Nuclear Science, 1982); H. Jack Geiger, "Fallout, the Medical Effect," *Common Cause,* August 1982, pp. 44–46; *New York Times,* April 28, 1982.

8. *Washington Post,* November 2, 1983; Paul Ehrlich, Carl Sagan, Donald Kennedy, Walter Orr Roberts, *The Cold and the Dark: the World After Nuclear War* (New York: Norton, 1984); Carl Sagan lecture on Public Broadcasting System, May 6, 1987; "Nuclear Winter," *Disarmament Forum* (Helsinki: World Peace Council), no. 1, 1985, p. 11.

9. On Kennedy see *Washington Post,* July 25, 1985; On Reagan see Mark Green and Gail MacColl, *Ronald Reagan's Reign of Error* (New York: Pantheon, 1983).

10. *Washington Post,* March 30, 1982. But when pressed for an on-record public statement, Reagan changed his tune, saying that "everybody would be a loser if there's a nuclear war," *New York Times,* April 1, 1982.

11. Quoted in Robert Scheer, *With Enough Shovels: Reagan, Bush and Nuclear War* (New York: Random House, 1982), p. 88.

12. Quoted in Fred Halliday, *The Making of the Second Cold War* (London: Verso, 1983), p. 232.

13. Scheer, *With Enough Shovels,* p. 138; originally quoted in *New York Times,* March 19, 1982.

14. *Washington Post,* August 15, 1982.

15. *New York Times,* April 8, 1982.

16. Quoted in Fred Kaplan, *The Wizards of Armageddon* (New York: Simon & Schuster, 1983), p. 228.

17. Scheer, *With Enough Shovels,* p. 29.

18. Quoted in the *Progressive,* June 1983, p. 22.

19. *New York Times,* July 22, 1982.

20. *Weekly Compilation of Presidential Documents,* (Government Printing Office, Washington, D.C.), May 13, 1982. For the Soviet response see the *Washington Post,* November 21, 1981.

21. *Wall Street Journal,* May 21, 1985.

22. Richard Halloran, *To Arm a Nation* (New York: Macmillan, 1986); Richard Stubbing, *The Defense Game* (New York: Harper & Row, 1986); "No Business Like War Business," *The Defense Monitor* (Center for Defense Information, Washington, D.C.), 16, no. 3, 1987.

23. Kennan in a forward to Norman Cousins, *The Pathology of Power* (New York: W. W. Norton, 1987).

24. Joseph Gerson, "What Is the Deadly Connection?" in Joseph Gerson, ed., *The Deadly Connection* (Philadelphia: New Society Publishers, 1986), p. 14.

25. Randall Forsberg, "Behind the Facade: Nuclear War and Third World Intervention," in Gerson, *The Deadly Connection*, pp. 26–28.

26. Quoted in Robert Borosage, "What Drives the Arms Buildup?" *E.N.D. Journal*, March 1984, p. 20.

27. Quoted in Jack Colhoun, "Reagan's Nuclear-tipped War Threats," *Guardian*, February 17, 1982.

28. Quoted in Robert Scheer, *With Enough Shovels: Reagan, Bush and Nuclear War* (New York: Random House, 1982), p. 13. Emphasis added.

29. Tony Palomba, "First Strike: Shield for Intervention," in Gerson, *The Deadly Connection*, p. 92.

30. Daniel Ellsberg, "Call to Mutiny," *Monthly Review*, September 1981, pp. 1–26, and the citations therein. also *New York Times*, February 2, 1980 and July 23, 1985.

31. Theodore Sorenson, *Kennedy* (New York: Harper & Row, 1965), p. 705; Robert Kennedy, *Thirteen Days* (New York: Norton, 1969); Kaplan, *The Wizards of Armageddon*.

32. Quoted in Christopher Paine, "On the Beach: The Rapid Deployment Force and the Nuclear Arms Race," in Gerson, *The Deadly Connection*, p. 113.

33. Melvin Leffler, "The American Conception of National Security and the Beginnings of the Cold War, 1945–48," *American Historical Review*, 90, February 1985, p. 366.

15

Can We Trust the Russians?

How do we prevent a nuclear holocaust? As the hardliners would have it: "The only way is by remaining so much stronger than the Soviets that they dare not attack us. And if we did not spend all that money on arms, all you peace advocates would not be able to reassure us that Soviet military superiority is a myth. As President Reagan said, it's better to put our trust in our military might than in the Russians." I would respond to this argument by first reiterating what was said earlier:

(1) We have an arms chase not an arms race, which we have repeatedly and unilaterally escalated—even before the Soviets had any strategic nuclear force to speak of. In most instances, Soviet escalations have been *in response* to US buildups. Unlike the United States, the Soviet Union has never striven for superiority and has sought only a sufficient deterrence or, at most, parity. This is why, in order to justify new US arms escalations that could not be justified by actual Soviet behavior, our leaders have had to fabricate stories about weapons gaps and windows of vulnerability.

(2) US arms escalation has been motivated principally by the profiteering interests of the US defense industry and by a long-standing desire to achieve a first-strike superiority that would allow our leaders to dictate terms in any crisis and intervene more freely to make the world safe for capitalism.

(3) The cold warriors assume that the Soviets are less human than we and therefore less readily deterred by the risks of nuclear war. As Reagan said: "We have a different regard for human life than those monsters do."[1] Presumably only a

massive superiority in US arms would deter them. But as we try to find security by making others feel insecure in the face of our superior might, we fail to recognize that others will react by continuing to build up their armaments—as has been the pattern over the last four decades. The result is less security for everyone.

In 1946, the US proposed the Baruch Plan, setting up an international commission, on which the United States would enjoy a controlling majority. The commission would have exclusive command of all atomic research, raw materials, and industries throughout the world. Under the plan, the United States could go on manufacturing atomic bombs until satisfied at some unspecified time that the US-dominated commission had attained total control of Soviet atomic research and production. In effect, the US would retain its monopoly of nuclear expertise and the Soviets would be forever foreclosed. Not surprisingly, Moscow turned down the offer. As Secretary of State Dean Acheson wrote, the American proposal was "almost certain to wreck any possibility of Russian acceptance."[2] But to this day, cold-war propagandists refer to Moscow's rejection of the Baruch Plan as proof of Soviet unwillingness to end the arms race and share in the peaceful development of atomic energy.

Peace advocates have urged that both sides engage in a mutual, gradual de-escalation of nuclear and conventional arms. What is usually overlooked by the US media and even by many persons in the peace movement (who strive for an appearance of evenhandedness by faulting both "superpowers" equally) is that this peace approach has been the Soviet position for the last forty years. In 1986, President Reagan stated that Mikhail Gorbachev was "the first Russian leader, to my knowledge, that has ever voiced the idea of reducing and even eliminating nuclear weapons."[3] In fact, Soviet leaders were calling for the reduction and elimination of nuclear weapons when Reagan was still making movies in Hollywood. Here is a partial listing.

In 1946, the USSR proposed a ban on the manufacture of atomic weapons and the destruction of all existing arsenals, along with reductions in conventional arms. In 1950 and again in 1951 and 1952 at the United Nations, the Soviets proposed banning the atomic bomb and asked for the establishment of an international agency to enforce the ban. The Soviets also called for a one-third reduction in the armed forces of both nations. In 1954, they proposed a mutual security pact with the Western powers. In effect, they were asking to join NATO. The proposal was turned down.

In 1954, the British and French offered a detailed plan for staged reductions of both nuclear and conventional forces, eventually leading to the elimination of all nuclear weapons. The following year the Soviet Union accepted the Franco-British plan, adding a proposal for permanent monitoring of nuclear and nonnuclear facilities. (Contrary to present-day misinformation, the Soviets did not agree to arms inspection for the first time in 1986, but have been for it since at least 1955.) Moscow's acceptance of the Franco-British plan took Washington by surprise. Against Soviet objections, US negotiators broke off talks.

In 1957 and again in 1961, Moscow proposed a nonaggression pact between NATO and the Warsaw Treaty Organization. The proposal was rejected by the United States. At various times throughout the 1960s, the Soviets proposed the banning of underground nuclear tests and a freeze on the production of nuclear weapons (long before the nuclear-freeze movement began in the USA), along with proposals that nuclear stockpiles be destroyed. In 1970, the Soviets made twenty-six separate overtures to limit the deployment of MIRV missiles. According to the *Christian Science Monitor*, "After heated internal debate, the White House . . . refused to regard the 26 contacts as serious, saying that it was a trick designed to dupe the US into delaying MIRV development."[4]

From 1971 through 1980, the Soviets submitted proposals to (a) prohibit the further testing, manufacturing, and deployment of nuclear weapons, (b) ban the production and stockpiling of chemical and biological weapons, (c) outlaw any forms of tampering with ocean beds, cloud streams, earth depths, the atmosphere, and the ozone layer for military purposes. In 1975, in a typical year at the United Nations General Assembly, the United States voted *against* a condemnation of nuclear tests and against a Soviet-supported proposal for a mutual cutback in nuclear missiles.

In 1979, Soviet leader Leonid Brezhnev announced a unilateral reduction of 20,000 troops and 1,000 tanks in Central Europe and invited the United States to reciprocate—even if on a smaller scale. In 1980, the Soviets reiterated their long-standing calls for a mutual halt of nuclear testing and a freeze on nuclear-weapons production. In 1982, Brezhnev proposed a two-thirds cut in the Soviet and American medium-range nuclear arsenals in Europe to be completed by 1990. Also in 1982, the Soviet Union and 118 other nations supported a UN General Assembly resolution calling for nations to stop making nuclear weapons and fissionable matter, ban all nuclear tests, and ban the deployment of nuclear arms; only the US and its NATO allies voted *no*. Another UN resolution outlawing nuclear testing was adopted by 111 nations to 1; only the USA voted against it.[5]

In 1983, Soviet leader Yuri Andropov offered to reduce the Soviet intermediate-range missile force from 600 to 162, matching the total of the French and British forces, if the US would refrain from deploying the cruise and Pershing missiles in Western Europe. Andropov also proposed a ban on all nuclear tests and on the production and deployment of new weapons.[6] The United States rejected both proposals.

Most dramatic of all were the disarmament efforts of Soviet leader Mikhail Gorbachev. Rather than working just through traditional diplomatic channels, Gorbachev presented his proposals directly to the international public, holding press conferences and buying space in Western newspapers to publicize the Soviet position on arms, so making it a little harder for the US to ignore Moscow's overtures. In January 1986, Gorbachev offered a sweeping proposal to rid the world of all strategic and medium-range warheads and delivery systems within fifteen years, to be accomplished through a series of graduated verifiable reductions by both nations.[7] Washington put the proposal "under study."

Later that year, the United States chose to respond only to Gorbachev's offer to eliminate medium-range missiles. When the Soviets agreed to negotiate the total elimination of medium-range arms, American hardliners then warned that this would leave the Soviets with an advantage in short-range missiles. When Gorbachev announced in 1987 that the USSR was ready to negotiate the elimination of all short-range missiles, the cold warriors fell back on a familiar refrain: take away our nukes and the Soviets will have a dangerous edge in troops and tanks. As already noted, Soviet conventional forces are *not* superior. In any case, for almost forty years Moscow has been calling for equitable cuts in conventional forces.[8] In addition, Gorbachev proposed the mutual withdrawal of US and Soviet fleets from the Mediterranean in 1986 and from the Arabian-Persian Gulf in 1987. Both overtures were rejected by the United States.

In September 1987, the Soviet Union and 129 other countries attended a United Nations conference to determine how monies saved from disaramament might be reinvested into Third World economic development. The United States boycotted the meeting, maintaining that disarmament and development were unrelated goals—a view not shared by Third World and Communist nations.

What good are Soviet peace proposals? Should we not judge nations by what they *do* and not by what they *say?* Maybe so, but what nations say is often part of what they do. What they propose in the diplomatic realm is often a reflection of their interests and represents a form of action. A nation that calls for mutual arms reductions and another that declines the offer are both dealing in something more than words. Both the overture and the refusal are actions; both reflect policy stances.

"Let them back up their words with deeds," said President Reagan. But when deeds *are* forthcoming, our leaders tend to look the other way or retreat into their own words. When Moscow did *act* in 1983, announcing a unilateral moratorium on antisatellite weapons testing (ASAT), saying it would refrain from testing as long as the US did, the White House refused to join the moratorium and continued to push Congress for ASAT funds. When the Soviets acted again in April 1985, announcing a seven-month moratorium on new missiles in Europe, saying it would deploy no more missiles as long as the US refrained from deployment, Washington again refused to join in the action, dismissing the Moscow initiative as a propaganda ploy.

Once more in August 1985, when the Soviets unilaterally embarked upon a five-month moratorium on underground nuclear tests, saying it would refrain from testing for as long as the United States did, our leaders again refused to join in. New weapons need to be tested; eliminate tests and you eliminate the arms buildup. Both sides knew this, but only one side seemed willing to act upon it. The other side, the Reagan administration, came up with a barrage of words, claiming it had to continue testing in order to be in a better position to engage in "realistic" arms reduction later on, dismissing the Soviet moratorium as just a trick to wreck a series of US tests scheduled for that year. The following year, with its tests completed, the White House still refused to join the moratorium even though the Soviets extended it two more times for a total of eighteen months.[9]

The USSR has pledged never to be the first to use nuclear arms. The United States has refused to follow suit. At first sight, the pledge may seem senseless, since both sides would very likely fire their missiles should a war start. But again, a nation's pronouncements often represent real policy positions. US leaders refuse to sign a no-first-use pledge because they want to be able to threaten first use. Were the US to sign, it would be undermining the very nuclear-threat "credibility" our leaders have tried so hard to implant in the minds of others, that is, an image of a nation willing to use nuclear weapons "if necessary." The Soviets have not only made a pledge, they also have never threatened anyone with first use. Again, for both nations, their words reflect real policies and interests.

Some people still think Soviet peace proposals and even unilateral disarmament actions are nothing more than propaganda ploys to conceal Moscow's real aims. But if the Soviets are bluffing, why not call their bluff and expose them as deceivers? Furthermore, on those occasions when the US *has* been willing to enter into agreements, the Soviets have not backed off. The two nations signed treaties outlawing nuclear weapons in the Antarctic and in outer space. They have entered treaties banning nuclear tests in the atmosphere, outer space, and under water. They have agreed to prevent the spread of nuclear weapons to other countries (the Nuclear Non-Proliferation Treaty of 1968). They signed the 1972 Strategic Arms Limitation Talks (SALT I) to limit offensive forces on each side, and the 1979 SALT II which the United States did not ratify but abided by until 1986, when President Reagan declared the treaty a dead letter and announced his unilateral intention to exceed its limitations.[10]

Reagan charged that the Soviets have a record of cheating on treaties. But he never produced that record. Arms-control experts, research scientists, former government officials involved in arms negotiations, members of Congress, and even high-ranking US military officers, have noted that the Soviet record on arms compliance has been a good one.[11] A close examination of the administration's charges show they are largely complaints about "possible" violations, "ambiguities," and "insufficient data."[12]

When one nation suspects the other of a treaty violation, the normal procedure is to refrain from public recrimination and bring the matter before the Standing Consultative Committee (SCC), a US-Soviet group set up to resolve any question concerning compliance. Experts say the SCC was one of the few success stories in arms control, effectively resolving often delicate and volatile matters in strict confidence. Every complaint the United States has brought before the commission has been resolved to its satisfaction. But the Reagan administration, in an unprecedented move, ignored both the SCC and the complaints the Soviets brought before that body regarding US radar violations.[13] Reagan preferred to pummel the Soviets in public for alleged violations rather than have his charges against them investigated and resolved.

Even if it can be demonstrated that the Soviets are eager for arms limitations and have a good compliance record, some people still worry about what the Kremlin might do at some future time when our guard is down. Can we trust the Russians? Though asked all the time, that question is really not relevant. No one is asking us to trust them. "Trust" implies placing one's faith and fate in the hands of another, as might a child with a parent or an adult with a close friend. There is no need to expect that kind of trust from either side. Agreements on arms reduction and arms elimination are to be bilateral and subject to verification. Instead of trusting the Russians, we will supervise them and they will supervise us in order to allay suspicions and insure compliance by both sides. But is the process of supervision itself reliable? Can we trust verification?

Generally, each nation is already fairly sure of what the other is doing. Even without special verification arrangements, it is impossible for one side to tip the nuclear balance by deploying a major new weapons system or a significant number of additional missiles without the other side knowing about it. Yet verification has often been a sticking point in arms negotiations. For instance, in the early 1980s, the US argued against a comprehensive test ban treaty because verification supposedly was impossible. But according to just about every American seismologist outside the administration, the technical capacity needed to police a comprehensive test ban, including explosions of a very small capacity, unquestionably exists.[14] In 1987, when the Soviets went on record supporting any and all systems of verification, including seismographic and satellite surveillance and comprehensive on-site inspection—the United States suddenly reversed its long-standing advocacy of thorough on-site inspection. The same thing happened with the comprehensive test ban, the ASAT, and other proposals *originally made by the United States:* in each instance, when the Kremlin surprised our policymakers by accepting their proposals, our leaders retreated from their positions, thus raising a question about the sincerity of the original proposals. Was it really the USSR that was bluffing or the USA?

By the late 1980s, the hardliners in Washington were arguing that we should scrap the SALT II treaty, the ABM treaty, and other arms accords because they were "ineffective." Far from being ineffective, past treaties stopped atmospheric testing, stopped deployment of an ABM system, and set limits on the number of warheads each side could have—which was the real reason US leaders wanted them out of the way. For instance, Article 5 of the ABM treaty rules out Reagan's Star Wars project, stating unequivocally that each nation "undertakes not to develop, test or deploy ABM systems or components which are sea-based, air-based, space-based or mobile land-based." The White House argued that this applied only to those weapons existing at the time the treaty was signed, which is like saying that a law prohibiting the dumping of toxic wastes applies only to toxins that existed when the law was passed. In fact, American and Soviet negotiators of the ABM treaty rather explicitly understood that the accord covered future as well as present weapons components.[15]

Maybe we should worry more about whether we can trust *our* leaders to negotiate arms reductions in good faith. An overview of US tactics, especially during the 1980s, offers cause for concern. Here are some standard ploys that have been used by US leaders to avoid ending the arms race.

False Offers and One-Sided Demands

The Baruch Plan remains as a model of the US offer that is so lopsidedly self-serving as to invite Soviet rejection. More recently, Reagan offered to negotiate a 50-percent reduction in ICBM land-based missiles but refused to include sea-based and bomber missiles—which is where most of our strategic force is—thus subjecting three-fourths of the Soviet strategic force to the cut and only one-fourth of the US missiles. The proposal also excluded any consideration of the SDI space-based system. So the Soviets were being asked to reduce their strategic arsenal drastically while we advanced our first-strike capacity by building an SDI system that could help wipe out their remaining strategic missiles. Not surprisingly they rejected the "offer."

In late 1987, the United States entered an agreement to eliminate intermediate-range and short-range missiles (the INF treaty), but only on very asymmetrical terms. The Soviets would have to dismantle 1,300, almost twice as many missiles as would the US and over four times as many warheads (1,565 to 364), leaving untouched over 4,000 NATO, Western allied, and US missiles on land and on ships and submarines around Europe. The weapons to be eliminated composed but 5 percent of the two nations' arsenals. Still, this represented the first time a treaty eliminated an entire class of weapons (except for the British and French intermediate-range missiles, which were left intact).

No Negotiating from Weakness or Strength

Through much of the 1980s, our leaders warned that if we negotiated from a position of weakness, we would be forced to accept disadvantageous terms. Furthermore, the Soviets supposedly would not negotiate seriously until they were pushed to the table by their fear of our stronger forces and by an American arms buildup that Moscow would find too costly to match.[16] Oddly enough, while *we* could not negotiate from a weak and threatened position, the *Soviets* would negotiate only when feeling weak and threatened.

But once we were stronger, it would be silly to negotiate away our advantage by agreeing to equitable arms reductions. In 1960, the United States refused to enter a mutual moratorium on the development of MIRVs and in 1986 refused to negotiate Star Wars because in each case we were so far ahead of the Soviets that we anticipated a continual superiority.[17] In sum, when we are "behind," it is too dangerous to negotiate; when ahead, there is no reason to.

Glorified Rigidity

The US approach, especially during the 1980s, was to protect all US advantages and new weapons programs while forcing the Soviets to abandon many of theirs. Negotiations were not a search for avenues of mutual interest—the traditional goals of diplomacy—but a way of extracting as many concessions from Moscow as we could while making as few of our own as possible. And when the Russians complained that Washington was stonewalling, we let them know they could take it or leave it—a stance that came easily to those who had little real interest in arms reductions. This rigidity was often characterized positively in the US press as showing "firmness" and "not yielding to Soviet demands."[18] By the end of 1986, as reported in the *Washington Post,* US officials were freely admitting that they were making "no new offers . . . and planned instead to 'listen' for new concessions by the Soviets."[19]

Spending Them into Compliance (Or Maybe into Aggression)

Soviet leaders have pointed out that a major reason they seek arms reductions is to have more resources available for domestic needs.[20] The cold warriors argue the reverse, that the Soviets want to improve domestic performance because a stronger economy would allow for a more aggressive Soviet foreign policy.[21] "The weakness of the [Soviet] economy is the most significant constraint on Soviet international activity," according to one writer.[22] It is argued that since the USSR's economic base is smaller than ours, we could use the arms race to force them to expend more on arms and thus spend themselves into poverty, thereby making them weaker and less dangerous.[23] This represents a departure from the usual and more obvious view that if they spent more on weapons, they would be more dangerous.

Another view, enunciated by former secretaries of state, Alexander Haig and Henry Kissinger while in office, and others is that internal weaknesses will cause the USSR to seek "foreign diversions" to distract its populace from domestic grievances and "will drive it to try to solve its problems through expansionism."[24] Thus, domestic weakness makes the Soviet Union feel *less,* not more, constrained abroad. In short, when the USSR grows stronger militarily it becomes (1) more dangerous, or (2) less dangerous because it becomes more impoverished domestically, which (3) constrains its aggression or (4) makes it more aggressive. When talking about the "Soviet Menace," our leaders feel free to say just about anything they want, as long as it is consistently negative rather than logically consistent.

Imputing Evil Intent

When the Soviets reject American proposals as too one-sided, this is treated as evidence of their hostile intent and unwillingness to negotiate. But when they offer dramatic concessions, they are accused of launching a "peace propaganda campaign." Everything they do may be treated as suspect. The cold-war psychology propagates the notion that not only do *we* know they are evil, but *they* know they are evil. Not only do *we* know we are good, but *they* know we are good. Therefore, if they oppose us in any way, it can only be out of wrongful intent.

When the Soviets' words are peaceful and positive, our leaders point to their supposedly evil *actions:* their arms buildup, their presence in Afghanistan, and so on. But when Soviet actions are peaceful, as with their unilateral moratoria on missile placements and nuclear testing, and unilateral cuts in conventional forces, our cold-war propagandists point to their threatening *words,* reminding us that Khrushchev said he would bury us. So actions speak louder than words except when words speak louder than actions. (In 1959, Khrushchev explained in a press conference with American reporters that his "we will bury you" statement did not mean the physical burial of the American people but was referring to his anticipation that the socialist system would historically outlive the capitalist system. Just as capitalism buried feudalism, so "socialism . . . would take the place of capitalism and capitalism thereby would be, so to speak, buried."[25] Yet today, Khrushchev's clarification is regularly ignored when the thirty-year-old quotation is dredged up out of context and taken as proof of Moscow's murderous intent.)

Infinite Linkage

When all else fails and the cold warriors are faced with the terrifying prospect of arms limitations, there is always "linkage," that is, the tying of arms reductions to other issues. Thus before, during, and after the 1986 Iceland summit, Reagan and other officials said we could not enter any agreement with the Soviets until they freed their dissidents, stopped jamming our Voice of America broadcasts, allowed Soviet Jews to emigrate in larger numbers, got out of Afghanistan, allowed more democracy in their internal affairs, and so on. (It should be noted that the Soviets have never demanded as a precondition for arms agreements that the FBI end its surveillance of American dissidents, that American Communists be granted regular access to the national media, that poverty and racisim in America be ended, and that the United States cease supporting counterrevolutionaries in Central America, Africa, and Afghanistan.) In December 1986, one senior US official, who called for "greater openness in Soviet society," pointed out that since such a goal could not be met "in the predictable future," the US position was that nuclear testing and nuclear weapons could never be eliminated.[26]

Not long after those remarks were made, the Soviets began an effort to develop greater democracy in all areas of life under Gorbachev's *glasnost* campaign; in short time they released over a hundred dissidents, they opened new areas of debate and criticism in the press, the party, the government, the workplace, and the arts; they allowed larger numbers of Jews to emigrate and began taking back those who wanted to return. But it really does not matter if they do these things, for the linkage is infinite. The hardliners will then demand that other ethnic groups be allowed to emigrate, that the *glasnost* is only a facade until the Communist Party relinquishes power to noncommunist parties, that an anticommunist government be installed in Afghanistan after the Soviet depart, and so on.

US officals have made much of the Soviet intervention in Afghanistan. Even some peace advocates in the United States have likened it to the US intervention in Vietnam and Nicaragua. One big difference is that the US intervenes to prevent fundamental changes in the social relations and class structures of Third World countries, while the Soviets intervened in Afghanistan to support the forces that were promoting such changes, meeting a fierce resistance from Islamic reactionaries, feudal landowners, tribespeople, and opium growers, a resistance richly supported with hundreds of millions of dollars in US aid and weapons. The Soviets intervened to save a faltering revolution in Afghanistan, supporting the side that worked for land reform, literacy, and an end to the wretched oppression of women, workers, and tenant farmers.[27] As of early 1988, Moscow sought to withdraw its troops from Afghanistan and end the bloody stalemate. The Soviets called for a nonsocialist, multiparty coalition government that would provide a major role for the rebels.

One nation's intervention into another nation is not inherently evil. If the Allied forces had intervened in Germany in 1933 and wiped out Hitler and his Nazis before they started World War II—even over the protests of a majority of Germans—it would not have been such a bad thing. The French intervened in support of the American Revolution, sending supplies and troops, yet probably no American thinks ill of them for doing so. There are many different roads to revolution. To their credit, the Cubans intervened in Angola to defend a revolution that was being threatened by reactionary forces from Zaire and South Africa. Interventions should be supported or opposed, depending on whether they support progressive or reactionary social forces. If the United States gave aid to revolutionary forces in reactionary countries, many of us would support rather than oppose US interventionism. But as already noted, given the global interests of its capitalist class, the United States consistently intervenes on the side of counterrevolution and against revolution.

In any case, the Soviet intervention in neighboring Afghanistan hardly looms as evidence of the Kremlin's intent to dominate the world nor as demonstration that peaceful coexistence and friendship with the USSR is a chimera. In both words and deeds, the Soviets have had a much more positive and activist overall record regarding arms limitations than the United States.

Notes

1. Quoted in Robert Scheer, *With Enough Shovels: Reagan, Bush and Nuclear War* (New York: Random House, 1982), p. 241.

2. Dean Acheson, *Present at the Creation: My Years in the State Department* (New York: W.W. Norton, 1969), p. 155.

3. *New York Times*, June 12, 1986.

4. *Christian Science Monitor,* May 12, 1970, cited in Daniel Rosenberg, ed., *Swords Into Plowshares: Soviet Initiatives for Peace, Security and Disarmament 1917–1982* (New York: National Council of American-Soviet Friendship, 1982), p. 19.

5. Most of the instances listed above are from Rosenberg, *Swords Into Plowshares.* On the UN votes see *New York Times,* December 10 and 13, 1982.

6. *Washington Post*, February 2, 1983.

7. Gorbachev's proposal was published in its entirety as a paid advertisement in the *New York Times*, March 21, 1986.

8. Rosenberg, *Swords Into Plowshares.* For Gorbachev's call for cuts in conventional forces in 1986 see *New York Times,* July 1, 1986; for an earlier instance, see *Washington Post,* March 6, 1984.

9. Georgi Arbatov, "Moscow's View on Nuclear Testing," *New York Times,* January 10, 1986; also *New York Times,* March 18, 1986.

10. *New York Times*, May 28, 1987; *Boston Globe*, July 25, 1986.

11. A good study of this question is Daniel Rosenberg, *The Unbroken Record, Soviet Treaty Compliance* (New York: International Publishers, 1985); see also Michael Gorden, "U.S. Aide Testified Soviets Kept Most Arms Pacts," *New York Times,* January 10, 1986; Admiral Noel Gayler, "The Way Out" in *The Nuclear Crisis Reader* (New York: Vintage, 1984), p. 235; Charles Mohr, "Soviet Arms Pact Breaches: Charges Questioned," *New York Times,* June 6, 1986; R. Jeffrey Smith, "Alleged Soviet Treaty Violations Rebutted," *Washington Post,* February 13, 1987; also the report by Center for International Security and Arms Control, released in February 1983.

12. Kosta Tsipis and Jerome Wiesner, "That Report on Soviet Treaty Violations: Guesswork?" *Washington Post,* November 15, 1986. The most notable charge

regarded a radar site in Krasnoyarsk which was said to violate the ABM treaty because it could track incoming missiles. The Soviets say it has no such capacity and is used to track satellites. Scientists say the necessary radar for missiles has not been installed. A delegation of US House members came to the same conclusion after an on-site visit to the facility: see *Washington Post,* September 10, 1987, and the MacNeil/Lehrer NewsHour, September 9, 1987.

13. Marta Daniels, "Reagan's Public Accusations of Soviet Treaty Violations," *Freeze Focus,* May 1984 (reprinted by Promoting Enduring Peace, Woodmont, Conn.).

14. See observations by seismologists Lynn Sykes and Jack Evernden quoted in Conn Hallinan, "Verification—The Last Refuge of a Scoundrel," *People's Daily World,* March 13, 1987.

15. *Washington Post,* February 6, 1987.

16. For an example of this reasoning see William Safire's column in the *New York Times,* June 22, 1987.

17. For a discussion of the US unwillingness to negotiate see John Anderson's criticisms in the *New York Times,* August 28, 1984; also Reagan's comments in *New York Times,* May 25, 1984.

18. *New York Times* editorial, April 10, 1985. Consider the discussion in Russell Leng, "Reagan and the Russians," *American Political Science Review,* 78, June 1984, pp. 339–340.

19. *Washington Post,* December 3, 1986.

20. See Khrushchev's remarks quoted in Fred Halliday, *The Making of the Second Cold War* (London: Verso, 1983), p. 147.

21. See the criticisms by Arthur Macy Cox in *Los Angeles Times,* July 26, 1987.

22. Stephen Burg, "Constraining Soviet Behavior," *International Review,* March 1984, p. 6.

23. Reagan's advisor Richard Pipes, for one, argued this position, claiming that the US could spend the Soviets so deeply into poverty as to bring down their regime: see Matthew Evangelista, "Soviet People Support Arms," *In These Times,* March 31–April 6, 1982, p. 11.

24. See Haig's comments in *Hartford Courant,* October 4, 1981; Kissinger as quoted by Bob Paine in *People's Daily World,* June 7, 1986.

25. Khrushchev's news conference in *Washington Post,* September 17, 1959.

26. The unnamed official was quoted in *Washington Post,* December 3, 1986.

27. Philip Bonosky, *Washington's Secret War Against Afghanistan* (New York: International Publishers, 1985), for information and opinion suppressed by the US news media. In retrospect, the *New York Times* reported (May 22, 1988): "The rebellion began when the Afghan Communists imposed land redistribution and literacy campaigns and encouraged women to cast off their veils, work and go to school." The *Times* might have added that the Communists' attempt to suppress the large and lucrative narcotics traffic was an additional cause rebellion by the Afghan "freedom fighters."

16

Against Imperialism

In this book I have traveled beyond liberal and conservative opinion in an attempt to show that over the centuries capitalism has been—and still is—a dynamic, expansionist, imperialist force, principally beneficial to the owning classes of the world and harmful to the earth's people, especially the masses of the Third World. More than a matter of "planting the flag," imperialism is a system of forcibly expropriating the land, labor, resources, and markets of other nations. Along with that, it is a coercive and often violent method of preventing competing economic orders from arising. There exists, answerable to no nation, a plutocracy that can go almost anywhere, transferring its operations from one country to another, punishing resistant governments and "rewarding" compliant ones. This plutocracy battens on tax-free investments and lavish subsidies from penurious Third World governments. It monopolizes the markets and resources of entire regions, and acts as a usurious creditor for increasingly indebted nations. Attached to no country, international finance capital is a distant ruler over outwardly sovereign states. Since the end of World War II, the burden of making the world safe for this plutocracy has been shouldered preeminently by the most powerful and richest of capitalist nations, the United States.

If the above assertions are just the imaginings of Marxist and neo-Marxist writers, then what is the evidence to support an alternative view? Why has the United States never supported social revolutionary forces against right-wing governments? Could it possibly do so? If not, why not? Why in the postwar era has the United States overthrown a dozen or more popularly elected, left-reformist democracies? Why has it warred against revolutionary movements? Why has it fostered close relations with just about all the right-wing autocracies on earth? If the explanations provided in this book are wrong, what are the correct answers to these questions?

191

The answers usually given, as already noted, have been found wanting. US foreign policy is neither shortsighted nor stupid as some liberal critics maintain, nor fainthearted and lacking in will as conservatives say. While it has suffered setbacks, US policy usually has been successful. It has been capable of a ruthless assertion of power, frequently unconstrained by humanitarian considerations. US imperialism has a harrowing arsenal of nuclear weaponry and a growing accumulation of conventional firepower that is approaching the nuclear level in its destructive capacity.[1] US policymakers have deployed troops, fleets, and bombers around the world, and waged one of history's most destructive wars in Indochina. They have promoted counterrevolutions, counterinsurgency, and political repression—complete with death-squad assassinations, torture, and terror—in scores of nations and have overthrown democratic governments in bloody coups. They have engaged in massive military spending programs, an outpouring of anti-Soviet invective, and frightening cold-war confrontations, saturating the American public with threatening images of a Red tide about to inundate us. All this hardly represents a policy of fainthearted appeasement.

Nor is US policy a captive of excessive moralism or utopian globalism; nor is it compelled by "the nation's vision of its role in history."[2] If there *is* a utopianism or an historical vision, by some strange coincidence it is always directed against popular revolution and socialism and is supportive of global capitalism. The "vision" may be universal and inspirational but it is also remarkably selective and class bound, capable of putting aside its democratic or utopian idealism to support the worst of facist regimes in the Third World. To be sure, fine-sounding ideology and idealism have played an important role in justifying imperialism's mean methods and exploitative goals. Far from dismissing the role of ideas and ideology, this book has dedicated its entirety to countering the prevailing ideology with a body of evidence and argument generally ignored or misrepresented by liberals and conservatives.

On earlier pages I noted that US leaders urge the populace to support existing (capitalist) governments in order to thwart Soviet expansionism. Whether there is or is not a Soviet threat is a question that would have to be settled by an investigation of actual Soviet behavior rather than by repeated assertion. Closer examination suggests that the primary purpose of US policymakers seems to be to use the "Soviet threat" as justification to shore up regimes that are friendly to capitalism and to prevent competing noncapitalist social orders from arising. The "Soviet threat" is also used to justify building a US military force of such superiority that it could secure US hegemony without having to go to war, or US victory if war becomes necessary. For all its ostensible insanity, then, the nuclear arms buildup has a "rational" dimension in that it reflects both the global containment interests of the US ruling class and the financial interests of a highly profitable defense industry.

I also observed that there *is* a real Soviet threat, the one that has existed since the first days of the Bolshevik Revolution, when a new system emerged that used the land, labor, markets, and resources of society in ways that might signal the end of capitalism. This system needed to be destroyed or contained not because of its alleged "totalitarian" features but because of its socialist agenda. *The containment of socialism remains to this day the basis of most US interventions throughout the world.*

But why has nothing been said on these pages about *Soviet* imperialism in such places as Eastern Europe and the Middle East? The answer should be clear enough: if imperialism is a system of economic expropriation, then it is hard to describe the Soviets as "imperialistic." They own not an acre of land, not a factory or oil well in the Middle East or Eastern Europe. Moscow's trade and aid relations with other socialist countries are decidedly favorable to those countries, contrary to the imperialist pattern in which wealth flows from the client states to the dominant nation. Indeed, living standards in much of Eastern Europe is higher than in the USSR. The contrast between US and Soviet "imperialisms" shows up in the vast differences in economic conditions between the Soviet "client states" of Eastern Europe and the US client states of the Third World, as measured by overall health and education standards, job opportunities, conditions of labor, and availability of human services. These differences are not to be lightly dismissed.

Some writers, who might agree with the above view that the Soviets have not been imperialistic (as the word is normally defined), have maintained that the Soviets are nevertheless "hegemonic" in their dealings with Eastern Europe, as evinced by their military interventions to suppress uprisings in Hungary in 1956 and Czechoslovakia in 1968.[3] The Soviets certainly have a record of intervening in Eastern Europe, a region that repeatedly has been an avenue of invasion and mortal threat to them. But it is one thing to criticize them for hegemonic behavior in not allowing hostile anticommunist regimes to reemerge on their borders and even for committing repressive acts and undemocratic abuses at home and in Eastern Europe, but something else to treat this as evidence that the Kremlin is bent on world conquest.

Nor should this hegemony be exaggerated. For years the mainstream press has told us that the "captive nations" of Eastern Europe were puppet regimes of the Kremlin. Yet Rumania has refused to go along with the USSR on a number of important foreign policy issues. Nor has such recalcitrance prevented Moscow from having friendly and equitable relations with Bucharest. In 1987, the East German, Czechoslovakian, Hungarian, and Rumanian governments were resistant to Gorbachev's *glasnost* proposals and in some instances even refused to publicize his views in their own media—an odd way for puppets to act. It was reported on National Public Radio (March 8, 1987) that Poland was totally supportive of the Gorbachev reforms not because Warsaw hoped to travel the same road but because it already *had*—a view that clashed with the usual image of a thoroughly repressed Poland.

As is well-publicized in the West, existing Communist nations are beset by problems of production, bureaucracy, corruption, faulty planning, shortages of goods, criminal abuses of power, and the suppression of dissidence. Less publicized by the media are the social gains made by people under Communism. Before World War II, Eastern European countries like Poland, Bulgaria, Hungary, and Rumania had right-wing political states that ruled over largely poor and politically backward populations. After the war, Communist governments transformed these countries into relatively prosperous nations, in which all the people could get a free education to the highest level of their abilities, and everyone had a right to free medical care, a job, and subsidized housing, utilities, and transportation. Whatever one's view of existing Communist countries, one might stop thinking of them as devoid of any possibility for change and development and as a threat to our security and world peace.

At this point opponents might argue: "This book offers nothing more than a conspiracy theory about 'global capitalism.' It argues that we are ruled by an all-knowing monolithic capitalist elite that commits no errors of judgment and suffers no confusions. This elite is supposedly all-powerful and immune to considerations beyond its own class interests. Such a view of an aggrandizing single-minded global capitalism is nothing more than a mirror image of the Right's conspiracy theory about an implacably aggrandizing monolithic global Communism."

Several responses are in order. First, even if the Left does have a view of global capitalism that bears resemblance to the rightist theory about Communism, the two theories thereby do not automatically cancel each other out. Both Jews and Nazis saw each other as diabolical entities bent on conquest and death. It so happened that the Nazis were preaching a grotesque propaganda about the Jews, while the Jews were quite correct about the Nazis. That two arguments have a similarity in *form* says nothing about whether the *content* of either is true or false. That question can only be decided by empirical investigation.

Second, conspiracies do exist. If we define conspiracy as planning in secrecy for illicit purposes while misleading the public as to what is happening, then there have been conspiracies aplenty. There was the secretly planned Bay of Pigs invasion of Cuba, initially presented to the public as a purely Cuban émigré venture; the fabricated story about a North Vietnamese Tonkin Gulf attack against US destroyers, designed to induce Congress to support greater military involvement in Indochina; the CIA's clandestine operations to assassinate foreign leaders and overthrow governments; the FBI's COINTELPRO program to use illegal methods to disrupt dissenting organizations in the USA; the Watergate break-in and the Watergate cover-up; and above all, the Iran-contra affair, involving the unlawful use of funds, secret bank accounts, the criminal destruction of government documents, the illegal financing of counterrevolutionaries in Nicaragua, the complicity of other nations, and a secret coterie of unsavory operatives— all covered over with lies and misrepresentations served up by the president of the United States and other top policymakers. Not all conspiracies are fantasies.

Third, nobody says that US policymakers are "all-knowing" and incapable of blundering. They have been taken by surprise at certain times and frustrated by unintended consequences. They may sometimes be confused and divided over tactics. But the fact that there is not *perfect* determinacy does not mean there is *no* determinacy of any kind. US leaders may not be omniscient but neither are they somnambulists, habitually bereft of aim and intent. US policy may not always be consistent but it is seldom directionless, especially in regard to its counterrevolutionary and cold-war commitments. Most political participants act with conscious intent, but when we ascribe such intent to those in power, oddly enough, we are immediately denounced as "conspiracy theorists."

Fourth, the Left does not claim that policy is made by a mysterious coterie. The people who make US foreign policy are known to us—and they are well known to each other. Top policymakers and advisors are drawn predominantly from the major corporations and from policy groups like the Council on Foreign Relations, the Committee for Economic Development, the Trilateral Commission, the Business Roundtable, and the Business Council. Membership in these groups consists of financiers, business executives, and corporate lawyers. Some also have a sprinkling of foundation directors, news editors, university presidents, and academicians.

Most prominent is the Council on Foreign Relations (CFR). Incorporated in 1921, the CFR numbered among its founders big financiers such as John D. Rockefeller, Nelson Aldrich, and J. P. Morgan. Since World War II, CFR members have included David Rockefeller, chairman of Chase Manhattan Bank (and erstwhile CFR president); Allen Dulles, Wall Street lawyer and longtime director of the CIA; and, in the 1970s, all the directors of Morgan Guaranty Trust; nine directors of Banker's Trust; five directors of Tri-Continental holding company; eight directors of Chase Manhattan; and directors from each of the following: Mellon National Bank, Bank of America, General Motors, Ford, Chrysler, Standard Oil of New Jersey, General Electric, General Dynamics, Union Carbide, IBM, AT&T, ITT, and the *New York Times* (a partial listing).[4]

One member of the Kennedy administration, Arthur Schlesinger, Jr., described the decision-making establishment as "an arsenal of talent which had so long furnished a steady supply of always orthodox and often able people to Democratic as well as Republican administrations."[5] President Kennedy's secretary of state was Dean Rusk, president of the Rockefeller Foundation and member of the CFR; his secretary of defense was Robert McNamara, president of Ford Motor Company; his secretary of the treasury was C. Douglas Dillon, head of a prominent Wall Street banking firm and member of the CFR. Nixon's secretary of state was Henry Kissinger, a Nelson Rockefeller protégé who also served as President Ford's secretary of state. Ford appointed fourteen CFR members to his administration. Seventeen top members of Carter's administration were participants of the Rockefeller-created Trilateral Commission, including Carter himself and Vice President Walter Mondale. Carter's secretary of state was Cyrus Vance, Wall Street lawyer, director of several corporations, trustee of the Rockefeller Foundation, and member of the CFR.[6]

Reagan's first secretary of state was Alexander Haig, former general and aide to President Nixon, president of United Technologies, director of several corporations including Rockefeller's Chase Manhattan Bank, and member of the CFR. Reagan's next secretary of state was George Shultz, president of Bechtel Corporation, director of Morgan Guaranty Trust, director of the CFR, and advisor of the Committee for Economic Development (CED). Reagan's secretary of defense was Caspar Weinberger, vice president of Bechtel, director of other large corporations, and member of the Trilateral Commission. The secretary of treasury and later chief of staff was Donald Regan, chief executive officer of Merrill, Lynch, trustee of the CED, member of the CFR and of the Business Roundtable.[7] Reagan's CIA director, William Casey, was director of the Export-Import Bank, head of the Securities and Exchange Commission under Nixon, and partner in a prominent Wall Street law firm. At least a dozen of Reagan's top administrators and some thirty advisors were CFR members.[8]

Members of groups like the Council on Foreign Relations and the Trilateral Commission have served in just about every top executive position, including most cabinet and subcabinet slots, and have at times virtually monopolized the membership of the National Security Council, the nation's highest official policymaking body.[9] The reader can decide whether they compose (1) a conspiratorial elite, (2) the politically active members of a ruling class, or (3) a selection of policy experts and specialists in the service of pluralistic democracy.

These policymakers are drawn from overlapping corporate circles and policy groups that have a capacity unmatched by any other interest groups in the United States to fill top government posts with persons from their ranks. While supposedly selected to serve in government because they are experts and specialists, they really are usually amateurs and "generalists." Being president of a giant construction firm and director of a bank did not qualify George Shultz to be Nixon's secretary of labor nor his secretary of the treasury. Nor did Shultz bring years of expert experience in foreign affairs to his subsequent position as Reagan's secretary of state. But he did bring a proven capacity to serve well the common interests of corporate America.

Rather than acting as special-interest lobbies for particular firms, policy groups look after the class-wide concerns of the capitalist system. This is in keeping with the function of the capitalist state itself. While not indifferent to the fate of the overseas operations of particular US firms, the state's primary task is to protect capitalism as a system, bolstering client states and opposing revolutionary or radically reformist ones. To do so, the state sometimes must violate the short-term interests of specific corporations, as when the government imposes embargoes on socialist countries with whom particular companies wish to trade.[10] More often the interests of individual firms coincide with the state's goals as when the US seeks to ward off the threat of socialism by moving against a country that tries to redistribute income and nationalize corporate holdings; likewise, when the US prevails upon a Third World government to take over a failing private company at much cost to that government and with generous compensation to the private investor.

In some instances, corporations play a rather direct role in the formulation of policy. After it expropriated some uncultivated lands belonging to the United Fruit Company, the democratically elected Arbenz government in Guatemala was overthrown in 1953 by a mercenary force financed and directed by the CIA. According to a former United Fruit Company official, "United Fruit was involved at every level" in the planning and execution of the coup.[11] The mercenary force was trained on one of the company's plantations in Honduras. The president who was installed by the coup promptly returned the expropriated lands to United Fruit and abolished the tax on dividend and interest earnings to foreign investors, a move that saved United Fruit about $11 million. United Fruit had been, and after the coup remained, Guatemala's largest landowner. In similar fashion, and for like reasons, International Telephone and Telegraph (ITT) and other large investors in Chile actively conspired with the CIA in planning the strategy that promoted a military coup in that country in 1973.[12]

Do capitalist rulers form a cohesive monolith? (A view attributed to the Left by its critics.) Not really. Conflicts arise repeatedly—which is one reason capitalists feel compelled to form policy groups whose task is to keep sight of their class's dominant concerns. Conflicts exist between heavy and light industries within a country, between multinational and domestic producers, between different capitalist nations such as Japan and the United States. There are ideological differences, as between the conservative Rockefeller groups and the ultraconservative Du Ponts and other more far-right true believers. But these intraclass conflicts have not caused serious disarray in ruling circles and thus far have not prevented policymakers from applying the political, economic, and military means needed to maintain imperialism.

Are the capitalist rulers all-powerful? (Another view attributed to the Left by its critics.) Far from it. The reason they must work so persistently, brutally, and deceptively to maintain the status quo is because the world is not really all that safe for imperialism. The monopoly in modern arms and systematic effort that imperialism once enjoyed no longer exists. Revolutionary movements in various countries now have a level of organization, political mobilization, and military capacity superior to what oppressed peoples possessed in earlier eras. One need only compare the sporadic Indian uprisings in seventeenth-century Mexico to today's well-organized liberation struggles in Central America, or the divided and deceived native resistance in Southwest Africa in 1904-07 to today's unified struggles in Namibia and South Africa, or the impassioned and doomed Boxer Rebellion of 1900 to the protracted and victorious Chinese Revolution of 1925–49, or the futile Vietnamese insurrections against the French in 1930 to the Vietnamese liberation movement that defeated the US militarists in the early 1970s.

Revolutionary—or at least anti-imperialist—consciousness today has spread throughout the world, among workers, peasants, students, and clergy. Even the "middle classes" within Third World countries, independent professionals and modest-level bureaucrats whose living standards are deteriorating, farmers and businesspeople dependent on local markets, and some of the more patriotic members of the military—while not necessarily looking to restructure their societies along revolutionary lines—believe they and their compatriots would be better off if they could be free of the onerous intrusions of foreign capital, including the crushing debt owed to Western banks. The resistance registered by these sectors might explain why large majorities of member states in the United Nations have failed to support the United States in almost 80 percent of the votes in UN General Assemblies in recent years.[13]

Not only in the Third World but in the capitalist nations of

Western Europe and North America, political, religious, labor, and community peace forces have mobilized in unprecedented numbers against US-sponsored wars and the nuclear arms race. In the United States itself, popular backing for President Reagan's increases in defense spending dropped from 71 percent in 1980 to 9 percent by 1985. In 1986, by 2 to 1, the American public opposed Reagan's plans to abandon the arms limitation agreements that existed between the US and the USSR. By 74 to 22 percent, Americans said they wanted all countries that had nuclear weapons to destroy them. And by large majorities, the public disapproved of US interventions in Lebanon and Central America, and the sending of more funds to the contras in Nicaragua.[14] The nuclear freeze was endorsed in the USA by 446 New England town meetings, more than 276 city councils, 11 state legislatures, and in 9 out of 10 statewide referenda.[15]

Socialist governments themselves have been a considerable force for peace, pushing hard for cultural exchanges and better trade relations, offering major arms proposals, taking unilateral steps toward disarmament, inviting Western observers to make on-site inspections, and the like. To the extent that these efforts evoke positive responses from the publics of Europe and North America, they exert a pressure on reluctant Western leaders to negotiate.[16]

Far from being powerless, the pressure of democratic opinion in this country and abroad has been about the only thing that has restrained US leaders from using nuclear weapons in Vietnam, and intervening with US forces in Angola, Nicaragua, and elsewhere. How best to pursue policies that lack popular support is a constant preoccupation of White House policymakers. President Reagan's refusal to negotiate with the Soviets in the early 1980s provoked the largest peace demonstrations in the history of the United States. Eventually he had to offer an appearance of peace by agreeing to negotiate. To give this appearance credibility, he actually had to negotiate and even reluctantly arrive at unavoidable agreement on some issues, including the 1987 INF treaty.

Evidence of the importance of mass democratic opinion is found in the remarkable fact that the United States has not invaded Nicaragua. Even though the US had a firepower and striking force many times more powerful than the ones used in the previous eleven invasions of Nicaragua, and a president (Reagan) more eager than any previous president to invade, the invasion did not happen. Not because it would have been too costly in lives but because it would have been *politically* too costly. President Reagan would not have balked at killing tens of thousands of Nicaraguans and losing say 5,000 Americans to smash the Red Menace in Central America. When 241 Marines were blown away in one afternoon in Lebanon, Reagan was ready to escalate his involvement in that country. Only the pressure of democratic forces in the USA and elsewhere caused him to leave Lebanon and refrain from invading Nicaragua. He did not have the political support to do otherwise. Invasion was politically too costly because it was militarily too costly even though logistically possible. It would have caused too much of an uproar at home and throughout Latin America and would have lost him, his party, and his policies too much support.

Critics voice concern about the Western peace movements' "one-sidedness," bemoaning the fact that no equivalent popular pressure for peace exists in the Soviet Union.[17] "We do not know what the peoples of the totalitarian states, including the people of the Soviet Union, may want. They are locked in silence by their government," says Jonathan Schell.[18] Actually it is Schell who is locked in ignorance. That he and others have never heard about the peace movements in socialist countries does not mean they do not exist. In 1982, in East Germany, several million persons took part in rallies and demonstrations against nuclear arms. That same year, tens of millions of Soviet citizens participated in some 14,000 mass demonstrations, rallies, and meetings for peace all over the USSR, calling for the end to nuclear arms both East and West.[19] The Soviet peace movement is funded privately by labor unions, churches, women's federations, youth groups, and others, yet it is dismissed by critics because it is supposedly "government sponsored." To be sure, it probably would not have been allowed to operate openly if it did not have the government's blessings, since public differences on foreign policy were not tolerated in the USSR until recent years. But is it such a bad thing that the Soviet government approves of its peace movement? (The critics would denounce Soviet authorities even more if they *opposed* the peace movement in their country.)

The question is, when is the *United States* government going to show friendliness toward peace advocates at home and abroad? A distinction should be made between the government in Washington that ignores, denounces, and red-baits peace proponents, and the government in Moscow that looks favorably upon peace movements in all countries.[20]

George Wald discerns "an astonishing unanimity" behind the view that the arms race and nuclear war can be prevented by the following measures: (1) a pledge of no first use; (2) a moratorium on testing nuclear weapons followed by a comprehensive test ban treaty; (3) no Star Wars and no antisatellite weaponry; (4) large reductions in the present stockpiles of nuclear weapons. What Wald fails to note is that the Soviet Union has already agreed to all four of these conditions—and to much more, including the total elimination of nuclear and chemical weapons.[21] Some peace advocates, afraid of being red-baited and concerned with maintaining their "credibility," strain for an appearance of evenhandedness by charging both nations with being equally intransigent and insincere.[22] The trouble with this position is that it is not true. There is no need to petition the USSR to pledge no first use or to accept a nuclear freeze or to stop testing. The Soviets already have done these things. Pretending that Moscow is equally to blame for today's dangers makes it harder for us to convince people that agreements can be reached with the Soviets. The false symmetry undercuts our very efforts at getting the United States to agree to peaceful settlements.

To claim that the Soviets too are in the grip of a "military-industrial complex" again is to play fast with the facts in order to maintain a false appearance of balance. To be sure, there are bureaucrats in the USSR who defend their domains and generals who worry about their promotions, but there are no giant private defense contractors raking in hundreds of millions of dollars in personal profits each year, no Soviet "iron triangle" of corporations that ladle out generous campaign contributions to politicians, who vote huge sums to military officers, who award lucrative weapons contracts to corporations in return for top positions in those same corporations when they retire from the military. If anything, in the Soviet Union the Communist Party exerts a tighter control over the military than ever. Nor does a Rambo bellicosity permeate Soviet popular culture or political life as it does our own. "Such a tendency would be anathema to the Soviet population, whose memory of World War II has given it a sobriety in matters of war and peace quite different from the lightminded belligerence that appears in much US debate."[23]

We live in a world where imperialism consigns hundreds of millions of people to lives of misery and oppression and where the shadow of nuclear death is cast upon us all, a world where the pursuit of profit is destroying the ecological conditions of life itself.

Latin American rain forests are being leveled at a rapid clip to raise beef for the fast-food market in the United States; the ozone layer is becoming dangerously depleted; the world's oxygen supply is threatened by pollutants; and the radioactive waste from European nuclear plants are being dumped into our oceans thereby killing them; industrial effusions from scores of nations are contaminating our land, air and water. "There is no security," noted Soviet leader Mikhail Gorbachev, "when currents of poison flow along river channels, when poisonous rains pour down from the sky, when an atmosphere polluted with industrial and transport waste chokes cities and whole regions, when development of nuclear power is accompanied by unacceptable risks."[24] The resources and energies of nations, Gorbachev urged, should be dedicated to the problems of global survival instead of global dominance and destruction.

The policies pursued by US leaders have delivered misfortune upon countless innocents, generating wrongs more horrendous than any they allegedly combat. The people of this country and other nations are becoming increasingly aware of this. The people know that nuclear weapons bring no security to anyone and that interventions on the side of privileged autocracies and reactionary governments bring no justice. They also seem to know that they pay most of the costs of the arms race and many of the costs of imperialism. From South Korea to South Africa, from Central America to the Western Sahara, from Europe to North America, people are fighting back, some because they have no choice, others because they would choose no other course but the one that leads to peace and justice.

Notes

1. The "firebreak" is the conspicuous divide between the most destructive conventional weapons and nuclear weapons; it is disappearing as the damage capacity of conventional weapons approaches the smaller nuclear weapons and the latter are developed to resemble conventional destruction. See Michael Klare, "Conventional Arms, Military Doctrine, and Nuclear War: the Vanishing Firebreak," in Joseph Gerson, ed., *The Deadly Connection* (Philadelphia: New Society Publishers, 1986), pp. 98–110.

2. As was claimed by Robert W. Tucker, *The Radical Left and American Foreign Policy* (Baltimore: Johns Hopkins University Press, 1971).

3. Albert Szymanski, *Is the Red Flag Flying?* (London: Zed, 1979).

4. Laurence Shoup and William Minter, *Imperial Brain Trust: The Council on Foreign Relations and U.S. Foreign Policy* (New York: Monthly Review Press, 1977).

5. Arthur Schlesinger, Jr., quoted in William Domhoff, *Who Rules America Now?* (New York: Simon & Schuster, 1983), p. 137.

6. Domhoff, *Who Rules America Now?* pp. 138–40.

7. Ibid.

8. Ron Brownstein and Nina Easton, *Reagan's Ruling Class* (Washington, D.C.: Center for the Study of Responsive Law, 1982); Anna Mayo, "Casey at the Bat," *Village Voice,* July 21, 1987, p. 21.

9. Holly Sklar, ed., *Trilateralism* (Boston: South End Press, 1980).

10. For instance, Maisie McAdoo, "An Embargo That Serves No Purpose," *Nation,* December 4, 1982, pp. 586–88; Joanne Omang, "Administration Worries as Banana Operation Closes in Costa Rica," *Washington Post,* January 16, 1985; Mark Potts, "Chevron's Purchase of Gulf Brought Assets and Headaches," *Washington Post,* May 31, 1987.

11. Quoted in Jeff McMahon, *Reagan and the World* (New York: Monthly Review Press, 1985), p. 13; also Stephen Kinzer and Stephen Schlesinger, *Bitter Fruit: The Untold Story of the American Coup in Guatemala* (Garden City, N.Y.: Doubleday, 1982).

12. See the discussion on Chile in Chapter 5.

13. *New York Times,* July 4, 1986.

14. *In These Times,* May 22–28, 1985; Harris poll, *Bulletin of Atomic Scientists* (August–September 1982); *Washington Post,* June 10, 1986, March 8 and 17, 1986, and June 3, 1987; *New York Times,* April 29, 1984.

15. *Economic Notes,* January 1983, p. 12; also *Voter Options on Nuclear Arms Policy* (New York: Public Agenda Foundation, 1984).

16. Gary Lee, "U.S. World Influence Seen Slipping in Gorbachev Era," *Washington Post,* May 29, 1987.

17. For instance, Theodore Draper, "How Not to Think About Nuclear War," *New York Review of Books,* July 15, 1982, p. 40.

18. Jonathan Schell, *The Fate of the Earth* (New York: Knopf, 1982).

19. Joell Fishman's report on the peace movement in the German Democratic Republic: *Daily World,* July 8, 1982; "Peace Marches Sweep USSR," *Daily World,* June 15, 1982.

20. Soviet authorities, however, have opposed the small groups of right-wing dissidents who suddenly sought to link the peace issue to the question of greater political freedom for themselves or the opportunity to emigrate to the United States.

21. George Wald, "The Arms Race: How to Stop It," statement published by Promoting Enduring Peace, Woodmont, Conn., c. 1987.

22. For instance, representatives of the European Nuclear Disarmament Movement such as Mary Kaldor and E. P. Thompson; see the latter's "East, West—Is There a Third Way?" *Nation,* July 10–17, 1982, pp. 48–52; and his comments in the *Nation,* December 6, 1986, pp. 634–35.

23. Fred Halliday, *The Making of the Second Cold War* (London: Verso, 1983), p. 135.

24. Quoted in Marilyn Bechtel, "For Peace, Eliminate Economic and Ecologic Threats," *People's Daily World,* September 30, 1987.

Selected Bibliography

For readers who wish to pursue further some of the subjects treated in this book, the following titles are recommended.

General treatments of imperialism:

Berberoglu, Berch. *The Internationalization of Capital: Imperialism and Capitalist Development on a World Scale.* New York: Praeger, 1987.

Lenin, V. I. *Imperialism, The Highest Stage of Capitalism.* New York: International Publishers, 1937.

Magdoff, Harry. *The Age of Imperialism.* New York: Monthly Review Press, 1968.

Marx, Karl, and Frederick Engels. *On Colonialism* (selected writings). New York: International Publishers, 1972.

Polyansky, F. *An Economic History, The Age of Imperialism (1870–1917).* Moscow: Progress Publishers, 1973 (available from Imported Publications, Chicago).

Rodney, Walter. *How Europe Underdeveloped Africa.* Washington, D.C.: Howard University Press, 1974.

Stavrianos, L.S. *Global Rift, The Third World Comes of Age.* New York: William Morrow, 1981.

Szymanski, Albert. *The Logic of Imperialism.* New York: Praeger, 1981.

US foreign policy and counterrevolutionary interventionism:

Blum, William. *The CIA, A Forgotten History.* London: Zed, 1986.

Chomsky, Noam, and Edward Herman. *The Washington Connection and Third World Fascism.* Boston: South End Press, 1979.

Chomsky, Noam, and Edward Herman. *After the Cataclysm.* Boston: South End Press, 1979.

Gettleman, Marvin, Jane Franklin, Marilyn Young, and H. Bruce Franklin, eds. *Vietnam and America, A Documented History.* New York: Grove Press, 1985.

Herman, Edward, *The Real Terror Network.* Boston: South End Press, 1982.

Morley, Morris, and James Petras. *The Reagan Administration and Nicaragua: How Washington Constructs its Case for Counterrevolution in Central America.* (Forward by Noam Chomsky and Afterword by Michael Parenti.) New York: Institute for Media Analysis, 1987.

On how the US news media distort and suppress information about US foreign policy:

Aronson, James. *The Press and the Cold War,* Boston: Beacon Press, 1970.

Parenti, Michael. *Inventing Reality: The Politics of the Mass Media.* New York: St. Martin's Press, 1986.

On the suppressed history of earlier East-West relations:

Alperovitz, Gar. *Atomic Diplomacy, Hiroshima and Potsdam.* rev. ed. New York: Viking, 1985.

Sevostyanov, Pavel. *Before the Nazi Invasion.* Moscow: Progress Publishers, 1981 (available from Imported Publications, Chicago).

Williams, William Appleman. "American Interventionism in Russia: 1917–20," in David Horowitz, ed. *Containment and Revolution.* Boston: Beacon Press, 1967.

The arms race and the cold war:

Aldridge, Robert. *First Strike!* Boston: South End Press, 1983.

Gerson, Joseph. ed. *The Deadly Connection, Nuclear War and U.S. Intervention.* Philadelphia: New Society Publishers, 1986.

Gervasi, Tom. *The Myth of Soviet Military Supremacy.* New York: Harper and Row, 1986.

Halliday, Fred. *The Making of the Second Cold War.* London: Verso, 1983.

Index